MOROCCO'S QUEST FOR STRONGER AND INCLUSIVE GROWTH

Editors

ROBERTO CARDARELLI
TALINE KORANCHELIAN

Cataloging-in-Publication Data
IMF Library

Names: Cardarelli, R. (Roberto), editor. | Koranchelian, Taline, editor. |
    International Monetary Fund, publisher.
Title: Morocco's quest for stronger and inclusive growth.
Edited by Roberto Cardarelli and Taline Koranchelian
Description: Washington, DC : International Monetary Fund, 2023. | 2023. |
    Includes bibliographical references.
Identifiers: ISBN:
      9798400225406   (paper)
      9798400225468   (ePub)
      9798400225574   (WebPDF)
Subjects: LCSH: Economic development—Morocco. | Economic policy—
    Morocco.
Classification: LCC HD70.M6 M67 2023

Recommended citation: Cardarelli, Roberto, and Taline Koranchelian, eds. 2023. *Morocco's Quest for Stronger and Inclusive Growth*. Washington, DC: International Monetary Fund.

ISBNs: 9798400225406 (paper)
      9798400225468 (ePub)
      9798400225574 (WebPDF)

Please send orders to:

International Monetary Fund, Publication Services
PO Box 92780, Washington, DC 20090, USA
Tel: (202) 623–7430 Fax: (202) 623–7201
E-mail: publications@imf.org
Internet: www.elibrary.imf.org
www.bookstore.imf.org

Contents

PART IV. PROMOTING INCLUSION

Foreword

Kristalina Georgieva
Managing Director, International Monetary Fund

The World Bank Group and International Monetary Fund convened their Annual Meetings in Marrakech in 2023—the first time in Africa since the meetings were hosted in Nairobi, Kenya, 50 years ago.

The setting for the 2023 World Bank-IMF Annual Meetings is relevant because Morocco's economic performance over the past few decades—characterized by significant economic stability and steadily improving living standards—holds inspiring lessons for other economies, particularly in the current highly uncertain geoeconomic environment. Moreover, Morocco's pursuit of ambitious reforms helped the country withstand serious shocks in recent years, including the COVID-19 pandemic, two severe droughts, and a terms-of-trade shock triggered by Russia's war in Ukraine.

This book, *Morocco's Quest for Stronger and Inclusive Growth*, explores the factors underlying Morocco's resilience. The book points to the numerous reforms Morocco began a few decades ago, including measures to open the country to international trade, invest in key infrastructure, reduce nontargeted subsidies, strengthen the independence of the central bank, build a strong financial supervisory framework, and modernize governance in both the public and private sectors. Morocco's success in these areas suggests that these reforms are essential for countries in search of macroeconomic stability as a precondition for growth.

For all the progress that has been made, more needs to be done to enable growth that is sustainable and inclusive. Recognizing this, Moroccan authorities designed a series of reforms amid the pandemic aimed at improving the social safety net, strengthening educational outcomes, promoting private entrepreneurship and access to finance, scaling up opportunities for women and youth, and mitigating the impact of climate change. This book describes several of these efforts, which could serve as good examples for other countries.

Morocco is a gateway to Africa, Europe, and the Middle East. The Marrakech 2023 Annual Meetings provide an opportunity to recognize Morocco's strong commitment to economic reforms and stability and to promote the country as an example of how to build trade and investment links in a fragmenting world. I hope this book will help us in this endeavor and, even more important, that in the coming years we will continue to salute Morocco's progress in its long quest for robust, inclusive growth.

Foreword

Aziz Akhannouch
Head of Government, Kingdom of Morocco

Morocco is at a crucial crossroads as we move into the third decade of the 21st century. After 20 years of ambitious and steady reforms under the leadership of His Majesty the King, we are now at the dawn of a new era—an era when we will accelerate and intensify our efforts toward a new development model based on human capital and ecological transition. In this context, the comprehensive and detailed analysis in this book helps reiterate the successes achieved in recent decades and provides welcome insight into the challenges ahead.

Morocco's responses to successive crises—particularly the COVID-19 pandemic and the 2022 inflation episode—have demonstrated our ability to preserve macroeconomic stability while responding in a unified and rational manner to powerful exogenous shocks. Targeted measures to support purchasing power and public health, deployed with unprecedented speed and efficiency, have strengthened our confidence in our ability to implement inclusive and transformative social policies. With this in mind, and in line with the Royal agenda, in the fall of 2021, the government launched a series of reforms to strengthen institutional solidarity and social protection systems.

These reforms place human capital at the heart of our development model and are inspired by international best practices, both in school learning and the fight against poverty. The ambitious social component of the ongoing reforms includes the expansion of social protection and the introduction of a program of direct social assistance for the vulnerable. This program is accompanied by an in-depth reform of Morocco's education and health systems. Together, these reforms carry the seeds of a modern social state that guarantees social justice, inclusive development, and a greater role for women.

The transition to a sustained growth regime also demands that we proactively improve the attractiveness of Morocco's business and employment environment to private investment. The government has begun a comprehensive investment policy reform to strengthen the business climate. Our new investment charter, which targets sustainable, job-rich economic projects and investment in technological and future sectors, is accompanied by an overhaul of investment processes, greater administrative devolution, an ambitious tax reform, and a modernization of the state as a shareholder.

Crucially, these prospects cannot materialize without a vigorous and sustained response to the major challenge of water availability, which is essential to both food sovereignty and economic growth. Following the Royal Vision, the government is deploying a proactive roadmap to build reservoirs, further rationalize water resources, and link surplus basins in the north with those in deficit in the south. Large-scale investment in nonconventional water production projects, whether from desalination or wastewater treatment, is also underway, including in the construction of 10 desalination plants, which will boost water output by 1 billion cubic meters.

To develop a resilient, low-carbon economy, Morocco is investing in producing competitive green energy on a large scale. Under Royal leadership, we aspire to triple our installed capacity of wind and solar energy and position Morocco in the green hydrogen sector. These objectives will strengthen the country's energy sovereignty and set new standards for environmental preservation for others to emulate.

Our steadfast commitment to fiscal discipline and structural reform places us on a path of macroeconomic stability. These are the foundation of the trust of our economic and financial partners, as demonstrated by the Flexible Credit Line granted to Morocco by the IMF, the volume and favorable terms of financing obtained on international markets, and the country's exit from the Financial Action Task Force grey list.

This book highlights the work done while recognizing the magnitude of the challenges that remain. I want to express my gratitude to everyone who contributed to this book. Your detailed and rigorous work is a valuable resource in reaching our objectives. By putting the kingdom's recent economic and social achievements into perspective, the book documents the rise of Africa.

I wish you pleasant reading!

Acknowledgments

This book is the result of collaboration among a number of IMF, World Bank, and Moroccan economists. We are particularly grateful to Minister Chakib Benmoussa for contributing to the book with a chapter edition of the *New Model of Development 2021* report. We are also grateful to Moëz Cherif, Javier Díaz-Cassou, and Carole Megevand for preparing a chapter version of the World Bank's 2022 *Country Climate and Development Report* on Morocco. Finally, we thank the Policy Center for the New South in Rabat for contributing to this book with a chapter and the always fruitful exchange of views on the country and the region. We thank Lorraine Coffey of the IMF's Communications Department for her excellent work managing the production of this book, and Absolute Service, Inc. for copyediting, proofreading, and typesetting.

Contributors

EDITORS

Roberto Cardarelli is Assistant Director in the Middle East and Central Asia Department of the IMF, and mission chief for Morocco. Within the IMF he has held positions in the Western Hemisphere Department, where he was chief of the North America Division and the Southern Cone II Division, and mission chief for Canada, Chile, and Argentina; in the Asia and Pacific Department, where he was chief of the Regional Studies Division; and in the Research Department, where he worked on the *World Economic Outlook*. He is an Italian national and holds a PhD in economics from the University of Cambridge in the UK.

Taline Koranchelian is Deputy Director in the Middle East and Central Asia Department of the IMF, where she oversees the regional work of the department as well as Algeria, Djibouti, Egypt, Iraq, Mauritania, Morocco, Tunisia, and Yemen. She holds a Diplôme d'Études Supérieures in international finance and a master's degree in economic policy from Saint Joseph University of Beirut. Before taking up this position, Ms. Koranchelian was the Director of the IMF's Middle East Regional Technical Assistance Center since June 1, 2016. Between 2012 and 2016, she was Assistant Director in the IMF's Strategy, Policy, and Review, leading the IMF surveillance policy and reviewing the work of the IMF for some 30 countries across all regions. Throughout her 20+ years of experience at the IMF, Ms. Koranchelian held various positions in the Middle East and Central Asia Department, Fiscal Affairs Department, Strategy, Policy, and Review Department, and the Executive Board of the IMF. She led missions to many countries in Africa, Central Asia, Europe, and the Middle East, and she led the preparation of various IMF policies. Before joining the IMF, Ms. Koranchelian worked at the Central Bank of Lebanon and was chief of cabinet and advisor to the Minister of Economy and Trade in Lebanon.

AUTHORS

Federica Alfani is an economist in the Poverty and Equity Global Practice of the World Bank. She works on Tunisia and her main scientific interests are in the fields of poverty, rural development, and labor markets. Previously, she worked at the International Fund for Agricultural Development and the Food and Agriculture Organization of the United Nations. She holds an MSc in development economics and international cooperation and a PhD in economics from the University of Rome Tor Vergata.

Abdelaaziz Ait Ali is a principal economist and head of the Research Department at the Policy Center for the New South. He joined the Center in 2014 after five years of experience at the Central Bank of Morocco. He worked as an economist in the International Studies and Relations Department and was analyzing the real estate price index and financial asset prices for monetary policy and financial stability purposes. Since then, he has focused on cyclical and structural issues of the Moroccan economy, including macroeconomic management and industrial policy design. Mr. Ali holds a master's degree in econometrics from Hassan II University in Casablanca.

Gregory Auclair worked as a research analyst in the Middle East and Central Asia Department of the IMF between 2014 and 2018. He is now completing a PhD in economics at the Geneva Graduate Institute.

Dániel Baksa is an economist at the Institute of Capacity Development (ICD) of the IMF. He has contributed to various capacity development projects in macro forecasting and policy modeling at central banks (in Jordan, Morocco, and the Philippines) and finance ministries (in Armenia, Cambodia, Georgia, and Israel). Prior to working at the Fund, he was a macroeconomic model developer and analyst at several European policy institutions, including the Fiscal Council of Hungary, the Central Bank of Hungary, OGResearch in Prague, the Bank of Lithuania, and the European Central Bank. His research focuses on DSGE-OLG models, monetary and fiscal policy interactions, and the impact of aging on medium-term economic development. Mr. Baksa is a Hungarian national and holds a PhD in economics from the Central European University.

Hippolyte Balima is an economist in the IMF's Middle East and Central Asia Department. Before joining the IMF, he worked in the World Bank's Macroeconomics and Fiscal Management Global Practice. He has published in top academic journals, including the *Journal of Development Economics, European Economic Review*, and IMF *Economic Review*, and has contributed to various IMF policy publications.

David Bartolini is a senior economist in the European Department (EUR) of the IMF. He has held positions in the Fiscal Affairs Department, where he contributed to the work on financing SDGs for low-income and emerging market economies, supported Morocco and Mali as a fiscal economist, and led a capacity development mission to Morocco on strengthening their medium-term fiscal framework. He joined the IMF after working for seven years at the Organisation for Economic Co-ordination and Development (OECD), in Paris, where he contributed to the work on taxation and inclusive growth and led the work on taxation and firms' productivity. Mr. Bartolini also contributed to the OECD work on the future of work, regional development, and fiscal federalism and participated in several country reviews. He holds a PhD in economics from Essex University in the UK.

Chakib Benmoussa is Morocco's Minister of National Education, Preschool and Sports from 2021. He has held several positions within the Ministry of Equipment (Director of Planning and Studies, and Director of Roads) and has served as Secretary General of the Prime Minister's Department between 1995 to 1998. He then spent a few years in the private sector as chairman of Sonasid, president of Tangiers Free Zone, and general manager of the group Brasseries du Maroc. In 2006, he was appointed as Minister of Interior and then, in 2011, as president of the Economic and Social Council of Morocco. Mr. Benmoussa served as Ambassador of His Majesty King Mohammed VI to France from March 2013 to October 2021. He was appointed by His Majesty King Mohammed VI on November 2019 as president of the Special Commission on the Development Model. Mr. Benmoussa holds engineering degrees from the École Polytechnique de Paris (1979) and the École Nationale des Ponts et Chaussées-Paris (1981). He also holds a Master of Science degree from the Massachusetts Institute of Technology (1983).

Olivier Bizimana is a senior economist in the IMF's Middle East and Central Asia Department, where he works on Morocco and in the Regional Analytics and Strategy Division. He previously served in the IMF's Research Department with a focus on G20 countries. Before joining the IMF in 2015, he worked in the Global Economics Team at Morgan Stanley in London. He was previously responsible for economic research for the euro area at Crédit Agricole Group in Paris. He has also taught postgraduate courses in macroeconomics at Paris Dauphine University for five years. His research interests include international finance, monetary policy, macro-financial issues, and business cycle fluctuations. Mr. Bizimana earned a PhD and an MPhil in economics from Paris Dauphine University and an MSc in economics and statistics from the École Nationale de la Statistique et de l'Administration Économique (ENSAE) in Paris.

Oumayma Bourhriba is an economist at the Policy Center for the New South. She holds a master's degree in applied economics and is currently a PhD candidate at Mohammed V University in Rabat. Her research areas cover macroeconomic management, international trade, and long-term economic growth. Previously, she has worked on issues related to trade services in Morocco and Africa, foreign direct investments in Morocco, economic development in the MENA region, as well as economic implications of COVID-19 and the war in Ukraine on Africa and Morocco.

Aleš Bulíř is Deputy Director of the IMF – Singapore Regional Training Institute (STI). Within IMF, his most recent positions were in the Policy Development and Review, Research, and Institute for Capacity Development Departments. His graduate degrees are from the London School of Economics and Prague University of Economics. Prior to joining the Fund, he taught economics in Prague and worked at the Czech National Bank. His research interests include the role of communication in monetary policy, macroeconomic modeling, and the role of development aid.

Moëz Cherif is the World Bank's program leader for infrastructure. With more than 20 years of experience in the energy and infrastructure sectors, he is currently focused on promoting investments in green energy and transport infrastructure, improving the performance of the energy sectors and the integration of cross-border electricity markets, as well as promoting access to competitive digital services. Previously, he worked as an infrastructure economist at the International Finance Corporation and then joined the World Bank in 2008, where he initially worked in sub-Saharan Africa on hydropower and gas-to-power project development, as well as on power utility turnaround and reform.

Fabio Clementi, PhD, is Professor of Economics at the University of Macerata, Italy. His main research interests focus on the size distribution of income, wealth, and firms; business cycle analysis; and the empirical validation of agent-based economic models with real-world data. He has published several papers in peer-reviewed international journals as well as book chapters on topics related to his scientific activity, and he serves as referee for various international journals. He has also been involved in several national and international research projects in the field of agent-based computational economics. Mr. Clementi presented communications at many international meetings, also as an invited speaker, and contributed as a member of the scientific and/or organizing committees of some international conferences. Most recently, he has acted as a consultant for the World Bank on matters related to income distribution, poverty, and inequality.

Ananta Dua is a research analyst in the Middle East and Central Asia Department of the IMF. Prior to this, she was in the Research Department, where she worked on several projects such as the *World Economic Outlook*, G-20 surveillance notes, and G-20 policy reports. She holds a master's degree in applied economics from Johns Hopkins University.

Javier Díaz-Cassou is the World Bank's senior country economist for Morocco, based in Rabat. Prior to joining the Bank in 2020, he was a lead economist at the Inter-American Development Bank, covering the Andean region. He has also held various positions at the London School of Economics, the Bank of Spain, and the European Central Bank. His main research interests lie in the areas of development economics, growth, climate change, and sovereign debt, with publications in various academic journals such as *World Development,* the *Journal of Banking and Finance, Oxford Academic Papers,* and the *Journal of Applied Economics.* He earned his PhD from the London School of Economics.

Michele Fabiani is a Research Fellow in Political Economy at University of Macerata, and he has been a consultant at the World Bank since 2018. He holds a PhD in quantitative methods for policy evaluation from the University of Macerata. His main research interests include income distribution and inequality.

Dominique Fayad is an economist in the Strategy, Policy, and Review Department of the IMF, working on climate issues. Previously, she covered several macroeconomic policy topics related to fiscal policy and governance, and monetary and external sectors in the Middle East and Central Asia, Eastern Europe, and Sub-Saharan Africa. She worked on growth and structural reform on Morocco from 2014 to 2016. She joined the IMF in 2014 as part of the Economist Program after receiving her PhD education at the University of Paris Sorbonne.

Lisa Kolovich is a senior economist in the IMF's Inclusion and Gender Unit and was one of the coauthors of the IMF's first gender mainstreaming strategy. She has also worked in the IMF's African and Research Departments and was the team manager for gender research under a joint IMF-DFID collaboration that focused on macro issues in low-income countries. Her research examines gender budgeting and fiscal policies initiatives as tools for reducing gender inequality, and she is the contributor and editor of the book *Fiscal Policies and Gender Equality*.

Chiara Maggi is an economist in the World Economic Studies division of the IMF's Research Department. Prior to this position, she worked as an economist for the Morocco desk in the IMF's Middle East and Central Asia Department and in the Structural Reforms Unit of the IMF's Research Department. She holds a PhD in economics from Northwestern University.

Carole Megevand has 25 years of professional experience in international development across various regions in the world. She is currently based in Rabat, Morocco, as the World Bank's Sector Leader for the Sustainable Development program in the Maghreb and Malta. Carole joined the Bank in 2002 and has led several complex operations on natural resources in various African and Latin American countries, always with a specific focus on intersectoral dimensions and governance issues. Among other positions, she has been the global lead on forests, leading the preparation of the Bank's Forest Action Plan. She holds two master's degrees, one in agricultural economics and one in environment/natural resources economics.

Vasco Molini is a program manager at the World Bank. Over more than a decade with the World Bank, he worked in Mozambique, Angola, São Tomé and Príncipe, Ghana, Nigeria, Morocco, Tunisia, and Libya, where he led country-level dialogues on jobs, poverty reduction, polarization, and conflicts and managed country-level statistical capacity-building initiatives. He has also published on these topics in more than 20 internationally peer-reviewed journals. He holds a PhD in economics from the University of Florence and a post-doc from the Free University of Amsterdam.

Anta Ndoye is the IMF Resident Representative for Mauritania in the Middle East and Central Asia Department. She worked previously as an economist on

Saudi Arabia and Morocco, where she participated in several research projects on inclusive growth and financial inclusion. She also has prior experience as an advisor to the Ministry of Economy of Senegal and at Bruegel, a Brussels-based think tank. She holds a PhD from the University of Strasbourg and an engineering degree in statistics from Toulouse School of Economics.

Lorraine Ocampos is an experienced policy-oriented economist with more than 30 years of extensive practice working with the IMF, central banks, and economic think tanks. From 2000 to 2021, she was a senior economist at the IMF in a variety of assignments with main topics of expertise in designing, negotiating, and reviewing Fund programs and fiscal policy issues, including fair taxation, public expenditure policy, and public financial management.

Maximilien Queyranne is a deputy division chief in the Fiscal Affairs Department (FAD) of the IMF. He previously worked on Morocco in the IMF's Middle East and Central Asia Department and on Senegal in the African Department. He was also an economist in FAD, working on Cote d'Ivoire, Portugal, and Myanmar, and was actively involved in delivering technical assistance on budgeting, reporting, and public investment management. Prior to joining the IMF, he served as a diplomat at the French Ministry of Foreign Affairs (2002–2004), a magistrate at the French Court of Accounts (2006–2010), and a public sector specialist at the World Bank (2010–2011). He is an alumnus of the National School of Administration (ENA).

Francisco Roch is an economist in the Systemic Issues Division at the Research Department of the IMF. Previously, he worked in the African, Western Hemisphere, and Strategy and Policy Review Departments. While on leave from the IMF during 2017–2019, he was deputy manager of the Research Department at the Center for Latin American Monetary Studies (CEMLA) in Mexico. His main research interests are in macroeconomics and international finance, with a focus on sovereign debt crises and monetary and macroprudential policies. Francisco has published in top academic journals, including the *American Economic Journal: Macroeconomics, Journal of International Economics,* and *Journal of Political Economy Macroeconomics.* He holds a PhD from the University of Chicago.

Enzo Valentini is Professor of Political Economy at the University of Macerata (Department of Political Science, Communication, and International Relations). His fields of research are labor economics, irregular economy, inequality, structural change, and consequences of robotization. He holds a degree in economics from the University of Bologna and a PhD from Marche Polytechnic University.

Abbreviations

BAM	Bank Al-Maghrib
CBAM	carbon border adjustment mechanism
CCDR	Country Climate and Development Report
COP26	UN Climate Change Conference
DRF	disaster risk financing
EMDE	emerging market and developing economy
EMEs	emerging market economies
EMs	emerging markets
FLFP	female labor force participation
FSGM	flexible system of global models
GDP	gross domestic product
GTAP	Global Trade Analysis Project
ICT	internal consumption tax
ILO	International Labour Organization
IMF	International Monetary Fund
LAC	Latin American countries
MCD	Middle East and Central Asia
MENA	Middle East and North Africa
MENAP	Middle East, North Africa, Afghanistan, and Pakistan
MFMod	World Bank's macrostructural model
MSME	micro, small, and medium enterprises
MVF	multivariate filtering
NAIRU	nonaccelerating inflation rate of unemployment
NDM	New Development Model
NEET	youth not in employment, education, or training
OECD	Organisation for Economic Co-operation and Development
OI	oil importers
PIRLS	Progress in International Reading Literacy Study
PISA	Program for International Student Assessment
PNE	National Water Plan
SCDM	Special Commission on the Development Model
SFA	stochastic frontier analysis
SMEs	small and medium enterprises
SOEs	state-owned enterprises
TFP	total factor productivity
TIMSS	Trends in International Mathematics and Science Study
VAT	value-added tax

Introduction

Roberto Cardarelli and Taline Koranchelian

Over the last three decades, Morocco had a remarkable journey to economic stability and development. Following the turbulent 1980s, when severe macro-economic imbalances required IMF-supported adjustment programs, the last three decades have been characterized by significant economic stability, and a steady progress in improving standards of living. This has been made possible by a conservative approach to fiscal policy, an effective program of public investment that improved the country's infrastructure, and a series of reforms that have (1) modernized the monetary policy and financial supervisory frameworks, (2) opened the country to international trade and attracted foreign investors, and (3) gradually strengthened the governance of public administration. It is not a coincidence that, because of this progress and in recognition of the efficiency of its economic institutions, Morocco secured a Flexible Credit Line arrangement with the IMF in 2023, a precautionary credit line reserved for countries with very strong policies and institutional frameworks.

Still, Morocco's quest for a strong, resilient, and inclusive growth is far from over. After accelerating in the first decade of the new millennium, income convergence with advanced economies has slowed over the last 15 years. And, although better than a decade ago, the benefits of economic development still remain elusive for a significant part of Morocco's population, particularly young people and women, given their high unemployment rate and the presence of a still-large informal sector.

Even though Morocco is not the only country in the world that struggles to ensure wider and fairer opportunities for all its citizens, what stands out from its experience is its policymakers' recognition that addressing these issues will require a new series of bold and ambitious reforms. Indeed, starting from 2020, and thus right into the middle of the pandemic and the largest recession in Morocco's recent history, the authorities announced a series of sweeping reforms that would enable the country's transition to a "new model of development." At the heart of this transition is the idea that future economic growth will need to increasingly come from private sector investment, a stronger accumulation of human capital, greater participation of women in economic life, a social protection system that efficiently targets those who are really in need of state support, a financial sector that combines stability with dynamism in allocating resources, and continued progress in strengthening the governance of public institutions.

This book provides a broad overview of both Morocco's economic progress in the past few decades and its economic modernization agenda going forward. To a certain extent, its success story makes Morocco a useful example for many developing economies still in search of building the foundations of macroeconomic stability. And the series of reforms that the country has begun to implement provides equally interesting ideas for all countries engaged in the quest for stronger and more inclusive growth.

The first chapter, by Maximilien Queyranne, focuses on the policies and reforms that allowed Morocco to maintain macroeconomic stability throughout the multiple negative shocks that have occurred in the past 15 years. In particular, the elimination of oil subsidies, the parametric pension reforms, and the adoption of a multiyear budgetary framework have helped to maintain fiscal discipline throughout the global financial crisis, the euro area crisis, the Arab uprisings, and the oil price shocks between 2008 and 2012. At the same time, opening the country to international trade, inserting itself into a few manufacturing global value chains (e.g., automotive, aeronautics, and electronic sectors), and developing non–tourism-related service exports (including banking and telecommunications) protected Morocco's external position over the same period. Having maintained domestic and external balances before the pandemic crisis provided the space for a strong policy response to the health crisis and the terms of trade shock that followed Russia's invasion of Ukraine.

However, the last 15 years have also witnessed slower economic growth. The impulse to development that came from rapid industrialization into new sectors and the accumulation of physical (infrastructure) capital begun to level off after the global financial crisis. The slower pace of economic growth is inconsistent with the absorption of new entrants into the labor markets, the gradual entry of women into the labor force, and the reduction of widespread informality. The Moroccan authorities correctly concluded that the traditional growth model had run out of steam and they began designing a new wave of structural reforms to catalyze a different model of development. In Chapter 2, Chakib Benmoussa, the president of the Royal Commission on the New Model of Development, explains the ambitious agenda of reforms elaborated in the report that the Commission published in the summer of 2021. The report sets a series of quantitative objectives, including 1) doubling gross domestic product (GDP) per capita and women's labor force participation rate by 2035, 2) reducing the share of informal jobs from 60 to 20 percent, and 3) increasing the share of energy consumption produced via renewable sources from 11 to 40 percent. Achieving these objectives would require making the private sector the key engine of growth by removing barriers to entry, improving competitiveness, and reforming state-owned enterprises (SOEs) to reduce their role in the economy. But these efforts are unlikely to succeed without a strong investment in human capital, including through high-quality education; a social protection system that enhances resilience and inclusion; and measures that multiply opportunities and means of participation, particularly for young people and women.

Morocco's transition to a new model of development would also require continued evolution of its macroeconomic policy framework, the theme of the second section of the book. In Chapter 3, Dániel Baksa and Aleš Bulíř discuss one aspect of this evolution, namely Morocco's planned transition to an inflation-targeting monetary policy regime. This transition began a decade ago (supported by IMF technical assistance) and has already gone through two steps: a first widening of the band (±2.5 percent) around the peg in 2018, and a second widening (to ±5 percent) in March 2020. The last step of the transition would be the removal of the peg and the free fluctuation of the exchange rate within a monetary policy regime that explicitly targets an inflation rate. The chapter explains the benefits of such a transition through model simulations showing that an inflation-targeting regime has the potential to cushion the Moroccan economy against real external shocks. Although the currency peg has helped Morocco maintain low inflation and an exchange rate in line with economic fundamentals and desirable policies over the last two decades, a more flexible exchange rate and active monetary policy guided by a formal inflation target could help the country's transition to a new model of economic growth, underpinned by stronger private sector investment.

In Chapter 4, David Bartolini, Chiara Maggi, and Francisco Roch discuss the potential evolution of another dimension of Morocco's macroeconomic policy framework—the adoption of a new fiscal rule based on a debt-to-GDP ratio as a medium-term anchor and an operational rule to guide fiscal policy in the short term. Morocco has significantly strengthened its fiscal policy framework over the last decade with the adoption of a new organic budget law in 2015 and the publication of a medium-term fiscal framework in 2022. Still, as the country embarks on a gradual process of fiscal consolidation following the increase in public debt in 2020, a new fiscal rule could help better shape expectations about future fiscal policy and reassure investors about Morocco's commitment to fiscal stability. Using a general equilibrium model calibrated to Morocco, the authors show that by working as a credible commitment device, a debt-anchor fiscal rule may correct the "time-inconsistency" problem associated with discretionary (period-by-period) fiscal policy, which may lead to overborrowing. By lowering the cost of debt, a credible debt-anchored fiscal rule may also reinforce policymakers' ability to ease fiscal policy when facing an economic downturn. Crucially, looking at past experiences of fiscal rules suggests that a key condition for their success is the presence of credible and effective fiscal institutions.

The third section of the book moves the focus to how to make the Moroccan economy more productive and resilient. In Chapter 5, Hippolyte Balima, Olivier Bizimana, and Ananta Dua first document the slowdown of Morocco's potential growth right after the global financial crisis, a phenomenon that they explain with the weakening of both labor force participation and capital productivity. The pandemic shock seems to have compounded this trend by affecting productivity dynamics. The reforms announced by the authorities in 2020 have the potential to reverse these trends. The authors first use a production function approach and then a general equilibrium model to quantify the potential impact of these reforms on output. Three messages stand out from their analysis. First, although the impact of the reforms is uncertain and highly dependent on their success to close Morocco's existing gaps with advanced economies, long-term output increases significantly (by between 5 and 10 percent) even in a median successful scenario. Second, the greatest impact on long-term output is produced by reforms that increase female labor force participation. Finally, the impact of the reforms on output is maximized when they are financed on a budget-neutral basis (i.e., through a reallocation of spending or higher tax revenues) rather than through higher public debt.

In Chapter 6, Abdelaaziz Ait Ali and Oumayma Bourhriba (from the Policy Center for the New South) discuss the extent to which Morocco's manufacturing sector can be an important source of jobs going forward. The fact that the share of manufacturing employment has declined in Morocco over the past two decades (as in several other advanced and emerging market economies) seems to cast doubt on this statement. The authors suggest that the deceleration in manufacturing employment can be largely explained by lower domestic demand and the rapid increase in labor productivity in manufacturing over the last 15 years (spurred by the transition from labor-intensive manufacturing sectors, such as textile, toward higher-technology sectors, such as automotive and electronics). Although a vibrant manufacturing sector continues to be an essential component of Morocco's growth and a potential engine of high-quality job creation, the authors conclude that more jobs will need to come from Morocco's service sector.

Any discussion of the structural transformation of the Moroccan economy cannot ignore the changing climate landscape, which is in turn a source of risks but also of significant opportunities. In Chapter 7, Moëz Cherif, Javier Díaz-Cassou, and Carole Megevand (all from the World Bank) first discuss the risks associated with more frequent droughts and increasing scarcity of water resources, which threaten to yield major GDP losses in the future (with a disproportionate impact on rural and urban vulnerable households). To confront this challenge, Morocco should continue to deploy water storage and infrastructure mobilization but also introduce demand management measures to rationalize the use of water. However, climate change also presents opportunities. Blessed with vast amounts of renewable energy sources, Morocco is particularly well-placed to reap the benefits of the global decarbonization agenda. Transitioning toward a green electricity generation matrix could bolster Morocco's comparative advantage, potentially turning the country into an exporter of green energy while boosting job creation in the industry and services that benefit from the decarbonization process. Because achieving these objectives would require significant investment, particularly from the private sector, a comprehensive policy approach would be needed to mobilize the resources required to finance this investment as well as to create an enabling environment for climate action to deliver transformative change.

The last section of the book deals with the inclusive nature of economic development in Morocco. Chapter 8, from Federica Alfani, Vasco Molini (both from the World Bank), Fabio Clementi, Michele Fabiani, and Enzo Valentini (all from the University of Macerata, Italy), discusses a well-known stylized fact of the Moroccan economy as well as many economies in the Middle East and North Africa region, namely the large share of young people who are unemployed, outside the school system, or not undergoing any training (the so-called "not in employment, education, or training," or NEETs). One striking result of the analysis is the gender dimension of this fact: although women's enrollment in secondary and tertiary education increased markedly in Morocco over the last two decades, the same positive improvement cannot be observed when it comes to participation in labor markets. In 2018, the NEET rate for women was still more than twice that for men. Indeed, the authors find that the probability of being NEET is higher for Moroccan women (particularly those married and/or with children) as well as for young people with lower levels of education, living in midsized towns, and coming from low-income families. The policy implication is clear: developing incentives and providing services to encourage Moroccan women to enter or remain in the labor market should be a top priority in the country's agenda of structural reforms.

The implications of a large gender gap, and the identification of policy measures to close it, is the topic of Chapter 9, by Lisa Kolovich and Anta Ndoye. Consistent with the findings in Chapter 5, Chapter 9 points to a large body of research that emphasizes the significant output costs of having high gender gaps in the labor markets. In particular, closing the gender gap in Morocco's labor force participation over the next 50 years would increase income levels by about 20 percent. The chapter summarizes the progress Morocco has made in terms of legal and policy reforms aimed at closing gender gaps, including through the introduction of a gender-focused budgeting framework in 2014 that integrates gender priorities throughout the budgeting process. Moreover, the chapter also points to several areas for additional reforms, including eliminating the legal barriers that hinder women's opportunities to participate in economic life, ensuring equal access to education, and redoubling efforts to close literacy gaps.

One key aspect of inclusion is equal opportunities to access financial products and services. Chapter 10, by Lorraine Ocampos, documents the considerable progress achieved by Morocco over the recent past in developing a comparatively deep and well-developed financial system. Still, despite these improvements, micro, small, and medium enterprises continue to have a relatively low access to credit, and large segments of the population (mostly female, the poor in rural areas, and young adults) have low access to financial services. Addressing these issues would require a comprehensive and holistic approach that could leverage recent fintech developments and the opportunities offered by digitalization, as envisaged in the National Strategy for Financial Inclusion launched by the Bank Al-Maghrib and Morocco's Ministry of Economy and Finance. In particular, the adoption of innovative technological solutions could help overcome traditional limits to the provision of financial services and credit to micro, small, and medium enterprises, including by facilitating credit information and reducing the financial and administrative costs linked to the low amounts and perceived risks of this type of lending.

The last chapter of the book, by Dominique Fayad, Gregory Auclair, and Ananta Dua, focuses on one of the most important challenges that Morocco faces going forward, namely the need to improve the quality of its education system. Although Morocco has made considerable progress in improving access to education, learning outcomes (as measured by students' scores on international tests and dropout rates) remain comparatively weak and skill mismatches are widely recognized as a key factor behind the elevated level of youth unemployment. The low fiscal space since the pandemic crisis means that improving the efficiency of public spending on education is key to boosting education results. The chapter shows that significant efficiency gains could be obtained by improving the quality of budget management, enhancing teachers' incentives and overall education levels, and strengthening institutional and governance quality. Encouragingly, these measures are included in the reforms announced by Morocco under the Education's Strategic Reform Vision 2015–2030 and envisaged in the *New Model of Development Report*.

These chapters describe most but not all of the dimensions of Morocco's planned transition to a new model of economic development. Among the new reforms that Morocco has launched recently and that, despite not being discussed in detail in this book, are an integral part of its transition to a new model of development are the following:

- *The reform of the social protection system.* This reform entails extending health care insurance to about 22 million Moroccans currently excluded, replacing the remaining subsidies with more targeted transfers thanks to the introduction of a unified social registry, strengthening the unemployment insurance system, and changing the pension system to bolster its financial viability with greater coverage for Moroccan elderly.

- *Health care reform.* The supply of health care is also undergoing a deep restructuring, with the introduction of new regional health care centers under the direction of a new national health authority, the reinforcement of health care supply through new hospitals and more personnel, and measures to improve system efficiency (e.g., encouraging the use of family doctors and local practices, and facilitating the exchange of patient information through better use of digitalization).

- *The overhaul of Morocco's SOEs.* This reform aims at refocusing the business model and strengthening the governance of Moroccan SOEs by eliminating those whose mission is deemed no longer essential and corporatizing those with commercial activities. The reform also introduces a national agency responsible for the valorization and strategic management of SOEs, as well as the continuous monitoring of their performance.

The IMF has been a close partner of Morocco throughout the last decade, including through four successive Precautionary and Liquidity Line arrangements from 2012 to 2019, and remains committed to supporting the implementation of this wide-reaching set of reforms in several ways.[1] By leveraging its expertise

---

[1] The first two-year Precautionary and Liquidity Line was approved in August 2012 and was followed by three arrangements until March 2020, when Morocco drew on all resources available (about US$ 3 billion) during the COVID-19 pandemic.

and drawing lessons from other countries that went through similar changes in the past, the Fund can help Morocco design a smooth transition to an inflation-targeting monetary policy regime and a debt-anchored fiscal rule. Regular surveillance activity can help to assess the macroeconomic impact of the reforms; this information can help to advise the authorities on policies, including, for example, to ensure that their funding will not jeopardize macroeconomic stability. On the financing side, the approval of a new precautionary Flexible Credit Line in April 2023 allows Morocco to benefit from an extra layer of insurance against the risk of severe adverse shocks, which could not only damage Morocco's economy but also hinder policymakers' ability to continue implementing their structural reform agenda. It is our hope that this book will also contribute to advancing the ongoing discussion around Morocco's quest for a more resilient and dynamic model of economic development—one where the benefits of economic growth are shared more equally across the entire population and all Moroccans have a fair shot at realizing their ambitions and fulfilling their aspirations.

PART I

Morocco: Past Reforms and Agenda for Change

CHAPTER 1

Morocco: 20 Years of Reforms

Maximilien Queyranne

INTRODUCTION

Morocco entered the new millennium having dramatically improved a vast set of socioeconomic indicators. Life expectancy had risen to levels close to advanced economies, and the infant mortality rate had fallen dramatically. Significant progress had been made in raising income levels, fighting poverty, and improving access to education. High levels of public sector investment had permitted building high-quality infrastructure, a necessary condition for the development of the private sector. A wave of reforms opened Morocco to international trade, attracted foreign investments in key global value chains, strengthened public finances, modernized the monetary policy framework, and improved governance in several sectors of the Moroccan economy.

But the last two decades have also exposed Morocco to a series of global and regional shocks that have severely tested its macroeconomic stability. Between 2008 and 2012, the global financial crisis, the euro area crisis, the increase in international prices of energy and food products, and regional tensions linked to the Arab Spring all challenged Morocco's macroeconomic stability and required decisive actions. The reforms cited earlier, and that will be described in this chapter, helped Morocco weather these shocks and gradually reabsorb the external and fiscal imbalances that they created.

Over the past three years, another series of severe negative shocks hit Morocco. The combined effect of the pandemic and the drought led to a historic contraction of economic activity and a sharp increase in the unemployment rate in 2020. A very successful vaccination campaign and prompt fiscal, monetary, and financial policy measures managed to mitigate the economic and social impacts of the shocks and paved the way for the strong economic rebound in 2021. As Morocco and the whole world were recovering from the health crisis, the economic fallout of Russia's invasion of Ukraine and another drought tested the resilience of the Moroccan economy once more in 2022, requiring new measures to protect the sectors most hit by the terms-of-trade shock and the resurgence of inflation.

Despite the remarkable resilience of the Moroccan economy, the latest shocks have emphasized that achieving stronger, more resilient, and more inclusive economic growth will require a new wave of reforms. Even before the pandemic, the reliance on public sector investment had become less effective in catalyzing economic growth and in generating employment opportunities. Raising living standards for all Moroccans would require accelerating the development of the private sector and strengthening Morocco's human capital. Cognizant of these challenges, the Moroccan authorities launched in 2020 a new series of deep structural reforms that are consistent with the gradual transition to a New Model of Development (see Chapter 2). Implementing such transition while rebuilding the macroeconomic policy space used between 2020 and 2022 will be a key challenge for Moroccan policymakers in the years to come.

This chapter first presents an overview of the progress achieved by Morocco in improving socioeconomic outcomes over the past few decades. It then examines the measures taken to address the macroeconomic imbalances that followed the shocks between 2008 and 2012; the strong policy response to the more recent challenges; and the reforms needed to catalyze a new growth model for Morocco to further enhance living standards and create opportunities for all.

IMPROVING ECONOMIC AND SOCIAL OUTCOMES

Living conditions have improved markedly in Morocco over the past decades (Figure 1.1). Life expectancy rose by almost 30 years since 1960 and is above the MENAP (Middle East, North Africa, Afghanistan, and Pakistan) average. The infant mortality rate also plummeted, as well as maternal death rates, which are now below the average in MENAP countries. This performance was achieved despite health spending below that in most MENAP countries, leading to a comparatively low supply of health services (as measured by hospital beds, physicians, and nurses) and high out-of-pocket spending. The ongoing efforts to provide

Figure 1.1. Living Conditions

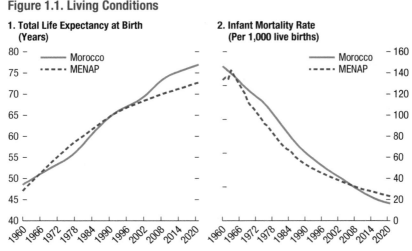

Sources: World Bank, World Development Indicators; and IMF staff calculations.
Note: MENAP = Middle East, North Africa, Afghanistan, and Pakistan.

universal health care insurance, along with the comprehensive reform of the governance of the health care system, are expected to improve access and quality of health care services and further strengthen health outcomes (see IMF 2023).

Morocco also has greatly improved living standards (Figure 1.2). Real gross domestic product (GDP) per capita almost doubled since the late 1990s, allowing Morocco to outpace lower-middle-income countries in the MENAP region. Poverty rates were reduced fourfold and were significantly lower than in the rest of the region in 2014. Morocco spends comparatively more on social assistance (2.5 percent of GDP in 2020) than the MENAP country average (1 percent of GDP), but this spending is dispersed around a myriad of programs that are not

Figure 1.2. Social Outcomes

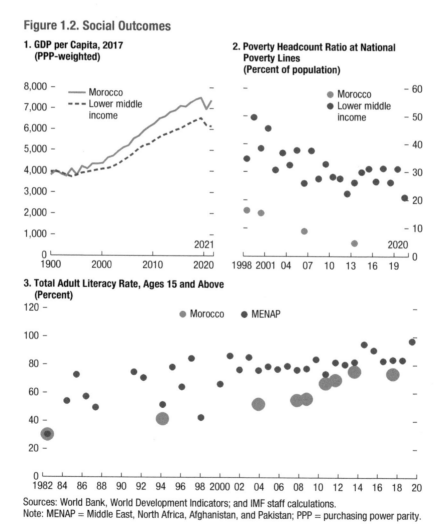

Sources: World Bank, World Development Indicators; and IMF staff calculations.
Note: MENAP = Middle East, North Africa, Afghanistan, and Pakistan; PPP = purchasing power parity.

Figure 1.3. Educational Outcomes

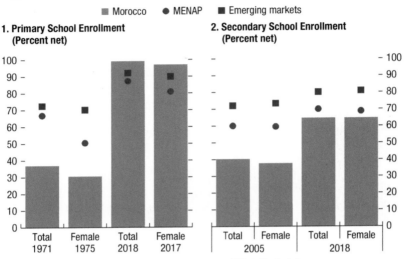

Sources: World Bank, World Development Indicators; and IMF staff calculations.
Note: MENAP = Middle East, North Africa, Afghanistan, and Pakistan.

necessarily well targeted. The authorities announced a reform of the social protection system aimed at harmonizing the existing programs into a major extension of the conditional cash transfer scheme (*allocation familiales*) particularly to low-income families with children, whereas the planned introduction of the Unified Social Registry in 2023 aims at targeting assistance to those who most need it (see IMF 2023).

Educational opportunities were expanded significantly. Adult literacy rates soared over the past 40 years (Figure 1.2, panel 3), although they were below the average for MENAP countries in 2018. Access to primary education has been extended significantly (Figure 1.3) and has become almost universal, with net enrollment rates above averages for the region and other emerging markets. Access to secondary school also improved considerably, although net enrollment rates are below regional averages. Despite these results, several indicators point to the need to strengthen the quality of human capital in Morocco and fill remaining education gaps (see Chapter 11).

Over the past few decades, Morocco accumulated a comparatively large capital stock and greatly improved the quality of its infrastructure. Public and private capital stock reached 286 percent of GDP in 2019, about 60 percent of GDP higher than MENAP countries on average (Figure 1.4). This reflects both sustained government investment and the central role of state-owned enterprises in infrastructure provision (recorded in private investment). As a result, Morocco's infrastructure quality is higher than regional peers and comparable to advanced countries in air transport, roads, and ports (Figure 1.5).

Figure 1.4. Investment and Capital Stock

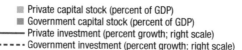

■ Private capital stock (percent of GDP)
■ Government capital stock (percent of GDP)
—— Private investment (percent growth; right scale)
- - - - Government investment (percent growth; right scale)

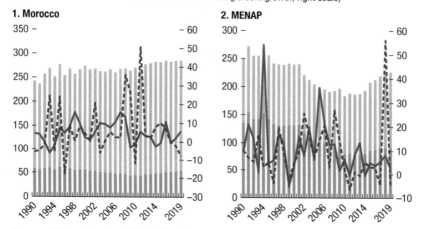

1. Morocco

2. MENAP

Sources: IMF Investment and Capital Stock Dataset; and IMF staff calculations.
Note: MENAP = Middle East, North Africa, Afghanistan, and Pakistan.

Figure 1.5. Capital Stock and Infrastructure Quality, Latest Value Available
(Ranking; 1 = best, 144 = worst)

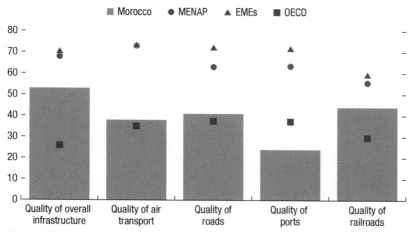

■ Morocco   ● MENAP   ▲ EMEs   ■ OECD

Sources: IMF, Investment and Capital Stock Dataset; and World Economic Forum.
Note: EMEs = emerging market economies; MENAP = Middle East, North Africa, Afghanistan, and Pakistan; OECD = Organisation for Economic Co-operation and Development.

REDUCING MACROECONOMIC IMBALANCES AND TRANSFORMING THE ECONOMY DURING 2012 AND 2019

From 2008 to 2012, Morocco experienced a series of negative shocks. The 2008 global financial crisis impacted Morocco mostly through the slowdown in external demand from Europe, its main trading partner, and rising oil prices (IMF 2015a). Financial channels played a limited role because the exposition of the Moroccan economy to international markets was limited. Although Morocco weathered this shock by easing fiscal and monetary policies, the debt crisis that took place in the European Union in 2009–10, the sociopolitical tensions that arose in 2011 in the context of the Arab Spring, and the significant rise in oil and food prices all caused large internal and external imbalances. Morocco's twin deficits surged as the negative terms of trade shock worsened the current account balance to 9.5 percent of GDP in 2012, while the surge in energy subsidies and wage spending pushed the fiscal deficit to 7.2 percent of GDP during the same year. As a result, in 2012 public debt rose to 58.2 percent of GDP (+16.7 percentage points of GDP from 2010) and international reserves declined to 4.1 months of imports and below levels considered as appropriate under the IMF's reserve adequacy metric (Figure 1.6). The emergence of macroeconomic vulnerabilities was met with a series of policies and reforms that modernized Morocco's economy, restored internal and external balances, and helped strengthen resilience.

Improving Morocco's External Position and Competitiveness

By 2019, Morocco's current account deficit fell by about 6 percentage points of GDP to 3.7 percent (Figure 1.7). While the fall in international energy prices in the second half of the last decade contributed to the adjustment by almost

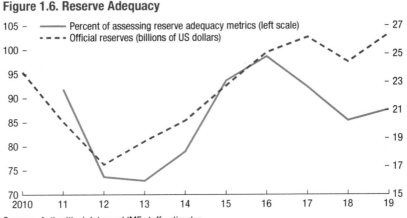

Figure 1.6. Reserve Adequacy

Sources: Authorities' data; and IMF staff estimates.

Figure 1.7. Cumulative Current Account Adjustment, 2012–19
(Percent of GDP)

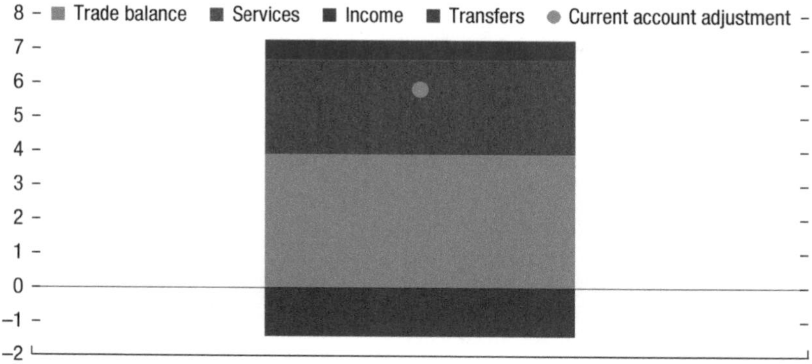

Sources: Authorities' data; and IMF staff estimates.

halving Morocco's energy bill, the improvement in the external position also reflected the impact of measures that have significantly changed the composition of Moroccan exports. In particular, the improvement in the current account deficit also reflected a much stronger contribution of net services. Although tourism remained Morocco's main export service, the positive contribution of net services to the current account adjustment also reflected the development of business services (including consultancy, and information and communication technology).

As Morocco rebuilt its external buffers, it gradually increased its capital account openness. In nominal terms, official reserves increased by more than 50 percent over 2012–19 and almost reached their pre–Arab Spring position as measured by the IMF's reserve adequacy metric. This comfortable external position allowed Morocco to gradually ease its system of capital controls for inward investments. This helped boost foreign direct investments, which averaged almost 4 percent of GDP over the period 2010–19, with a growing share benefiting manufacturing (from 15 to 37 percent of total foreign direct investments over the same period).

The greater openness to foreign direct investments and trade accelerated the process of diversification of Morocco's export base as the country joined highly sophisticated global value chains, such as automotive, aerospace, and electronics. This reflected relatively low production costs but also an extremely efficient and proactive set of industrial policies, which included setting up special economic zones, tax incentives, investment subsidies, and training incentives but also the conclusion of free trade agreements with the EU and the US. The Industrial Acceleration Plan launched in 2014 was aimed at better integrating global value chains into the domestic economy, increasing job creation and the domestic value-added content in exports. This strategy has completely changed

Figure 1.8. Export Diversification

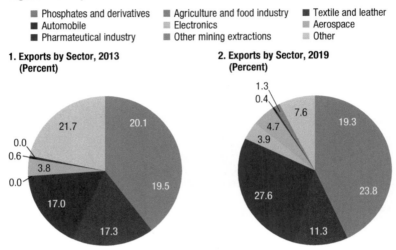

■ Phosphates and derivatives ■ Agriculture and food industry ■ Textile and leather
■ Automobile ▩ Electronics ■ Aerospace
■ Pharmateutical industry ■ Other mining extractions ▩ Other

**1. Exports by Sector, 2013
(Percent)**

21.7 20.1 0.0 0.6 3.8 0.0 19.5 17.0 17.3

**2. Exports by Sector, 2019
(Percent)**

1.3 0.4 7.6 4.7 3.9 19.3 27.6 23.8 11.3

Sources: Authorities' data; and IMF staff estimates.

Morocco's gross export composition, with machinery and electrical goods and transportation goods becoming the dominant exports (accounting for 40 percent of total exports in 2019 compared to 3 percent in 1995), replacing textiles (accounting for 12 percent of total exports in 2019 compared to about 20 percent in 1995). The three global value chain sectors (automotive, aerospace, and electronics) accounted for 36 percent of exports in 2019 versus 21 percent in 2013 (Figure 1.8).

Strengthening Public Finances

On the fiscal front, spending rationalization allowed to reduce the overall deficit. The budget deficit fell by 3.5 percentage points of GDP over 2012–19, mostly reflecting lower current expenditure (–4.9 percentage points of GDP), as public investment was broadly stable and tax revenues fell. The subsidy reform brought most of the savings, with efforts to contain public wage bill contributing to a lesser extent.

Between 2000 and 2012, prices of fuel products in Morocco were administered and set below international market prices by the government, with infrequent and ad hoc price adjustments. In 2012, as rising international oil prices drove the cost of fuel and food subsidies to 6.5 percent of GDP, the government decided to phase out subsidies (Figure 1.9). A first increase in the retail prices of diesel, gasoline, and fuel prices was introduced in 2013, yielding an estimated saving of 0.7 percent of GDP. As international energy prices fell, the government accelerated the removal of subsidies on gasoline, industrial fuel, oil, and diesel,

Figure 1.9. Change in Fiscal Deficit, 2012–19
(Percent of GDP)

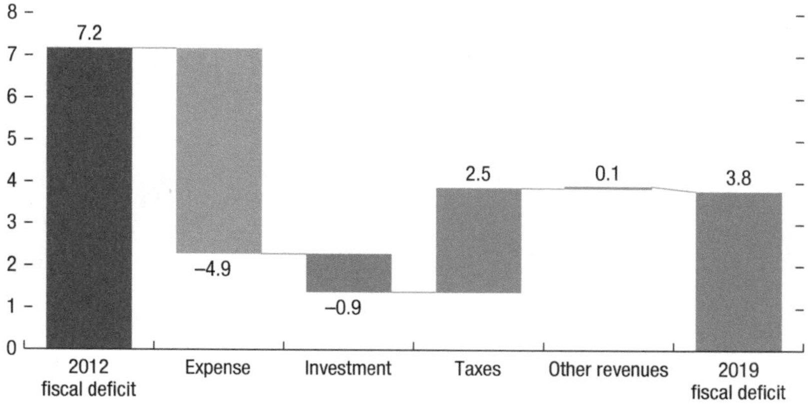

Sources: Authorities' data; and IMF staff estimates.

which were completely deregulated in 2015 (IMF 2015b). To mitigate the social impact of this reform, the government developed a diversified set of social programs, including for education (Tayssir) and health care (RAMED), while maintaining subsidies to wheat, sugar, and butane to protect the most vulnerable populations. As a result, energy subsidies declined by 4.6 percentage points of GDP and were brought below 1 percent of GDP on average from 2015 to 2019. In addition, across-the-board wage and recruitment containment measures gradually reduced the public wage bill spending by 1.4 percent of GDP between 2012 and 2019, although Morocco fell short of undertaking a comprehensive civil service reform that would generate more permanent savings and increase the efficiency of public services.

From public pension to expenditure management, fiscal structural reforms were also accelerated. In 2015, Morocco introduced parametric changes to improve the viability of the government employees' pension system (*Caisse Marocaine de Retraites*), by gradually increasing contributory rates (from 11 percent to 14 percent of salary), the retirement age (from 60 years old to 63 years old), and reference wages (from the last 2 years to the last 8 years of work). The authorities also adopted the new Organic Budget Law in 2015, which provided the legal backing for multiyear budget planning, program budgeting, and accrual accounting. Fiscal decentralization was accelerated with the adoption of the Organic Budget Law for local government in 2015 and of the law to strengthen the role of Regional Investment Centers in 2018. Finally, Morocco put in place the first and most developed gender budgeting initiative in the Middle East and Central Asia region to make fiscal policy more inclusive.

Figure 1.10. Treasury Bonds Yields and Spreads

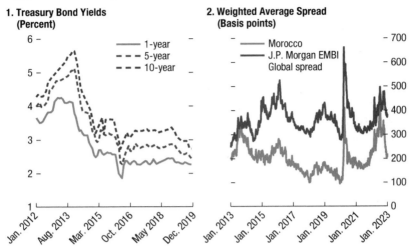

Sources: Haver; Bloomberg; and IMF staff calculations.
Note: EMBI = Emerging Market Bond Index.

As a result of these efforts, the ratio of central government debt to GDP fell from about 62 percent in 2013 to about to 58.5 percent in 2015 and remained relatively stable thereafter. During this period, Morocco also improved the structure of its public debt by reducing both the share of short-term debt (from 6.5 to 1.5 percent of total debt) and that of external debt (from 23.5 to 21.5 percent). The government yield curve in the domestic market also fell and flattened at the long end, pointing to more favorable sentiments toward sovereign risks (Figure 1.10). The authorities tapped international markets four times over this period both in US dollars (3 billion) and euros (3 billion) and benefited from a gradual decline in Morocco's international sovereign bond spreads, which were consistently lower than other emerging markets on average.

Upgrading the Monetary Policy Framework and Financial Sector Supervision

In the 2000s, Morocco's central bank gained a high level of autonomy and successfully anchored inflation expectations while easing financial conditions. The central bank's charter adopted in 2017 provides Bank Al-Maghrib (BAM) with an effective governance structure and operational independence to pursue its mandate while ensuring adequate accountability and transparency. The charter made price stability the primary monetary policy objective of the central bank, ruled out monetary financing of the deficit, and granted the Board full decision powers on monetary policy without interference from the government. BAM built strong credibility in keeping inflation low and stable and in anchoring inflation expectations around 2 percent from 2012 to 2019 (Figure 1.11). It gradually reduced its policy rate by 100 basis points and reserve requirements from 6 to 2 percent, which brought down interbank money market rates. Deposit rates steadily declined in line with the policy rate without hurting bank funding (Queyranne and others 2021), and lending rates became more supportive to borrowing by households and firms.

Figure 1.11. Monetary Developments

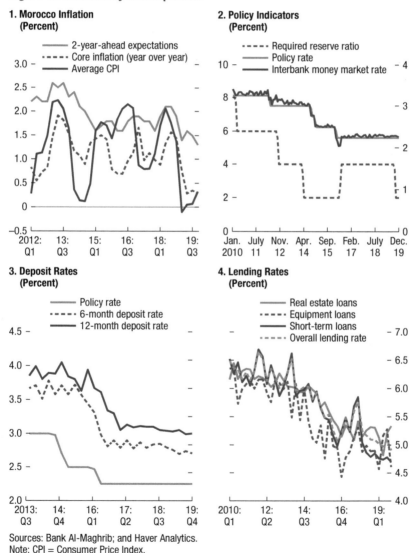

Sources: Bank Al-Maghrib; and Haver Analytics.
Note: CPI = Consumer Price Index.

At the same time, Morocco started a gradual transition to greater exchange rate flexibility and made progress in developing the fundamental elements of an inflation-targeting framework. As part of such a transition, the authorities increased the exchange rate band to ±2.5 percent from ±0.6 percent in January 2018 vis-à-vis a basket comprising the euro and the US dollar. During this period, spot exchange rate volatility gradually increased, and Morocco developed a solid hedging market (relative to its financial development). Limited currency mismatch in the financial sector and modest unhedged exposures to exchange rate risk in the nonfinancial private sector also provide a conducive environment to stronger exchange rate flexibility.

With IMF technical assistance, BAM developed tools to produce macroeconomic forecasts and policy simulations (Achour and others 2021) and implemented comprehensive transparency practices, including by improving communication with external stakeholders on its policy framework, objectives, and governance structure. This enhanced level of transparency enabled BAM to strengthen the trust of the stakeholders and its own autonomy (IMF 2022a).

Several reforms improved the resilience of Morocco's banking sector. The implementation of Basel III standards from 2013 improved banks' capital and liquidity ratios, whereas the adoption from 2018 of IFRS9 criteria on loan classification and provisioning helped maintain comfortable levels of provisioning against persistently high levels of nonperforming loans (Figure 1.12). In the past

Figure 1.12. Financial Sector Developments

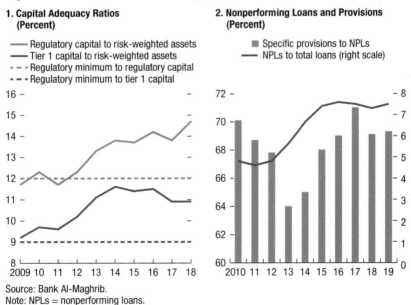

1. Capital Adequacy Ratios
(Percent)

— Regulatory capital to risk-weighted assets
— Tier 1 capital to risk-weighted assets
- - - Regulatory minimum to regulatory capital
- - - Regulatory minimum to tier 1 capital

2. Nonperforming Loans and Provisions
(Percent)

■ Specific provisions to NPLs
— NPLs to total loans (right scale)

Source: Bank Al-Maghrib.
Note: NPLs = nonperforming loans.

decade, the largest Moroccan banks expanded their operations abroad, particularly in sub-Saharan Africa, bringing new business opportunities and promoting greater diversification of the financial sector. BAM played a major role in guiding and supervising this expansion, helping Morocco develop into an international financial hub while ensuring appropriate risk control.

Finally, more stringent regulatory and macroprudential supervision reinforced financial stability. Solid progress was made to strengthen financial sector oversight with the adoption of the Banking Law in 2014, the establishment of the Systemic Risks Coordination and Monitoring Committee, and the development of a macroprudential policy framework that includes systemic risk mapping, stress-testing, and an emergency liquidity assistance framework. BAM assumed a leading role in ensuring financial stability, because the governor chairs the Systemic Risks Coordination and Monitoring Committee, which coordinates financial institutions' supervision and regulation, assesses and prevents systemic risks, and coordinates crisis resolution measures. The stress-testing framework was strengthened following the 2015 Financial Stability Assessment (IMF 2016), and BAM began to run and regularly publish macro stress tests in its reports. Between 2013 and 2016, Morocco also reinforced the independence of the capital market authority and created new supervisory authorities for insurance and pensions.

Modernizing the Moroccan Economy

Ambitious reforms were launched to improve the business environment. A competition council was instituted in 2014 and became fully operational in 2019 to help limit anti-competitive behaviors and monopolies. Morocco also enacted a new bankruptcy law in 2018 and dematerialized administrative process in areas such as starting a business or transferring property. Efforts to improve small and medium enterprises' (SMEs) access to credit were accelerated, with BAM granting advances and refinancing banks that provide investment loans to SMEs from 2013. These reforms provided a more business-friendly environment that allowed the number of new entrants to increase in retail, construction, real estate, and services during the last decade (World Bank 2019).

Finally, Morocco also made progress in enhancing public sector governance, transparency, and accountability, including (1) the adoption of the National Strategy Against Corruption in 2015, which set up a new National Agency for the prevention of and fight against corruption; (2) the passing of a new information access law in 2019, which required public entities to publish more information and granted citizens the right to request access to public documents; (3) the design of the National Plan for the Reform of Public Administration (2018–21), which improved budgetary and human resource management and led to a simplification of administrative procedures also based on the digitalization of public administration (including through the introduction of a unified internet portal for Moroccan citizens and the centralization of data from different registries such as the ones on population, justice, land, and property); and (4) the implementation of the

Organic Budget Law approved in 2015, which included measures to strengthen the oversight role of parliament and the Court of Accounts (*Cour des Comptes*), thereby reinforcing public accountability.

MOROCCO'S RESPONSE TO THE 2020–22 SHOCKS

The reforms undertaken between 2012 and 2019 help explain Morocco's resilience to the numerous shocks that hit its economy over the past three years. Before the pandemic, inflation was low and stable (1 percent at end-2019), the current account deficit had fallen to around 3.5 percent of GDP with international reserves at about 7 months of imports, and the fiscal deficit and public debt were stabilized at around 3½ and 60 percent of GDP, respectively.

In 2020, Morocco experienced the most severe economic recession in its recent history, with real GDP contracting by 7.2 percent, as the drought severely curbed agricultural production and the COVID-19 crisis curtailed both external and domestic demand, particularly in a key sector of Morocco's economy such as tourism.

The authorities responded promptly to these shocks, using the macroeconomic policy space built in the past. In addition to the successful vaccination campaign, the policy response included a mix of fiscal and monetary measures that contributed to alleviate the social and economic impact of the crisis:

- *Fiscal policy:* The fiscal response was both innovative and efficient because it targeted those sectors and households that were affected most by the crisis while minimizing the burden on the budget. This was possible thanks to the creation of a special COVID-19 fund, of about 3 percent of GDP, financed mainly by voluntary contributions from public and private entities. This fund covered the additional health care costs related to the pandemic and funded cash transfers to about 5 million households in the informal sectors, which were reached by using mobile payment technology. Other forms of support included (1) the deferment of tax and social contribution payments, (2) wage subsidies for employees who were temporary furloughed, and (3) accelerated payment to government suppliers. In addition, Morocco introduced funding-for-lending schemes that provided about 5 percent of GDP in loans to SMEs at subsidized interest rates with government guarantees.

- *Monetary and financial policy:* BAM took unprecedented measures to support the economy, ensure financial stability, and strengthen Morocco's external position (Figure 1.13). The central bank reduced its policy rate by 75 basis points in 2020 and increased liquidity provision to the banking sector by easing refinancing conditions and bringing reserve requirements to zero. BAM also temporarily eased the liquidity coverage ratio requirements and reduced capital requirements by lowering the capital conservation buffer by 50 basis points, while restricting banks' dividend payments. In the

Figure 1.13. Bank Al-Maghrib's Monetary Interventions
(Billions of dirhams)

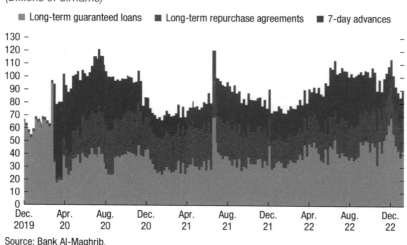

■ Long-term guaranteed loans   ■ Long-term repurchase agreements   ■ 7-day advances

Source: Bank Al-Maghrib.

wake of the pandemic, the authorities broadened the dirham's fluctuation band to ±5 percent (from ±2.5 percent) and purchased all available resources (about 3 percent of GDP) under the Precautionary and Liquidity Line arrangement. All in all, BAM's balance sheet expanded by 25 percent at the end of 2020 compared to the year before.

These strong policy actions allowed Morocco's economy to rebound quickly from the pandemic. In 2021, GDP grew at 7.9 percent and recovered most of the ground lost the previous year. The return to average good weather conditions and the strong increase in remittances provided a substantial boost to private consumption. The strong expansion in foreign demand and the gradual recovery of world trade led to a sharp rebound in goods exports, particularly automotive and electronic products. The current account deficit (that had collapsed to 1.2 percent in 2020 largely due to import compression) widened again but remained well below pre-pandemic levels, and international reserves increased by US$11 billion relative to the end of 2019.[1]

Just as the country was recovering from the pandemic, a new round of negative shocks hit Morocco's economy in 2022 (IMF 2023). The third drought in five

---

[1] This is despite Morocco's early repayment to the IMF in 2021 of about one third of the amount withdrawn under the Precautionary and Liquidity Line arrangement in March 2020 and reflects (1) the issuance of US dollar-denominated Treasury bonds in international markets at the end of 2020, (2) the purchase of foreign currency from BAM in the second half of 2021 (as the dirham appreciated at the lower end of the band), and (3) the allocation of additional special drawing rights from the IMF.

years resulted in a sharp decline in cereals production, while the spillovers from Russia's invasion of Ukraine reduced external demand and increased inflation pressures. As a result, economic growth slowed to 1.1 percent and the current account deficit widened to 4.3 percent of GDP, while inflation accelerated to 8.3 percent year over year at the end of 2022.

The authorities responded by tightening both their fiscal and monetary policy stances while protecting the most vulnerable populations from the impact of these new shocks. The central bank increased its policy rate by 100 basis points to 2.5 percent in December 2022 to keep inflation expectations well anchored in a context of high levels of inflation. Fiscal policy was aimed at mitigating the impact of the shocks through a series of measures that included higher energy and wheat subsidies, cash transfers to the transportation sector (to prevent a greater pass through of higher energy prices), and credit support to the agricultural sector.

Although the strong response of Morocco's policymakers has managed to mitigate the economic and social impact of the recent shocks, this resilience came at the cost of a significant erosion of the country's macroeconomic policy buffers. Monetary policy is focused on its primary objective to reduce inflation, and it will have limited room to support the economy. Fiscal policy will need to balance its support to growth with the need to rebuild the fiscal space used over the past few years and bring government debt toward pre-pandemic levels. In this context, accelerating the reforms to modernize the Moroccan economy is key to safeguard resilience and further improve living standards.

CONCLUSION

The last two decades have witnessed not only Morocco's strong resilience but also increasing evidence that its traditional growth model has run out of steam. The shift from agriculture to manufacturing and services, which typically characterizes economic development and brings about lower growth volatility, greater job opportunities, and higher overall productivity, has leveled off starting from 2010 (Pinto Moreira 2019). Although large public investment (mostly undertaken by state-owned enterprises) (IMF 2021) has developed the country's infrastructure network, the growth return on this type of investment is weaker than in comparable countries and has worsened over the past decade (Figure 1.14). GDP growth has slowed from an average of about 5 percent between 2000 and 2009 to 3.5 percent in the following decade. To some extent, this also reflects the more frequent occurrence of droughts in this period, which has reduced the contribution to growth from the agricultural sector.

Slower growth also means that Morocco's labor market has struggled to create a sufficiently large number of jobs. The intensity of growth in employment has declined over the last decade, with a 1 percent output growth generating around 60,000 net jobs during the 2010s compared with around

Figure 1.14. Morocco's Growth Model

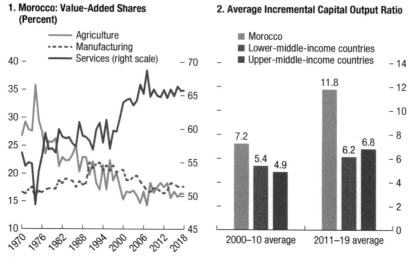

**1. Morocco: Value-Added Shares
(Percent)**

— Agriculture
- - - - Manufacturing
— Services (right scale)

2. Average Incremental Capital Output Ratio

■ Morocco
■ Lower-middle-income countries
■ Upper-middle-income countries

Sources: Haver Analytics; Moroccan authorities; and IMF staff estimates.

150,000 net jobs in the 2000s. As a result, the job market was unable to absorb the increase in the working-age population (World Bank 2022). The overall unemployment rate has stabilized at an average of about 10 percent over the past two decades, whereas labor force participation declined to particularly very low levels for women and youth. Finally, the informal sector is estimated to represent about 80 percent of total employment and one-third of output, reflecting the large role of the agricultural sector, a still-low level of education, the country's relatively young population, and remaining policy distortions (IMF 2022b).

To address these challenges, a new wave of structural reforms is needed to catalyze a different growth model. In 2021, the Royal Commission on the New Model of Development proposed an ambitious agenda of reforms to modernize the Moroccan economy (Commission on the New Model of Development 2021, and Chapter 2). It aims to make the private sector the new engine of growth by removing barriers to entry, improving competitiveness, and reforming state-owned enterprises to reduce their role in the economy. The report also recommends improving human capital and youth and women, encouraging formalization, and reinforcing inclusion to boost productivity and support Morocco's economic development. Implementing these reforms while navigating the still-uncertain global outlook and rebuilding the space needed to face future shocks will define Morocco's policies over the next few years.

REFERENCES

Achour, Aya, Ales Bulir, Omar Chafik, and Adam Reno. 2021. "The Morocco Policy Analysis Model: Theoretical Framework and Policy Scenarios." IMF Working Paper 21/122, International Monetary Fund, Washington, DC.

Commission on the New Model of Development. 2021. "The New Development Model—Releasing Energies and Regaining Trust to Accelerate the March of Progress and Prosperity for All." General Report. Kingdom of Morocco. https://www.csmd.ma/documents/CSMD_Report_EN.pdf.

International Monetary Fund (IMF). 2015a. "Morocco: Ex Post Evaluation of Exceptional Access Under the 2012 Precautionary and Liquidity Line Arrangement." IMF Country Report 15/231, International Monetary Fund, Washington, DC.

International Monetary Fund (IMF). 2015b. "Morocco: 2014 Article IV Consultation—Staff Report." IMF Country Report 15/43, International Monetary Fund, Washington, DC.

International Monetary Fund (IMF). 2016. "Morocco: Financial System Stability Assessment." IMF Country Report 16/37, International Monetary Fund, Washington, DC.

International Monetary Fund (IMF). 2018. "Public Wage Bills in the Middle East and Central Asia." IMF Middle East and Central Asian Department Paper, International Monetary Fund, Washington, DC.

International Monetary Fund (IMF). 2021. "State-Owned Enterprises in Middle East, North Africa, and Central Asia: Size, Costs, and Challenges." IMF Departmental Paper 21/019, International Monetary Fund, Washington, DC.

International Monetary Fund (IMF). 2022a. "Morocco: Central Bank Transparency Code Review." IMF Country Report 2022/380, International Monetary Fund, Washington, DC.

International Monetary Fund (IMF). 2022b. "Informality, Development, and the Business Cycle in North Africa." IMF Departmental Paper 22/011, International Monetary Fund, Washington, DC.

International Monetary Fund (IMF). 2023. "Morocco: 2022 Article IV Consultation—Staff Report." IMF Country Report 23/042, International Monetary Fund, Washington, DC.

Morocco's High Committee for Education, Training and Scientific Research. 2018. "Morocco 2018 PISA National Report."

Pinto Moreira, Emmanuel. 2019. "Morocco's Growth and Employment Prospects—Public Policies to Avoid the Middle-Income Trap." Policy Research Working Paper 8769, World Bank Group, Washington, DC.

Queyranne, Maximilien, Daniel Baksa, Vassili Bazinas, and Azhin Abdulkarim. 2021. "Morocco's Monetary Policy Transmission in the Wake of the Pandemic." IMF Working Paper 21/249, International Monetary Fund, Washington, DC.

World Bank. 2019. "Creating Markets in Morocco—A Second Generation of Reforms: Boosting Private Sector Growth, Job Creation and Skills Upgrading." Country Private Sector Diagnostic, World Bank Group, Washington, DC. https://documents1.worldbank.org/curated/en/228331567687617816/pdf/Creating-Markets-in-Morocco-a-Second-Generation-of-Reforms-Boosting-Private-Sector-Growth-Job-Creation-and-Skills-Upgrading.pdf.

World Bank. 2022. "Paysage de l'Emploi au Maroc—Recenser les Obstacles à un Marché du Travail Inclusif. " World Bank Group, Washington, DC. https://openknowledge.worldbank.org/handle/10986/35075?locale-attribute=fr.

CHAPTER 2

Morocco's New Development Model: Charting the Course for a Human-Capital–Led Development

Chakib Benmoussa

INTRODUCTION

In November 2019, a Special Commission on the Development Model (SCDM) was established by King Mohammed VI of Morocco to think through and elaborate a new development model for the country. This chapter discusses the features of this commission, its unique process, and how it led collectively to proposing a new human-capital-led development model.

Morocco's rethinking of its development model did not start with the SCDM. It dates back to 2017, when King Mohammed VI highlighted the country's slow development and limited growth and called on all stakeholders to rethink Morocco's development model. Since then, several contributions and debates have focused on the topic, confirming the country's capacity to look inward. Ten years after adopting a new constitution, Morocco stands as a pioneer in rethinking its development model and charting the course for promising development perspectives.

The SCDM's mandate was to review the state of Morocco's development through a co-construction and participative approach involving all of its economic, political, civil, and social stakeholders. This review had to be (1) strategic, focusing on identifying and resolving systemic issues, particularly those behind the fatigue of the current development model; (2) global and integrated, focusing on development through its various dimensions, in concert with the principles and values stated by the constitution of Morocco; (3) forward looking, taking stock of mid- to long-term evolutions of the national and international contexts; and finally, (4) citizen centered, taking into account the country's realities, its assets, and its particularities.

The new development model (NDM) is the result of a participatory approach where Morocco's driving forces contributed through different channels. The NDM report, "Releasing Energies and Regaining Trust to Accelerate the March

---

The author is President of the Special Commission on the Development Model and current Minister of National Education, Preschool and Sports.

of Progress and Prosperity for All,"[1] brings a bold ambition that requires the full mobilization of the entire nation to be achieved.

The NDM report outlines a new development model, sets out a national ambition by 2035, and charts a realistic and achievable path for change. This ambition would allow the country to reach a new level of inclusive and sustainable growth.

Its objective is to suggest guiding principles and building blocks for an inclusive and transformative development strategy around which key players can rally. It is a vision meant as a catalyzer for reform to accelerate the rollout of priority development strategies to meet the desired goal.

The NDM takes the current constitution, voted on in 2011, as its framework. Its proposals fit under the spirit and content of the constitution, particularly in terms of its choice of democracy, separation and extent of institutional powers, values and norms, and development objectives.

The NDM report also draws on Morocco's millennial history, which has shaped the national identity and enriched it with a wide range of cultural influences. This depth of history underpins Morocco's distinctive nature as a crossroads of civilizations and a land of peace, dialogue, and coexistence, and predisposes the country to actively contribute to building this thriving new world.

ELABORATING THE NEW DEVELOPMENT MODEL

The NDM was elaborated by leveraging three perspectives. The first is a frank and clear-sighted diagnosis to identify the main bottlenecks explaining Morocco's slowdown in development. This diagnosis was made both using current analyses as well as consultations by citizens, institutional and economic stakeholders, and experts.

The second is a highlight of key citizens' expectations and aspirations for the future, as expressed during the consultation and hearings process. During this process, the SCDM sought to gather the country's achievements as perceived by citizens, and it heard about the obstacles hindering the country's development path through the eyes of Moroccans and in connection with their aspirations.

The third is a forward-looking approach to identify structural trends and transformations that are expected in the medium term, both at the national and international levels. The objective was to reposition all national evolutions into a deeply changing global context, and to consider the complexity and uncertainties such transformations entail.

Morocco's development trajectory witnessed a sustained development momentum starting in the mid-1990s before experiencing a slowdown in the late 2000s. Infrastructure modernization, the launch of ambitious sectoral strategies, and Morocco's commitment to an extensive renewable energy program provided sound economic policies and paved the way for the future. However, despite bold reforms undertaken to answer popular and political expectations in the wake of the 2011 Middle East and North Africa region upheavals and following the 2008

---

[1] The Special Commission on the Development Model, April 2021. www.csmd.ma/rapport-en.

> ### Box 2.1. Four Systemic Bottlenecks That Are Hindering Morocco's Development
>
> 1. The lack of vertical coherence between the development vision and the announced public policies, and the weak horizontal convergence between these policies
> 2. The sluggish pace of the economy's structural transformation, hampered by high input costs and barriers to entry for innovative and competitive new players
> 3. Limited public sector capacity in providing and ensuring access to high-quality public services in critical areas for citizens' daily lives, well-being, and empowerment
> 4. A sense of legal insecurity and unpredictability that limits initiatives, as a result of a perceived disconnect between legal "gray areas" and social realities on the ground, and because of a lack of citizens' trust in the justice system, a burdensome bureaucracy, and ineffective appeals
>
> Source: Author, based on Morocco's New Development Model, April 2021.

global financial crisis, a lack of trust gradually took hold in the country, fueled by the slowing economic growth and growing social inequalities.

This diagnosis was based on a review of the current development model to identify strengths, weaknesses, and areas for improvement, particularly through consultations with stakeholders and leveraging of existing literature. The diagnosis led to the identification of four systemic bottlenecks impeding Morocco's development (Box 2.1).

In line with the royal orientations of King Mohammed VI, the SCDM conducted extensive consultations with citizens and key players to ensure that all views and critical feedback from citizens were taken into consideration in designing the new model. It met with nearly 10,000 people over the 12 regions of the country, as well as Moroccans living abroad. During this process, a majority of citizens voiced concerns and expectations in these areas: the quality of public services, the access to economic opportunities and employment, and the effectiveness of good governance principles.

The NDM also took into consideration domestic and global changes projected by 2035, integrating associated risks and opportunities. Considering the upcoming complexity and uncertainty that the world is facing, there is a need for renewed governance models combining agility and anticipatory risk management.

At the national level, significant demographic, social, and environmental changes are projected. At the international level, fundamental changes are also likely to occur, some of which were accelerated by the COVID-19 pandemic. On the economic front, the world order is likely to undergo major changes, as competition between major powers intensifies and multilateralism weakens. The COVID-19 crisis and recent geopolitical tensions are likely to lead to shorter and regionally refocused global value chains, which will present important opportunities for Morocco.

Finally, regional and global epidemic risks are set to become frequent, which requires greater effectiveness and efficiency in meeting health care needs in an

> **Box 2.2. A Snapshot from the Main New Development Model Indicators**
>
> - The transition to a new level of GDP growth, of 6 percent on average annually, driven in particular by the added value of medium- and high-technology industrial activities (50 percent of industrial value added)
> - Doubling the GDP per capita by 2035 to reach 16,000 (dollars/purchasing power parity)
> - Raising the share of formal employment to 80 percent of total employment and doubling the activity rate of women to bring it to 45 percent
> - Mastery of basic learning by 75 percent of pupils at the age of 15
> - Raising the share of renewable energies to 40 percent of total energy consumption
> - The development of the digital sector to bring its share in the GDP to 5 percent
>
> Source: Author, based on Morocco's New Development Model, April 2021.

anticipatory approach. This also calls for renewing the business models of severely impacted sectors, such as tourism, and for greater sovereignty over key sectors, such as agriculture.

THE FOUNDING PILLARS OF THE NEW DEVELOPMENT MODEL: FROM AN AMBITION TO STRATEGIC DEVELOPMENT CHOICES

The NDM suggests a strong ambition for the country by 2035. Considering Morocco's assets, this ambition is within reach and can help mobilize the nation's driving forces. It can be summarized as follows:

> In 2035, Morocco is a democratic country where everyone can fully take control of their future and realize their potential, and live with dignity in an open, diverse, just, and equitable society. It is a country that creates value and develops its potential in a sustainable, shared, and responsible manner. Capitalizing on its significant progress at the national level, Morocco is established as an exemplary regional power at the forefront of the major challenges facing the world.

Achieving this ambition calls on simultaneously pursuing the following five objectives:

1. A *prosperous Morocco*, creating wealth and quality jobs to match its potential

2. A *skilled Morocco,* where all citizens have the capacities enabling them to take charge of their lives and contribute to value creation

3. An *inclusive Morocco*, offering opportunities and protection to all, where social ties are consolidated

4. A *sustainable Morocco*, where resources are preserved across all territories

5. A *bold Morocco*, as a regional leader in promising areas of the future

These objectives are backed by ambitious, yet achievable, quantitative targets (Box 2.2), which are likely to position Morocco into the first half, or even the upper third, of the main international rankings by 2035.

A New Organizational Doctrine as a Base for the Development Framework

The NDM brings about a new development framework that suggests renewed ways of doing things and of continuing its development. It also emphasizes the required capacities and means to reach higher levels of success in implementing reforms and projects and delivering results for citizens. This development framework is based on a new organizational doctrine that can federate common action and seal the stakeholders' commitments. This new doctrine redefines the role of the state and clarifies the stakeholder's responsibilities. It advocates for a complementarity and a balance between (1) a strong democratic state and (2) a strong plural society:

1. A state with reinforced strategic capacities, materialized by the effectiveness and efficiency of its policies, which guarantees the security, dignity, and freedoms of Moroccans and protects them in the face of weaknesses and crises

2. A plural society, fully mobilized and empowered, which values and leverages the capacities of the individuals and groups that compose it, is committed to defending the general interest, and devotes its efforts to promoting the values of good and responsible citizenship

The balance between a strong state and a strong society has implications for the roles of the main stakeholders: public, private, or third sector. It strengthens their legitimacy as well as their representativeness. It widens their scope of intervention and space for contribution to the creation of material and immaterial wealth. It empowers them in implementing the new model while promoting complementarity among the various stakeholders for increased effectiveness of the collective action.

This new organizational doctrine comes with common principles that should guide the action of all stakeholders. These principles aim to guarantee an effective and systematic implementation of the proposed doctrine and to ensure joint progress toward the development objectives. They embody the method, the *how*, of the NDM around five interconnected principles of action:

1. Focusing the action on citizen impact with results-driven actions

2. Adopting a systemic, co-constructive, and collaborative approach to development

3. Developing capacities of all stakeholders

4. Encouraging subsidiarity and territorial development

5. Ensuring environmental and financial sustainability of development projects

This new organizational doctrine calls for a framework of trust and responsibility to secure the stakeholders' commitments and to guarantee transparent rules that apply to all. It is based on (1) an independent and efficient justice that protects freedoms; (2) integrity, exemplarity, and ethics of the bearers of a public mission; (3) independent and efficient governance and economic regulation institutions; (4) access to information and accountability; and (5) a reinforced representative democracy that is in complementarity with the participative democracy and a larger citizen participation. The overall objective is to establish trust among citizens and institutions, between the political and economic spheres, and between the state and the civil society.

The Four Strategic Transformation Pillars of the Development Model

The NDM has identified four strategic pillars (Table 2.1) that stand as priority areas to meet the urgent needs of the citizens. These pillars are meant to trigger a new dynamic of value creation that structurally includes all citizens and territories, sustainably harnesses the country's potential, and seizes available opportunities. A number of these options consolidate current practices and accelerate ongoing reforms, whereas others break with the past, at least in method if not in direction, and require fundamental changes in mentality and approach.

TABLE 2.1.

		Overview of the New Development Model's Strategic Proposals		
Transformation priority area	**Pillar 1:** Toward a productive and diversified economy that creates value and quality jobs	**Pillar 2:** Toward enhanced human capital that is better prepared for the future	**Pillar 3:** Toward opportunities for inclusion for all and a stronger social bond	**Pillar 4:** Toward sustainable and resilient territories, where development sets deep roots
Strategic choices	1. Make the entrepreneurial initiative secure. 2. Steer economic stakeholders toward productive activities. 3. Achieve a competitiveness shock. 4. Establish a macroeconomic framework dedicated to growth. 5. Emergence of the social economy as an economic sector in its own right.	1. Quality education for all 2. A system of university education, vocational training, and research centered on performance and spurred by autonomous governance that promotes responsibility 3. Quality health services and health protection as fundamental rights of citizens	1. Empower women and ensure gender equality and participation. 2. Promote the inclusion of young people and their fulfillment by multiplying opportunities and means of participation. 3. Build on cultural diversity as a lever for openness, dialogue, and cohesion. 4. Develop a common base for social protection that enhances resilience and inclusion and gives substance to solidarity among citizens.	1. Bring forth a prosperous, dynamic "Morocco of the Regions." 2. Ensure an innovative reengineering of the territorial hierarchy. 3. Promote integrated territorial organization, improve the housing and the living environment, and improve connectivity and mobility. 4. Preserve natural resources and enhance the resilience of territories to climate change. 5. Safeguard water resources through better use of the resource and more rigorous management of its scarcity.

Source: Author.

Pillar 1: Toward a Productive and Diversified Economy That Creates Value and Quality Jobs

Morocco's economic growth has significantly accelerated over the past two decades thanks to major efforts to modernize the economy, the conduct of structural reforms, greater economic openness, and significant investment in infrastructure. Despite these efforts, the Moroccan economy witnessed a slower pace of growth over the last decade, which strongly exposes Morocco to the risks of the middle-income trap.

The analysis of the current structure of the Moroccan economy reveals factors behind the slow pace of its structural transformation. First, the economy's modernization still has room for improvement. Of all Moroccan companies, 64 percent are very small businesses with fewer than 10 employees. Similarly, only 10 percent of Moroccan companies operate in the industry sector, whereas 21 percent are in construction, 28 percent in trade, and 41 percent in services. Second, the economy is not diversified enough, which requires opening up to new activities and new skills. Third, more efforts should be geared toward upscaling the economy to increase local content and added value. Fourth, the productive system strongly relies on the domestic market with a limited number of exporting companies. Hence, guiding Moroccan businesses toward exports is essential to fuel the economy's openness. In this perspective, the NDM's aim is to increase the number of exporting companies to 12,000 (vs. 6,000 as of 2022) and to raise Morocco to among the top 50 countries in the Economic Complexity Index ranking.

The NDM's objective is to lay the foundations for strongly accelerating the pace of economic growth and achieving a successful economic takeoff with diversified sources of growth. The NDM targets a GDP growth of 6 percent on average annually, driven in particular by the added value of medium- and high-technology industrial activities (50 percent of industrial value added). Such growth will stimulate the creation of decent jobs and finance the NDM's ambitions, particularly when it comes to social sectors.

Morocco's economic growth is expected to be more efficient and more resilient. It should rely more on productivity gains with a better allocation of investment toward productive capacities. It should also have a more diversified productive base that offers formal and skilled jobs, especially for youth and women. However, economic growth cannot be driven only by the state's effort. The role of the private sector is essential when it comes to value creation. Hence, achieving a productive transformation requires an entrepreneurial and innovative private sector that is capable of taking risks and exploring new sectors and markets while withstanding international competition.

Such an objective requires actions intended to secure entrepreneurial initiatives as well as steering economic stakeholders toward productive activities, through a regulatory framework ensuring fair competition and promoting the entry of new innovative and competitive players. Five proposals are suggested to achieve a productive and diversified economy.

Making the entrepreneurial initiative secure. Considering the current obstacles to entrepreneurship, the NDM's aim is to guarantee stable and impartial rules for all economic operators, who must find a trusted partner in public administration. This calls for significantly improving the business environment to lift obstacles, reduce uncertainty, and eliminate corruption. In this regard, there should be a systemic elimination of administrative and regulatory barriers to simplify relevant measures and procedures. Guaranteeing a healthy, competitive functioning of markets is also a precondition for boosting private initiative. Businesses should be protected effectively by granting access to a transparent, impartial justice system that can enforce judgments.

Steering economic stakeholders toward productive activities. Public interventions should encourage private operators to invest in new activities conducive to modernization, diversification, upscaling, and internationalization. The NDM suggests concrete proposals for achieving this objective. They include developing a national economic transformation policy to unleash Morocco's growth potential in all sectors but also setting up a harmonized steering and implementation mechanism to achieve strategic sectoral ambitions.

The NDM also recommends revisiting the incentive framework to steer investors toward productive activities and to support the development of small and medium enterprises more actively. It is also about supporting businesses in strengthening their managerial, organizational, and technological capacities. There is also the need to establish a framework conducive to promoting innovation within companies and facilitating the emergence of regional and global start-ups.

Guiding Moroccan businesses toward exports is also essential to fuel the economy's openness. In this regard, the NDM's aim is to increase the number of exporting companies to 12,000 (vs. 6,000 as of 2022) and to raise Morocco to among the top 50 countries in the Economic Complexity Index ranking. Last, the NDM also calls for the integration of the informal sector through an incentive-based, gradual approach suited to the nature of stakeholders.

Achieving a competitiveness shock. Despite Morocco's numerous competitive advantages, production factors remain relatively expensive. Those costs hinder the competitiveness of Moroccan companies and undermine the country's attractiveness with foreign investors.

Hence, structurally transforming Morocco's economy requires strong action on the cost of production factors by reducing costs linked to energy and logistics. Thus, the NDM calls for achieving a significant leap in competitiveness and allowing the production system to meet the challenges of competition in domestic and international markets.

When it comes to energy, it is essential to reduce costs by reforming the sector and using renewable and low-carbon energy. In this sense, the NDM calls for a major reform of the electricity sector that should be combined with a short-term effort of production cost reduction. In 2018, Morocco's energy bill amounted to 82 billion Moroccan dirhams, of which 80 percent represents the oil bill. This is in a context where the demand for energy is increasing (it was multiplied by 1.5

Box 2.3. The New Development Model's Bets for the Future: Morocco as a Regional Financial Hub

The new development model's aim is to make Morocco an attractive financial center, where large and small Moroccan and African businesses with high growth potential can raise financing—a center that attracts substantial financial flows in search of profitable investments in promising areas for the future. In addition to meeting internal needs for traditional or alternative financing, Morocco would be able to capture market shares in Africa (beyond the banking sector), particularly with regard to the financing of major projects. The status of regional financial center, that is increasingly dematerialized to be at the forefront of technological innovation in the financial sector, could also be consolidated by confirming Morocco as a regional platform for commodity trading in cooperation with certain international reference centers in this field.

Source: Author, based on Morocco's New Development Model, April 2021.

---

between 2007 and 2019). Hence, the NDM suggests reducing the energy cost for energy-intensive industries to 0.5 dirham/kilowatt-hour.

As for logistics, it is also important to restructure the sector. Achieving this mostly depends on the ability to modernize and structure the logistics sector to improve its quality of service and performance and to reduce costs. The NDM's aim is to lower the cost of transport and logistics to 12 percent of GDP by 2035.

Establishing a macroeconomic framework dedicated to growth. Morocco enjoys a stable macroeconomic environment and financial system that can be improved further to stimulate economic growth. Three proposals summarize the NDM's vision for the macroeconomic framework. First, it calls for optimizing budgetary expenditure through new management instruments. Second, it suggests reducing the tax burden weighing on productive and competitive activities. Third, it recommends accelerating efforts toward diversifying mechanisms for financing the economy, including banks, capital markets, fintech, and all innovative nonbank solutions. In particular, the NDM advocates for creating the right conditions for further development of capital markets (Box 2.3).

Emergence of the social economy as a full-fledged economic sector. No less important, strong action should be geared toward the emergence of the social economy whose turnover only represents 2 percent of Moroccan GDP and less than 4 percent in terms of jobs. The NDM proposes to increase its share in GDP to 8 percent by 2035. This implies ending with a vision of the social economy being dominated by low-added-value activities in order to have it emerge as an economic sector in its own right.

The social economy presents high potential for creating added value and jobs, particularly at the territorial level. It can provide jobs to complement positions in the commercial and public sectors. It can also be a producer of public services, particularly in health and education, through an experimental approach. Achieving this requires adopting a founding framework for the new social economy and developing innovative social entrepreneurship.

Pillar 2: Toward Enhanced Human Capital That Is Better Prepared for the Future

The NDM puts a strong emphasis on the urgent need to consolidate Morocco's human capital to enable all citizens to shape their own future, realize their potential in full autonomy, and contribute to their country's development and its integration into the global knowledge-based economy. The goal is also to jump-start the social elevator, ensuring equal opportunity for young Moroccans and thereby strongly mitigating the weight of the economic and social inequalities.

Aware that the education sector stands as a primary concern for citizens and Moroccan society, the NDM's ambition is to launch a genuine Moroccan educational renaissance. Moroccan schools should enable every student to acquire fundamental skills to promote the nation's academic and professional success and to ensure its socioeconomic integration. One of the targets projected by the NDM is that by 2035, more than 90 percent of students should have acquired these fundamental academic skills by the end of primary school, compared to less than 30 percent in 2020.

The NDM advocates focusing on four fundamental levers of an educational renaissance, complementing Vision 2030[2] and subsequent legislation:

1. Investing in teacher training and motivation to enable teachers to become guarantors of learning

2. Reorganizing the school curriculum and assessment system to ensure the success of every student

3. Renovating academic content and methods for effective and fulfilling teaching

4. Empowering schools to become drivers of change and stakeholder engagement

Achieving this educational renaissance calls for establishing specific steering and implementation systems, supported by strong political will and commitment to partnership among all stakeholders; aligning resources with objectives; and enhancing stakeholders' capacities and the autonomy of local stakeholders as well as academies and schools. The quality of higher and vocational education and the development of scientific research are also essential to speeding up Morocco's development and establishing it as a competitive nation in the long term.

The NDM also recommends an in-depth modernization of public and private higher education institutions and faster development of vocational training courses and hybrid and work-study learning methods; the primary objective is to provide young Moroccans with the means to acquire skills and improve their job market prospects.

---

[2] The Strategic Vision for Education Reform 2015–2030 was elaborated by the Higher Council on Education, Training and Scientific Research, https://www.csefrs.ma/wp-content/uploads/2017/09/Vision_VF_Fr.pdf.

Access to affordable and quality health care is also among the pressing demands of Moroccan citizens. The NDM stresses the need to ensure access to quality health services and health protection as a fundamental right of citizens. Furthermore, new challenges raised by the COVID-19 crisis and the risk of future health crises require urgent measures to strengthen the health care system with regard to monitoring, prevention, and resilience.

To this end, the NDM puts forward major policy proposals with the following aims:

- Accelerating universal access to basic medical coverage
- Substantially strengthening the overall supply and quality of care, specifically through investing in human resources, upgrading health professions, enhancing public hospitals, and optimizing patient care
- Strengthening the overall system efficiency by overhauling health system governance so as to make all public and private actors accountable, overseeing and normalizing operations, including at the territorial level, by digitizing all health system management processes
- Ensuring a more transparent and rigorous regulation of the pharmaceutical sector so as to promote a competitive local industry, particularly for generic drugs

Pillar 3: Toward Opportunities for Inclusion for All and a Stronger Social Bond

The third NDM pillar relates to opportunities for inclusion for all and the imperative of consolidating social ties. Gender equality and the political, economic, and social participation of women are major challenges for modern Moroccan society, as both are essential conditions for an open, cohesive, and supportive society. The new model seeks to substantially raise levels of participation of women in economic, political, and social spheres.

The NDM also advocates for strengthening the inclusion and development of young people through an integrated policy that is specifically dedicated to them. Morocco's development hinges on free, fulfilled, competent, and enterprising youth. Morocco's youth aged 15–34 account for 33 percent of the population, of which more than 4.5 million are inactive (that is, neither in employment, nor in education, nor in training). Providing young people with the skills and opportunities to improve their future prospects, and with the space for expression, civic participation, and initiative taking, thereby strengthening their civic mindedness and attachment to the nation's fundamentals, as well as actively involving them to serve their country's development, are all critical challenges for Morocco.

Inclusion also implies ensuring social protections that strengthen the resilience and inclusion of the most vulnerable and engenders solidarity among citizens. Finally, the quest for an inclusive Morocco also requires mobilizing cultural diversity as a lever for openness, dialogue, and social cohesion for the purpose of consolidating the foundation of a peaceful and harmonious life together.

Pillar 4: Toward Sustainable and Resilient Territories Where Development Sets Deep Roots

The NDM brings about a new vision on the role of territories as spaces for the codesign and implementation of public policies alongside the state. This vision enshrines the centrality of territories as sources of tangible and intangible wealth creation, the emergence of participatory democracy, and the rooting of resource sustainability and resilience to climate change effects.

In accordance with the constitution, the NDM advocates for a "Morocco of regions" to ensure the convergence and efficiency of public policies at the territorial level. This requires state territorial reform and enhancing the capacities of territorial stakeholders to meet their responsibilities.

Among the proposed actions, the NDM calls for accelerating the advanced regionalization with effective deconcentration and overcoming any reluctance restraining it. The NDM also suggests an innovative territorial reorganization to provide efficient access to public services closer to the citizens. This reorganization is based on the *douar* as the basic territorial unit and capitalizes on the *cercle* administrative level for coordinating and optimizing public services in an intermunicipal approach.[3] Putting participation at the forefront of the NDM priorities, the report recommends the creation of regional economic, social, and environmental councils to promote territorial stakeholder contribution to public development policies.

The NDM also stresses the need for integrated territorial planning that is focused on improving the citizens' living conditions (housing, connectivity, and mobility). The sustainability of territories also requires the conservation of natural resources, particularly water, and enhancing resilience to climate change. For this purpose, it is essential to strengthen the governance of natural resources by monitoring the stakeholders' consistency of actions. Taking water scarcity as an example where the situation continues to worsen in Morocco, the NDM calls for fully accounting for water scarcity and optimizing water use for current and future generations.

The valorization of natural capital must also be understood in light of the opportunities that it presents for developing both domestic and international tourism. In addition, the full potential of the green economy and the blue economy should be mobilized to strengthen value creation in all territories. In the same perspective, the water–energy couple should get special attention by promoting the use of renewable energies, in particular for seawater desalination and wastewater treatment, which would allow supplying coastal areas with water for drinking and irrigation at better cost, and to reduce pressure on water availability.

---

[3] The *cercles* represent an intermediate territorial administrative level, placed between provinces and municipalities. The *douar* are small communities where the most part of rural population lives in Morocco.

Box 2.4. The New Development Model's Pledge for the Future—Morocco: A Champion of Competitive and Green Energy

By working toward this goal for the future, the aim is to make Morocco's energy supply a major determinant of its economic attractiveness, building on competitive energy mainly from renewable sources. Morocco's accelerated transition to a low-carbon, competitive economy that is attractive to industry would make Morocco a benchmark in terms of low-carbon, responsible, and sustainable production methods. This would make it possible to broaden the accessibility of Morocco's exports to promising markets and attract foreign investors looking for opportunities in green economy sectors. A major reform of the energy sector is necessary to take advantage of the technological revolutions underway in renewable energy and to develop a market that is open to domestic and foreign investment.

Source: Author, based on Morocco's New Development Model, April 2021.

Finally, the NDM's aim is to consolidate efforts to develop a modern, socially and environmentally responsible agriculture that fully recognizes and integrates sustainability constraints. Very small farming units (*agriculture solidaire*) and family farming need greater support and development through more efficient support mechanisms for small-scale farming, to address the strong duality between commercial and solidarity farming, with a view to consolidating rural resilience. Water use in agriculture needs to be optimized, with a priority for national food security and fair use of water in the exportable offer. Finally, modernizing agriculture requires the mobilization of technology for sustainability, strengthening human skills in the sector, and investing in research and innovation in agriculture and agribusiness.

Alongside the four pillars identified by the NDM, five bets for the future are proposed as the foundation of a bold Morocco. The aim is to make Morocco one of the most dynamic and attractive economic and knowledge hubs at the continental level. These bets for the future include training research action at the service of the territories, low-cost and low-carbon energy (Box 2.4), digital platforms and broadband coverage, diversified mechanisms for financing the economy, and "made in Morocco" as a means of valuing production and as leverage for Morocco's integration into global value chains.

ACTIVATING DRIVERS OF CHANGE TO ACCELERATE THE NEW DEVELOPMENT MODEL'S IMPLEMENTATION

Achieving the NDM's ambition and structural transformations requires substantial technical, human, and financial capacities, particularly in the start-up phase. For this purpose, the report placed the emphasis on two main drivers of change to support successful implementation of the NDM: reforming the administration and relying on digital technology.

A Renovated, Efficient, and Honest Administrative Apparatus, Focused on the Quality of Services to Citizens and Businesses

In order to accelerate change, it is essential to update the administrative apparatus both in skills and in methods. The implementation of the NDM requires a renewed and modern administrative apparatus that is committed to the general interest. The administration should place greater emphasis on service quality for citizens and enterprises. This calls for a skilled and empowered administration that is oriented to performance and results. The administration should be accountable for its actions and able to take initiative and support change.

Improving the administration's performance also requires simplifying and streamlining internal management procedures that enable the administration to focus on crosscutting missions and objectives. The administration should be expediting the simplification and full digitalization of administrative processes, and granting access to public data to allow users to assess the quality of services and to have recourse in case of dispute or abuse.

In addition, regular renewal of senior national and local civil servants and managers of strategic public enterprises and establishments is a challenge that should be addressed. It is essential to put in place mechanisms of attractiveness, to identify a pool of skills, and to encourage leadership skills development.

Digital Technology as a Driver for Structural Transformation

The NDM sets digital technology as a crucial driver for change and development. Indeed, digital technology is likely to restore trust between citizens and the state; reduce corruption; and promote economic, social, and territorial inclusion of large segments of the population. Simplified and clarified procedures and better-quality services will make the state–citizen and state–business relationships more fluid and transparent.

The NDM considers that Morocco can aim to be an "e-nation" by 2025. For this purpose, the country's digital transformation requires swift upgrading of digital infrastructure, broadband connection throughout the country, extensive skills training, and completion of the legislative and interoperability framework to enable end-to-end digitization of public services and boost digital confidence.

In parallel with these important levers, the NDM stresses the importance of Moroccans of the world as full players in the implementation of the suggested transformative projects. Indeed, beyond the cash transfers they make to the country as remittances, and that represent a strategic financial windfall, the large-scale use of their skills would certainly constitute a powerful lever to strengthen the quality of Morocco's human capital.

The NDM also reaffirms Morocco's irreversible choice of openness to the world by highlighting the role of international partnerships to serve the country's new ambition. The NDM is also in line with Morocco's commitment to defending multilateral causes and providing responses to global challenges. Thus, this contributes to Morocco's outreach by leveraging its specificities and its constants, in particular with respect to its sovereignty and its territorial integrity.

Finally, the NDM's implementation needs a strong action to mobilize all national players around a national development compact as well as to establish a monitoring and steering mechanism to follow up on the NDM's transformative projects and the processes leading to change.

FINANCING THE DEVELOPMENT MODEL: THE NEED FOR ADDITIONAL RESOURCES TO FUEL A WEALTH-CREATING DYNAMIC

The COVID-19 crisis affected government resources and priority budget spending. This emphasizes how the NDM's success hinges on a sound approach to financing. Preliminary estimates established by the SCDM on the funding required to implement the NDM are 4 percent of GDP annually in the start-up phase (2022–25) and 10 percent of GDP in the maintenance phase by 2030.

This is a rough estimate that is aimed essentially at identifying the magnitude of the costs of the NDM's flagship projects and strategic bets for the future. Meeting these needs in terms of financial resources will require a specific financing strategy. The NDM suggests a financing strategy that hinges on four complementary areas (Figure 2.1).

The first area looks at possibilities for widening the state's budgetary space by working actively in favor of the mobilization of the fiscal potential, estimated at between 2 percent and 3 percent of the GDP. This mobilization of the fiscal potential can be achieved by means of a greater formalization of economic activities and an optimization of tax incentives by removing unproductive ones or those that contribute to favoring rent positions. This would also involve building the capacity of the tax administration to fight tax fraud and tax evasion.

The widening of the state's budgetary margins requires, in the short term, carrying out a general review of public expenditures aimed at optimizing the state's way of life, eliminating sources of waste, and strengthening the targeting of this spending to maximize the economic and social impacts. Budgetary savings that can be potentially mobilized could be allocated to the NDM's priority projects.

The second area focuses on stimulating private investment, both national and international, through a transparent and attractive business climate, guaranteeing free competition and promoting the entry of new innovative and competitive players. The national policy of economic transformation advocated by the NDM is fully in line with this perspective as long as it relates to new sectoral ambitions and innovative action levers for their implementation.

The impetus for private investment would also depend on the mobilization of state-owned enterprises and institutions, given their role as an engine of private initiative, a catalyst for the structural competitiveness of the national economy, and a lever for revitalizing territorial ecosystems. The reform at work of the state-owned enterprises and institutions, in the wake of the restructuring of the public

Figure 2.1. The NDM's Financing Strategy: Generating an Inclusive and Virtuous Dynamic Guaranteeing Sustainability

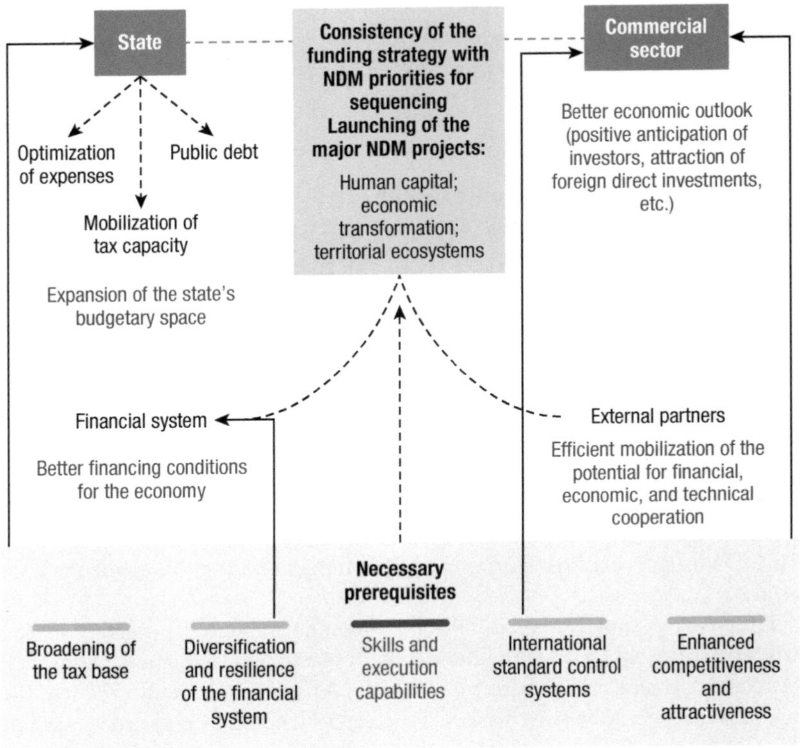

Source: Author.
Note: NDM = new development model.

portfolio and the optimization of the state' shareholder policy, would make it possible to create space for the benefit of national and foreign private investment. The launch of reforms in certain key sectors (for example, energy, water, digital, logistics) would be a necessary prerequisite for achieving this.

In addition, the new dynamic to be instilled in private investment could be based on the role of the Mohammed VI Investment Fund in financing productive diversification and the economy's upscaling. This Fund's operations can be conducted through equity investments in the capital of private companies with high growth potential. This would exert a leverage effect allowing companies to obtain additional financing from market players while promoting better development of the sectoral potential of Morocco's economy in promising sectors.

The third area relates to the multiplication of actors and the diversification of financing instruments to meet the needs of private firms, particularly very small and medium businesses. The entry of new players in both traditional financial activities and more innovative activities, in connection with fintech and other financing solutions, would be appropriate to create competition in the banking market, favoring both quality of services and cost reduction.

Broadening the financing spectrum to benefit private actors and operators calls for boosting the capital markets development and setting its regulation to the highest international standards. One of the key recommendations to achieve this objective is revitalizing Casablanca's stock exchange. In fact, the global Moroccan market capitalization stood at 54 percent of the GDP in 2019, which can be further extended. Compared with other developing countries and considering Morocco's untapped potential, the NDM aims to increase the total market capitalization to 70 percent of GDP in 2035 (vs. 54 percent of GDP as of 2022) and to increase the number of listed companies from 76 in 2019 to 300 in 2035.

In this regard, some priority actions should be deployed, including the acceleration of the legislative process to change the legal and regulatory framework of the capital markets, the broadening of the base of issuers and investors by initial public offerings of public companies, and the creation of a market dedicated to raw materials. In addition, developing the private-debt market and introducing new financial instruments and products would be likely to increase the market's liquidity and strengthen its attractiveness to international investors in search of profitable investments.

The fourth area consists of leveraging opportunities for mobilizing international financial partnerships at bilateral, regional, and multilateral levels, which cover several areas matching the NDM's priorities (for example, energy sustainability, human capital, development of financial markets).

Alongside these potential sources of funding, the NDM will also be able to contribute to its self-financing due to the additional growth it can generate. This contribution appears particularly through (1) the additional tax revenue due to the transition to a new level of growth that allows the favorable recovery of economic activity and (2) the increased attractiveness of direct foreign capital and portfolios, enabling Morocco to meet the financing needs of the national economy.

The transformation projects that underlie the ambition of the NDM are likely to accelerate the development trajectory of the country and raise it to the ranks of prosperous nations. In addition to the required agility to carry out these projects, there is also the need to promote a macroeconomic framework that is closely aligned with development objectives at the economic, social, territorial, and environmental levels. To meet this requirement, Morocco must meet three major conditions:

1. Macroeconomic management combining agility and flexibility in the short-to-medium term and exploiting all possible room for action while remaining vigilant about the macroeconomic framework's sustainability in the long term

2. Macroeconomic policies (monetary, fiscal, exchange rate policy) at the service of a strong, healthy growth with diversified sources, with a view to making them drivers for the creation of added value and jobs

3. Macroeconomic balances that must be reinforced by the internal performance of the NDM. This is a prerequisite to reinforce the national economy's resilience capacity in the face of exogenous shocks. The reinforced competitiveness of the productive system and the expected strong attractiveness of foreign investments will allow the economy to meet its financing needs.

CONCLUSION

The NDM is designed by Moroccans, with Moroccans, and for Moroccans. It results from extensive interaction with many segments of the population about their realities and aspirations. This model embodies a new way of looking at development, one that is more participative and involves all stakeholders. It is a proposal of an ambitious development path and a call on all to rally and work jointly to build the desired Morocco.

Considering the country's multiple assets, and its citizens' capacities, Morocco is fully capable of embarking on a new development stage under the leadership of King Mohammed VI. Achieving the NDM's ambition requires a renewed collective organization enabling all Moroccan women and men; public, private, and civil society; at central and local levels; and in all their diversity and richness, to work toward the same goals.

The NDM's success also hinges on fostering international partnerships. The transformative projects underlying the NDM offer investment opportunities as well as partnership prospects in promising fields (for example, education, health, energy, logistics). Mobilizing international partnerships is also the key to promoting technology transfer and providing technical support for development projects in the spirit of co-development.

Strengthening cooperation with international partners, including international financing partners and development agencies, can only be encouraged, especially by targeting the priorities and areas identified by the NDM.

PART II

Strengthening Macroeconomic Resilience

CHAPTER 3

Moving to an Inflation-Targeting Regime

Dániel Baksa and Aleš Bulíř

INTRODUCTION

Morocco is expected to adopt an inflation-targeting framework after measured preparations, having carefully weighed pros and cons. Other countries adopted inflation targeting because "monetary targets abandoned them," the country needed a disinflation mechanism, a financial crisis made a peg noncredible, or because other monetary frameworks failed to provide macroeconomic stability. In contrast, over the past two decades, in Morocco the exchange rate peg has not been under pressure (except some tensions at the onset of the COVID-19 pandemic) and the economy has shown remarkable nominal stability, with consumer prices only marginally more volatile than in the euro area.

Rather, the Moroccan authorities signaled as early as the mid-2000s their intention to move toward a more flexible exchange rate regime and eventually to inflation targeting, as part of a more general series of reforms aimed at reinforcing the Moroccan economy's resilience and growth potential. The main motivation has been that such a regime would increase the maneuvering space for macroeconomic policies and cushion the economy from real external shocks while keeping the dirham competitive.

The authorities understood early on that a successful regime switch will require three basic elements, namely (1) the various policymaking institutions must accept the need for reform and support the reform steps, (2) the reforms involve many interlinked steps under an overall framework, and (3) the staff in the government agencies must be trained and equipped with appropriate technical tools.

Although progress on these fronts slowed during the global financial crisis, it was rekindled in the early 2010s, supported by extensive domestic consultation and IMF-led technical assistance, including on a new policy modeling framework (Benlamine and others 2018). The preparatory work has continued in the aftermath of the COVID-19 pandemic crisis, again supported by IMF-led technical

We are grateful to Roberto Cardarelli for comments. Jing Xie provided excellent research assistance.

assistance in 2020–22. On the policy front, in January 2018 Morocco changed its official arrangement from "conventional peg" to "pegged exchange rate within horizontal bands" when the fluctuation band for the dirham was widened to ±2.5 percent; in March 2020 the band was further widened to ±5 percent.

In this chapter Morocco's monetary policy trade-off is outlined and the gradual process of external liberalization and transition to inflation targeting is mapped. The chapter then sketches the innovative features of the Morocco Quarterly Projection Model designed to capture monetary policy independence under a peg and capital controls. In the analytical section, the macroeconomic stabilization advantage of a counterfactual floating regime over the current peg regime is shown by exploring both deterministic and stochastic simulations of a scenario with initial conditions like those of 2020. The final section offers a conclusion.

MOROCCO: MONETARY INDEPENDENCE UNDER A PEG AND CAPITAL CONTROLS

Following the creation of the dirham in the 1950s, Morocco has combined a fixed exchange rate and capital controls to retain a degree of monetary policy independence. Presently, Morocco pegs the dirham against a basket of the euro and US dollar, and it limits capital account transactions to keep control over short-term domestic interest rates and other instruments of monetary policy, such as reserve requirements.[1] Some fluctuation of the dirham is allowed within a band, which the Moroccan authorities have widened first from ±0.3 percent to ±2.5 percent in January 2018 and then further to ±5 percent in March 2020. Even though these adjustments are a part of the gradual process toward a more flexible exchange rate and inflation targeting, the exchange rate continued to serve as the main nominal anchor, pinning down the aggregate price level and wage growth.

The choice of such a monetary policy framework reflected the empirical observation that no country can achieve simultaneously a fixed exchange rate, free capital mobility, and an independent monetary policy dedicated to domestic goals (Obstfeld, Shambaugh, and Taylor 2005; Rey 2013). The so-called impossible trinity argues that to retain control over short-term interest rates, the authorities have two options. The first is to float the exchange rate and identify an alternative nominal anchor, such as an inflation target. Arbitrage based on flow of capital will ensure that the depreciation or appreciation of a country's currency vis-à-vis another will reflect the nominal interest rate differential between these countries. The second is to continue pegging the exchange rate and suspend the uncovered interest rate parity condition by limiting the flow of capital in and out of the country. If the capital controls are sufficiently restrictive, a differential between

---

[1] The Moroccan dirham was pegged to the French franc from the time of independence in 1956 until the Bretton Woods system collapsed in 1973, followed by a peg to a basket of eight currencies. In the early 2000s the basket was narrowed to the euro and US dollar with respective weights of 80 percent and 20 percent, and in 2015 these weights were changed to 60 percent and 40 percent.

the domestic and world rates can persist without putting pressure on the peg and the country's international reserves.[2]

Morocco started relaxing its comprehensive system of foreign exchange controls in the 1980s, removing most barriers related to exports and imports of goods and services. Still, the less-visible system of import tariffs and import controls has remained in place. Outward capital transactions were relaxed for residents, and remittances of capital and related nonresident incomes were liberalized; however, foreign-currency denominated loans need to be authorized by the Moroccan Office of Foreign Exchange. Whereas restrictions related to inward investments were relaxed, outward restrictions remain binding (Taamouti 2015; IMF 2015), and the 2018 update of the Chinn-Ito financial openness index ranks Morocco in the second most restrictive group.[3]

Morocco's monetary policy choice has reflected the authorities' preference for a relatively tightly controlled economic system for capital flows. On the one hand, this approach has contributed to the overall macroeconomic stability experienced by the country from the late 1990s: during this period, Morocco has been largely insulated from the global financial cycle, avoiding financial bubbles, the build-up of unsustainable private, foreign-currency debt, and other issues often observed in emerging market countries with unrestricted flows of capital (Reinhart and Reinhart 2008). Predictably, nominal stability came at the expense of the ability to adjust to real shocks. For example, the negative productivity shock at the onset of the global financial crisis resulted in real effective depreciation of the dirham to the tune of about 9 percent by 2012 as compared to the pre–global financial crisis period (see IMF 2016 and *International Financial Statistics*). With a stable nominal exchange rate, the adjustment came about through the internal devaluation process, namely price and wage growth below the rate of Moroccan trading partners.

On the other hand, Morocco's monetary policy and exchange rate regime may have limited Morocco's ability to meet the international competitiveness challenges and to absorb external shocks.[4] Indeed, over the last two decades the active stabilization role of monetary policy in Morocco has been less pronounced than in countries with a floating exchange rate and an open capital account. Domestic policies have been focused instead on the achievement of the dual external objectives of exchange rate stability and sustainable international reserves. For example, the Bank Al-Maghrib (BAM) policy rate moved only 13 times during 2000–20, whereas most small open-economy central banks made three times as many adjustments to their key interest rates. BAM has instead relied on non-interest instruments of monetary policy, such as reserve requirements.

---

[2] From 2006, the operational target of the central bank has been the interbank weighted average rate, which the central bank has managed using two tools: adjusting the key policy rate and changing the required reserve ratio of the banking sector (Taamouti 2015). The interbank rate has been set with a broad view of achieving price stability, without an explicit inflation target, and supporting economic growth. The partly closed capital account has supported the Bank Al-Maghrib's efforts to keep the interbank rate at the desired level.

[3] http://web.pdx.edu/~ito/Chinn-Ito_website.htm.

[4] See Bank Al-Maghrib (2016, 21).

BAM was able to mount an effective response to the financial and liquidity tension created by the COVID-19 shock, and the widening of the band around the peg has allowed monetary policy to play a more active stabilization role than in the past. Still, even with the wider band, it remains the case that keeping the peg on the dirham could constrain the authorities' range of policy options to respond to future real shocks and, in particular, to those (like terms of trade and real interest rate shocks) that can result in changes of the equilibrium real exchange rate. Under a peg, the adjustment in the real exchange rate will need to take place mainly through changes in domestic nominal prices and domestic wages, which tend to be associated with deeper and longer contractions of economic activity (Edwards and Levy Yeyati 2005).[5]

The consensus view is that the economy's transmission mechanism tends to be less effective in the case of a peg and closed capital account than under a flexible exchange rate regime and free capital flows. Interventions in foreign exchange markets leave less scope for the functioning of the conventional interest rate channel and the asset channel, whereas the nominal port of the exchange rate channel is closed. Regarding the asset channel, capital controls are likely to slow down the development of well-functioning markets for fixed-income securities, equities, and real estate. Furthermore, effectiveness and reliability of the bank lending channel can be constrained by the oligopolistic structure of the banking sector due to barriers to entry into the domestic capital market (Benazzi and Rouiessi 2017).

A MONETARY POLICY MODEL FOR MOROCCO

In this section a trend-gap macroeconomic model is introduced that is then used in the next section to simulate developments under the current regime and an alternative policy regime, where the central bank targets inflation and the exchange rate is floating. The model is a somewhat simplified version of the framework used in BAM. The Morocco Quarterly Projection Model was developed during 2015–16 with the help of IMF-led technical assistance to support BAM's monetary policy decision making during the transition toward a more flexible exchange rate regime and eventual adoption of full-fledged inflation targeting (Benlamine and others 2018).

To this end, the model was designed to accommodate both the existing fixed exchange rate framework with capital controls and an alternative of a floating exchange rate and gradually increasing capital mobility. The main difference between the two regimes is in their choice of the long-term nominal anchor (Table 3.1). In the current fixed exchange rate regime, the fluctuation corridor

---

[5] Policy recommendations differ between flexible and fixed regimes. Let us consider a situation when the expected domestic output gap turns negative. Under a float, the authorities will be expected to loosen monetary policy, quickly depreciating both the nominal and real exchange rate as inflation expectations remain anchored. Under a peg, the authorities typically choose to tighten monetary conditions to protect the peg, with inflation eventually declining beyond the recession-induced developments, thus depreciating the real exchange rate.

TABLE 3.1.

Modeling Solutions to Regime Differences		
	Fixed Exchange Rate Regime with Capital Controls	**Flexible Exchange Rate Regime**
Nominal exchange rate	The nominal exchange rate is an exogenous policy choice variable, and without an ad hoc policy decision its value does not change.	The nominal exchange rate is determined by investors' portfolio choice, reflecting the expected relative return of domestic assets, proxied by the money-market interest rate differential adjusted for the risk premium. The arbitrage condition is described by the risk-adjusted uncovered interest rate parity condition.
Domestic interest rate	Limited capital mobility gives the central bank some independence to influence the money-market rates. The policy reaction function is (1) highly persistent, (2) inflation aversion is relatively weak, and (3) the overall interest rate is a hypothetical "rate" that reflects the fact that most domestic agents borrow at "domestic" rates whereas some can borrow at "foreign" rates.	The domestic interest rate is the main policy instrument and it is modeled as the standard inflation forecast–based reaction function (Berg and others 2006; Clark and others 2001). It describes a policymaker stabilizing inflation around the target and minimizing shortfalls in capacity utilization.

Source: Benlamine and others (2018).

notwithstanding, the anchor is the nominal exchange rate, whereas other nominal variables—inflation and nominal interest rates—are determined endogenously. In the flexible regime, it is the long-term rate of inflation, as defined by an explicit inflation target, that serves as the nominal anchor, and the interest rate, exchange rate, and inflation are determined endogenously. The key differences between the two regimes are captured in two blocks of the model: the exchange rate and interest rate equations.

The model structure and its calibration reflect a few well-known features of the Moroccan economy. First, Morocco is a small open economy, highly sensitive to external developments, especially in the euro area. This feature requires that the forecasting framework accounts for developments in foreign demand and commodity prices, especially oil and food. Second, domestic agriculture is an important source of output volatility, warranting a decomposition of GDP to agricultural and nonagricultural sectors. Third, the structure of Moroccan value added has begun to change as the automobile and other export-oriented sectors grow faster than domestic demand. Fourth, whereas investment has been linked to centralized infrastructure projects and foreign direct investment inflows, consumption has been driven by household decisions linked to agricultural production and inflows of remittances.

Fifth, Morocco has had low headline inflation, comparable to developed economies, averaging only 1.5 percent (Figure 3.1). The sizable weight of volatile food items—at 39 percent in the 2007 basket, the share of food in the Consumer Price Index basket is more than twice the share as in the euro area basket—and items with regulated prices warrant a decomposition of the Consumer Price Index to core inflation and other subindexes. Sixth, given the

Figure 3.1. Inflation and Monetary Transmission

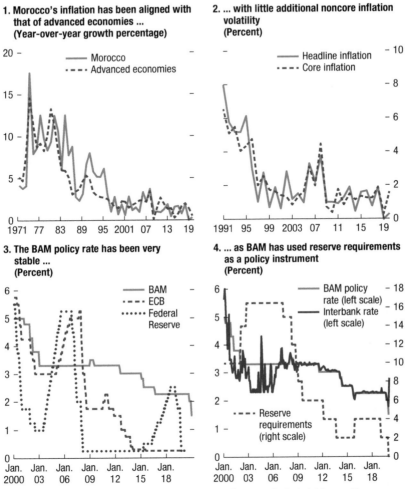

1. Morocco's inflation has been aligned with that of advanced economies ...
(Year-over-year growth percentage)

2. ... with little additional noncore inflation volatility
(Percent)

3. The BAM policy rate has been very stable ...
(Percent)

4. ... as BAM has used reserve requirements as a policy instrument
(Percent)

Sources: IMF, International Financial Statistics and World Economic Outlook databases; Morocco Quarterly Projection Model database; and national data.
Note: BAM = Bank Al-Maghrib; ECB = European Central Bank.

sizable weight of the euro in the basket, any change in the euro-to-dirham exchange rate is quickly translated into core inflation. Seventh, the changes in the interbank rate, which has evolved in line with the BAM policy rate, have been relatively quickly translated into lending rates. The last two stylized facts thus suggest the presence of both significant exchange rate and interest rate channels in Morocco.

COMPARISON OF THE FIXED AND FLOATING POLICY REGIMES

In this section is demonstrated the stabilization advantage of the floating regime over the peg by exploring two impulse-response functions and a stochastic simulation of a scenario with the 2020 initial conditions. For the sake of simplicity, the model structure and calibration are kept identical under both regimes, except for two equations: the uncovered interest rate parity and the policy reaction function. This approach follows the two-regime version of the Morocco Quarterly Projection Model (Benlamine and others 2018) and the modeling framework in Baksa, Bulíř, and Cardarelli (2021). The general finding is that the model economy, which is designed to mimic the key features of the Moroccan economy, is easier to stabilize with a flexible exchange rate than with a fixed one.

A Deterministic Comparison: Impulse Response Functions

We start by comparing key macroeconomic developments in a deterministic setting. The impulse response functions plot the response of the model economy to temporary 1 percentage point shocks to: (1) core inflation (Figure 3.2) and (2) domestic demand (Figure 3.3). These results broadly replicate the standard results found in the policy modeling literature while considering Morocco-specific calibrations.

Both regimes are comparable in stabilizing inflation; however, stabilization is delivered through different channels. Under the peg, the exchange rate does not move and the domestic interest rate moves only very little because it supports the objective of exchange rate stability. The interest rate channel plays only a minor role in responding to inflation and aggregate demand shocks. The policymaker relies instead on the exchange rate channel operating through the inflation differential vis-à-vis the trading partners. Real exchange rate misalignments are addressed through internal devaluation that returns the price level to its initial value, necessitating a long-lasting period of inflation and output below the steady state.

Under the floating exchange rate regime and inflation targeting, the policymaker is free to adjust both the interest rate and the exchange rate. The interest and exchange rate channels both operate and there is no need for a long period of internal devaluation—the nominal exchange rate adjusts quickly. The real exchange rate misalignment is addressed through nominal depreciation, with the price level settling at a new steady state. Crucially, the period needed to bring inflation and output back to their long-term trends under the float is shorter than under the peg.

A Stochastic Simulation of an Adjustment Scenario

The stochastic simulations confirm the intuition from the previous section—a pegged regime as compared to a floating regime results in (1) larger output losses when the economy is exposed to a negative demand shock and (2) larger volatility

Figure 3.2. A Positive 1 Percent Shock to Domestic Costs
(All variables are expressed as deviations from the steady state)

A temporary positive 1 percentage point shock to core inflation leads to higher headline inflation and causes the real exchange rate to appreciate.

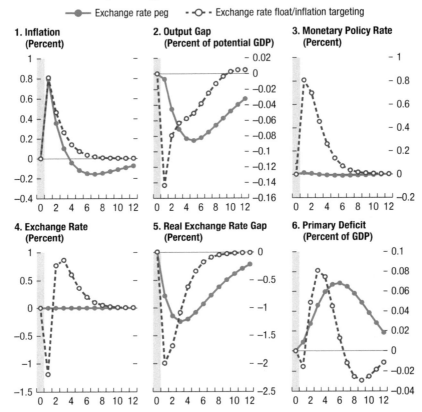

Source: Authors' simulations.
Note: Under a flexible exchange rate regime and inflation targeting (dashed red line), the policymaker tightens monetary policy but allows the exchange rate to depreciate in nominal terms, quickly extinguishing the initial exchange rate overvaluation. Under a peg (solid blue line), the policymaker keeps the nominal rate unchanged, and the initial overvaluation is addressed through internal devaluation—a long-lasting period of output below its trend level is needed to keep inflation below the steady state and to return the economy to the initial price level. Inflation is the year-over-year percent change in the Consumer Price Index; the output gap is defined as the percent deviation of actual GDP from its potential; the exchange rate is the dirham-to-euro rate, with a positive value indicating depreciation and a negative value indicating appreciation; the real effective exchange rate gap is defined as the percent deviation of the actual real exchange rate from its trend value; and the primary deficit is measured as revenue minus expenditure, excluding interest payments, adjusted for the business cycle. All variables are in annual frequency and are expressed as deviations from the steady state.

Figure 3.3. A Positive 1 Percent Shock to Domestic Demand

(All variables are expressed as deviations from the steady state)

A temporary positive 1 percentage point shock to nonagricultural GDP overheats the economy, creates inflationary pressures, and appreciates the real exchange rate.

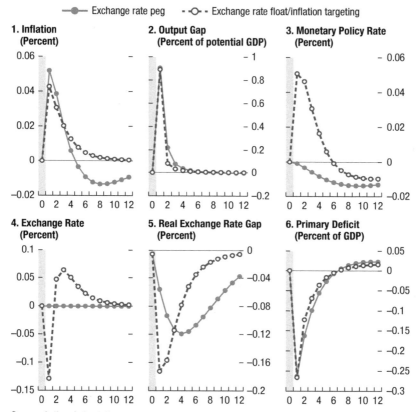

Source: Authors' simulations.
Note: Under a flexible exchange rate regime and inflation targeting (dashed red line), the policymaker briefly tightens monetary policy to close the output gap but allows the exchange rate to depreciate in nominal terms after the first year to offset the initial real appreciation. Under a peg (solid blue line), the policymaker keeps the nominal rate unchanged, and overvaluation is extinguished through long-lasting internal devaluation. Inflation is the year-over-year percent change in the Consumer Price Index; the output gap is defined as the percent deviation of actual GDP from its potential; the exchange rate is the dirham-to-euro rate, with a positive value indicating depreciation and a negative value indicating appreciation; the real effective exchange rate gap is defined as the percent deviation of the actual real exchange rate from its trend value; and the primary deficit is measured as revenue minus expenditure, excluding interest payments, adjusted for the business cycle. All variables are in annual frequency and are expressed as deviations from the steady state.

of the output gap and inflation. The interest and exchange rates are more volatile under the float; however, they are on average closer to the steady state—a result stemming from the faster adjustment under the float.

The previous simulation is extended for two additional features: namely, the simulation is initiated away from the steady state and the economy is hit with shocks afterward. Specifically, the behavior of the model economy is explored—under the two policy regimes—(1) when faced with a set of initial adverse conditions similar to those prevailing in 2020 (that is, a post–COVID-19 recovery path) and (2) when buffeted with normally distributed random shocks to external and domestic demand, fiscal variables, inflation, and the country risk premium. These shocks are auto- and cross-correlated and broadly reflect past domestic and external developments. The initial conditions encompass the collapse in global and domestic demand, an increase in the country risk premium, a sharp drop in oil prices, and a massive fiscal impulse that pushed the debt-to-GDP ratio over the fiscal target. The simulations were run for 15 years for both regimes, repeated 1,000 times, and the sample results were averaged for the first and second moments of the key variables of interest (the output gap, headline and core inflation, the nominal interest and exchange rate, and the cyclically adjusted primary fiscal deficit in percentage of GDP). Hence, relative to the previous section, not just the levels but also the variability of the key variables were compared.

Recall that the exchange rate moves only under the float and that the movement in the domestic interest rate under the peg is limited in order to support the exchange rate. Both regimes must deal with the rapidly increasing debt, and it was assumed that the authorities will attempt to bring the debt-to-GDP ratio back to the target of 60 percent over the medium term while considering the demand effects of the fiscal consolidation. The fiscal reaction function is identical for both regimes and is of the type proposed by Plödt and Reicher (2015).

These simulation results expand on the general point that the model economy would stabilize faster and with lesser output cost under a flexible exchange rate regime than under a peg (Table 3.2). Cumulative output losses are higher by one-third under the peg: the 15-year average of the output gap is –0.8 percent and –0.5 percent under the peg and float, respectively. Output is also marginally more volatile under the peg during this period. Similarly, inflation is expected to undershoot the 2 percent inflation objective more when the exchange rate is fixed, and it is expected to be more volatile. These results hold for both headline and core inflation. The nominal interest rate is on average higher by some 30 basis points under the peg as it must offset the initially higher risk premium, albeit it should be less volatile later in the sample period. In real terms, the interest rate is on average some 50 basis points higher under the peg. The exchange rate is the shock absorber under the float—it depreciates marginally in nominal terms, but it is much more volatile. The fiscal results are virtually identical under either regime as the fiscal rule ensures a gradual return to the debt target.

The results of the stochastic simulations corroborate the findings from the impulse response functions, namely that the Moroccan economy should benefit from a more flexible exchange rate and active monetary policy. Output and

TABLE 3.2.

Stochastic Simulation Scenario: Peg versus Float Comparison
(Sample average of 1,000 stochastic simulations)

	Peg	Float/IT
Averages		
Output gap	−0.8	−0.6
Headline inflation	1.5	1.7
Core inflation	1.5	1.7
Nominal interest rate	1.9	1.6
Nominal exchange rate (positive number implies depreciation)	−0.1	0.1
Primary fiscal deficit	0.3	0.4
Standard Deviations		
Output gap	3.8	3.6
Headline inflation	1.1	0.9
Core inflation	1.6	1.4
Nominal interest rate	0.8	1.4
Nominal exchange rate	0.2	3.3
Primary fiscal deficit	7.6	7.6

Source: Authors' simulations.

Note: The initial conditions of the simulation resemble developments in mid-2020 (a collapse in global and domestic demand, an increase in the country risk premium, a sharp drop in oil prices, and a massive fiscal impulse). Over the simulation period the model economy is also buffeted with normally distributed random shocks to external and domestic demand, fiscal variables, inflation, and the country risk premium. These shocks are auto- and cross-correlated, and these correlations broadly reflect past domestic and external developments.

Inflation is the year-over-year percent change in the headline Consumer Price Index; core inflation excludes food and energy; the output gap is defined as the percent deviation of actual GDP from its potential; the nominal interest rate is the three-month interbank rate; the exchange rate is the dirham-to-euro rate; and the primary deficit is measured as revenue minus expenditure, excluding interest payments, adjusted for the business cycle. All variables are in annual frequency. IT = inflation targeting.

inflation stabilization gains under the float more than offset the costs of exchange rate and interest volatility. Neither regime is superior with respect to the fiscal balances that will have to be repaired after the COVID-19–related debt shock in 2020.

CONCLUSION

The simulations presented in this chapter, which use alternative modeling frameworks, show that the Moroccan economy would benefit from a more flexible exchange rate and active monetary policy guided by a formal inflation target. The output and inflation stabilization gains under the inflation-targeting monetary policy regime with floating exchange rates more than offset the additional costs of exchange rate and interest volatility. Although BAM remains committed to an eventual switch to a floating exchange rate and inflation targeting, the switch needs to be carefully administered and reflected in the BAM modeling framework. The policy reaction function will need to be refined as the policymaker's past behavior under the fixed exchange rate regime will provide limited guidance for the new regime. The legacy of the COVID-19 pandemic and the war in Ukraine, and the resulting shifts in world demand for Moroccan exports, as well as the structural reforms launched by the Moroccan authorities, will have had profound, long-lasting impacts on economic growth and employment, necessitating a thorough review of the relationships embedded in the forecasting and policy analysis system.

REFERENCES

Baksa, Dániel, Aleš Bulíř, and Roberto Cardarelli. 2021. "A Simple Macrofiscal Model for Policy Analysis: An Application to Morocco." IMF Working Paper 21/190, Washington, DC. https://www.imf.org/-/media/Files/Publications/WP/2021/English/wpiea2021190-print-pdf.ashx.

Bank Al-Maghrib. 2016. "Strategic Plan 2016–2018." http://www.bkam.ma/en/content/download/18448/2700740/PS%202016-2018%20ANG.pdf.

Benazzi, Sara, and Imane Rouiessi. 2017. "Analyse de la concurrence bancaire au Maroc : Approche de Panzar et Rosse." Bank Al-Maghrib Working Paper. http://www.bkam.ma/content/download/537373/5660379/version/1/file/Document+1-Analyse+de+la+concurrence+bancaire+au+Maroc++Approche+de+Panzar+et+Rosse.pdf.

Benlamine, Mokhtar, Aleš Bulíř, Meryem Farouki, Ágnes Horváth, Faical Hossaini, Hasnae El Idrissi, Zineb Iraoui, Mihály Kovács, Douglas Laxton, Anass Maaroufi, Katalin Szilágyi, Mohamed Taamouti, and David Vávra. 2018. "Morocco: A Practical Approach to Monetary Policy Analysis in a Country with Capital Controls." IMF Working Paper 18/27, Washington, DC. http://www.imf.org/-/media/Files/Publications/WP/2018/wp1827.ashx.

Berg, Andrew, Philippe Karam, and Douglas Laxton. 2006. "Practical Model-Based Monetary Policy Analysis — Overview." IMF Working Paper 06/80, Washington, DC. https://www.imf.org/external/pubs/ft/wp/2006/wp0680.pdf.

Clark, Peter, Douglas Laxton, and David Rose. 2001. "An Evaluation of Alternative Monetary Policy Rules in a Model with Capacity Constraints." *Journal of Money, Credit and Banking* 33 (1): 42–64.

Edwards, Sebastian, and Eduardo Levy Yeyati. 2005. "Flexible Exchange Rates as Shock Absorbers." *European Economic Review* 49 (November): 2079–105.

International Monetary Fund (IMF). 2015. *Annual Report on Exchange Arrangements and Exchange Restrictions*. Washington, DC.

International Monetary Fund (IMF). 2016. *Morocco: 2015 Article IV Consultation—Staff Report*. Washington, DC.

Obstfeld, Maurice, Jay C. Shambaugh, and Alan M. Taylor. 2005. "The Trilemma in History: Tradeoffs among Exchange Rates, Monetary Policies, and Capital Mobility." *Review of Economics and Statistics* 87 (3): 423–38.

Plödt, Martin, and Claire A. Reicher. 2015. "Estimating Fiscal Policy Reaction Functions: The Role of Model Specification." *Journal of Macroeconomics* 46: 113–28.

Reinhart, Carmen M., and Vincent R. Reinhart. 2008. "Capital Flow Bonanzas: An Encompassing View of the Past and Present." NBER Working Paper 14321. http://www.nber.org/papers/w14321.pdf.

Rey, Hélène. 2013. "Dilemma not Trilemma: The Global Financial Cycle and Monetary Policy Independence." Proceedings - Economic Policy Symposium - Jackson Hole, Federal Reserve of Kansas City Economic Symposium, 285–333. https://www.kansascityfed.org/Jackson%20Hole/documents/4575/2013Rey.pdf

Taamouti, Mohamed. 2015. "Background Paper on Monetary Policy—The Kingdom of Morocco." Proceedings - Central Bank Papers on Monetary Policy Frameworks in the Arab Countries – Abu Dhabi, AMF-BIS Working Party Meeting on Monetary Policy in the Arab Region, 160–175.

CHAPTER 4

A New Fiscal Rule for Morocco?

David Bartolini, Chiara Maggi, and Francisco Roch

INTRODUCTION

Morocco's fiscal policy response to COVID-19 has helped to minimize the health-related, social, and economic impacts of the crisis. A special fund of about 3 percent of gross domestic product (GDP) was set up in 2020 to finance higher health expenditures, support the households and businesses most affected by the crisis, and maintain public investment. The impact of the fund on the budget was limited because its resources came from voluntary contributions (registered as fiscal revenues) from Morocco's private sector and several public sector agencies, and from the reallocation of spending within the 2020 budget.

Although the fiscal response to the pandemic was budgetary prudent, the severe economic recession together with the full application of automatic stabilizers (mainly from the tax revenue side) inevitably worsened Morocco's fiscal position, as occurred in many other countries. The general government[1] debt ratio, which was slightly below the average for emerging markets before the pandemic, rose to about 63 percent of GDP in 2020 from 53 percent in 2019 (Figure 4.1). Citing the deterioration of public finances, two rating agencies downgraded their outlook for Morocco's sovereign rating in October 2020.

As Morocco was recovering from the social and economic impacts of the pandemic, the economic fallout from Russia's invasion of Ukraine presented new challenges. Rising food and energy prices boosted spending pressures, with subsidies almost doubling in 2022 compared with the previous year. New spending pressures also originated from the gradual implementation of the reforms of the health care, education, and social protection systems. Only the strong performance of revenues (partly a lagged response to the economic rebound of 2021) managed to offset these pressures and caused the overall deficit to fall in 2022. The 2023 budget envisages a gradual return of the fiscal deficit toward its pre-pandemic level by 2025, with the public debt ratio remaining relatively stable over the next three years.

---

[1] General government debt consolidates central government debt and the debt from social security public entities.

Figure 4.1. General Government Gross Debt
(Percent of fiscal year GDP)

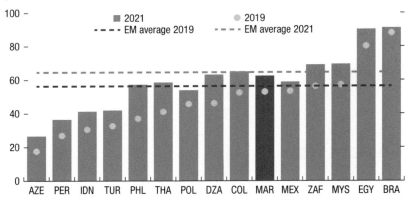

Sources: IMF, World Economic Outlook database; and IMF staff calculations.
Note: MAR represents Morocco's general government debt. AZE = Azerbaijan; BRA = Brazil;
COL = Colombia; DZA = Algeria; EGY = Egypt; EM = emerging market; IDN = Indonesia;
MEX = Mexico; MYS = Malaysia; PER = Peru; PHL = Philippines; POL = Poland; THA = Thailand;
TUR = Turkey; ZAF = South Africa.

Going forward, Morocco's fiscal policy faces a difficult trade-off between supporting growth and funding the cost of structural reforms on one side and the need to rebuild the fiscal space on the other by placing the debt ratio on a downward path toward pre-pandemic levels (International Monetary Fund [IMF] 2023). Of course, Morocco is not alone in facing this challenge, which is shared by many other countries that saw their fiscal position deteriorate during the COVID-19 pandemic. A large body of literature exists (see, for example, IMF 2021) suggesting that a transparent and credible fiscal policy framework may improve the terms of this trade-off. Convincing markets that the government has a clear plan to reduce the fiscal deficit and is committed to meeting its debt obligations could lower the economic cost of fiscal consolidation and build space for a countercyclical fiscal policy (Caselli and others 2022; Eyraud and others 2018).

Building on the literature, this chapter asks whether the adoption of a new debt-anchored fiscal rule could help Morocco address its fiscal challenge. To do so, first cross-country empirical evidence on the impact of fiscal rules in reducing deficit and the cost of debt is presented, using data on a large panel of countries over the last two decades. Then, a general equilibrium model calibrated to the Moroccan economy is used to assess the impact of a fiscal rule with a medium-term debt anchor on the cost of public debt and the effectiveness of fiscal policy (defined as the extent to which it can be countercyclical).

The rest of the chapter is organized as follows. The second section provides an overview of Morocco's current fiscal framework. The third section provides an overview of fiscal rules, including their design and effectiveness. The fourth section presents some empirical evidence on the impact of fiscal rules on fiscal discipline and the cost of debt, and the fifth section describes a general equilibrium model and simulation results. The final section presents the conclusion.

OVERVIEW OF MOROCCO'S FISCAL POLICY INSTITUTIONAL FRAMEWORK

Over the past decade, Morocco has taken important steps in the direction of strengthening its fiscal framework. These steps include the implementation of the Organic Budget Law, the adoption of the Framework Law on tax reform, and the reform of the subsidy system:

- The Organic Budget Law *(Loi organique n. 130-30)*, adopted in 2015, aimed at reforming Morocco's budgeting framework over a five-year horizon by (1) strengthening the budget performance in managing public resources, (2) improving transparency and predictability of budgeting procedures, and (3) reinforcing the role of the Parliament in the definition and approval of the annual budget law. The law indicates that the annual budget should be consistent with triennial budget projections and prescribes a clear indication of the timing and process for the approval of the annual budget law. With the presentation of the 2023 budget to the parliament, the authorities have begun publishing a medium-term fiscal framework containing their macro-economic and fiscal projections over the following three years. Finally, the law prescribes that only investment spending can be financed with new debt, a golden rule that intends to preserve growth-friendly spending while imposing limits on current spending.

- The Framework Law on tax reform *(Loi cadre n. 69-19)*, approved in 2021, proposes a set of principles and prescriptions that should guide a complete overhaul of the tax system in order to make it more efficient and equitable. The law entails, among other things, a rationalization of tax expenditures, a more progressive taxation of personal income, a more efficient taxation of corporate income, a harmonization of the value-added tax system (currently fragmented across several rates), and the possibility of introducing a carbon tax. Some of the elements of the Framework Law were introduced in the budget laws of the last three years, including a comprehensive reform of the corporate income tax system announced in 2022 (see IMF 2023).

- The reform of the Compensation Fund (Caisse de compensation) in 2012 reduced the number of goods and services subject to subsidies to three main categories (gas butane, soft wheat, and sugar), lowering the cost of subsidies from a peak of 6.5 percent of GDP in 2013 to 2 percent of GDP on average in the following decade (see Chapter 1). The authorities are planning to phase out remaining subsidies by 2024, replacing them with more targeted cash transfers to vulnerable households (based on income and number of dependent children).

An important component of the Moroccan institutional fiscal framework, the Court of Auditors (Cour des comptes), is responsible for overseeing the legitimacy of the budget law and the transparency of the fiscal framework. This control has generally been exercised on an ex-post basis, mainly through the publication of an annual report on the execution of the budget law. However, more recently, the court has extended its activities to several phases of the preparation of the budget law so that its role has become more akin to that of a fiscal council (and so it could also involve an assessment of the government pluriannual budgetary projections and policies).

Despite these improvements there is still scope for strengthening Morocco's fiscal framework and making it more effective, transparent, and credible. Although it had been adhered to before the pandemic, the golden rule hasn't been able to prevent the increase in debt and financing needs following the 2020 recession and it is not consistent with a particular pace of debt consolidation going forward. A well-designed fiscal rule based on a medium-term debt anchor could help better shape expectations about future fiscal policy, further improve transparency, and reassure international investors regarding the commitment of the Moroccan authorities to fiscal stability. With technical assistance from the IMF, the authorities have started working on the design of a new fiscal rule based on a medium-term debt anchor and an associated operational rule that would guide fiscal policy in the short term toward its medium-term objective.

FEATURES, CHALLENGES, AND EFFECTIVENESS OF FISCAL RULES

Over the last decade, an increasing number of countries adopted some type of a fiscal rule (Figure 4.2). In the late 1990s to the early 2000s this trend was led by advanced economies (mainly EU countries); however, the past ten years have seen a marked increase in the number of emerging market economies adopting a fiscal rule. The IMF dataset on fiscal frameworks across countries (Davoodi and others 2022a) distinguishes four types of fiscal rules:

- *A debt-anchored rule*, which sets an explicit ceiling for public debt-to-GDP ratio over the medium term. While in principle it is easy to communicate and monitor, its implementation requires clear guidance on how to react to shocks that drive fiscal policy off the path consistent with the medium-term anchor. Hence, this rule is generally complemented by operational rules that guide short-term fiscal policy based on fiscal flow variables (Eyraud and others 2018).[2]

- *A balanced-budget rule*, which targets the main fiscal variable affecting debt and is largely under the control of policymakers. It could refer to several

---

[2] As described in IMF (2018), operational rules can be linked to (a) the overall fiscal balance, (b) the fiscal balance net of capital expenditure (so called "golden rules"), (c) the primary balance, (d) the cyclically adjusted balance, (e) the structural balance (which corrects the cyclically adjusted balance for one-off fiscal measures), (f) the over-the-cycle budget balance (which averages over the years and thus encompasses different stages of the business cycle), (g) expenditures, and (h) revenues.

Figure 4.2. Adoption of Fiscal Rules across Countries over Time
(Number of countries)

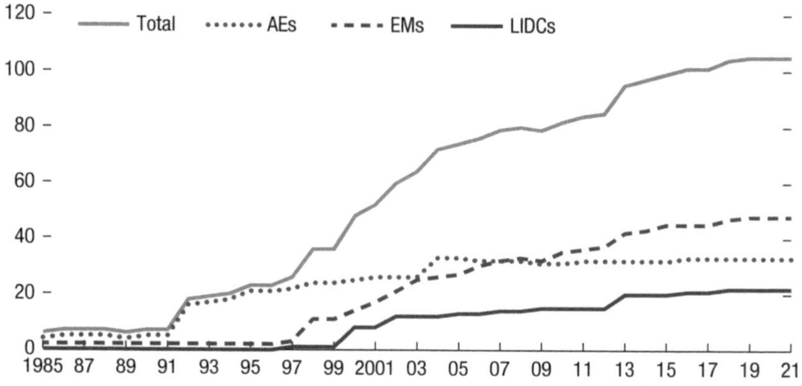

Source: IMF, Fiscal Rules Dataset.
Note: AEs = advanced economies; EMs = emerging economies; LIDCs = low-income developing countries.

fiscal aggregates, namely the overall budget balance, the primary balance, or the cyclically adjusted balance. While the latter allows one to distinguish discretionary policies from automatic stabilizers, it is more complex to implement because real-time cyclical adjustments of output, revenues, and spending are generally subject to high uncertainty and large revisions.

- *A spending rule,* which focuses on fiscal variables that governments can control directly, like total, primary, or current spending, defined in terms of level, percent of GDP, or growth rate. Although this rule is relatively easy to communicate and monitor, it is not directly linked to debt accumulation.

- *A revenue rule,* which sets a ceiling or a floor on revenues. As with the spending rule, this rule is not directly linked to public debt accumulation and is generally used to either incentivize revenue mobilization or prevent an excessive tax burden.

Data show that, as of 2020, 105 countries have adopted at least one type of rule, and most countries adopted two or three rules (Figure 4.3, panel 1). Most of the countries adopting a fiscal rule have chosen either a debt rule or a balanced budget rule, although the number of countries adopting an expenditure rule has increased sharply over the past decade (Figure 4.3, panel 2).

The increased popularity of fiscal rules could be explained by the need to mitigate the tendency of governments to run large fiscal deficits leading to high and increasing public debt levels—the so-called "deficit bias" (Alesina and Tabellini 1990; Persson and Svensson 1989; and Persson, Persson, and Svensson 2006). The literature has identified three broad possible explanations for this bias: (1) government's "short-sightedness": policymakers tend to run excessive deficits in anticipation of being replaced by different governments in the future;

Figure 4.3. Fiscal Rules Characteristics across Time and Countries

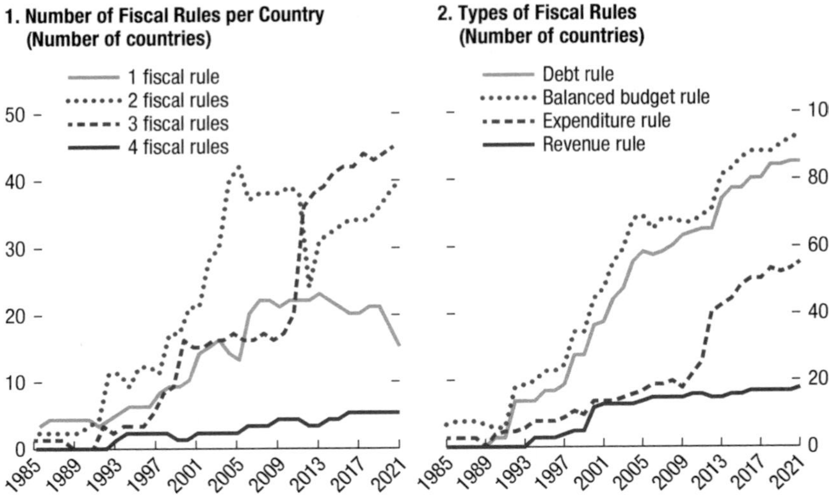

1. Number of Fiscal Rules per Country
(Number of countries)

- 1 fiscal rule
- 2 fiscal rules
- 3 fiscal rules
- 4 fiscal rules

2. Types of Fiscal Rules
(Number of countries)

- Debt rule
- Balanced budget rule
- Expenditure rule
- Revenue rule

Source: IMF, Fiscal Rules Dataset.

(2) a "common pool" problem: fiscal deficits reflect the interest of specific constituencies in using general taxation to finance spending that benefits them; and (3) a "time-inconsistency" problem: governments fail to commit to fiscal discipline given the incentives to stimulate aggregate demand in the short term.

In trying to address these issues, the adoption of a fiscal rule needs to balance the often-competing objectives of flexibility, simplicity, and enforceability. A flexible rule, which readily adapts to macroeconomic shocks, is likely to be complex in its design, making it harder to monitor and enforce (IMF 2018). In the past decade, so-called "second-generation" fiscal rules have expanded their flexibility provisions (that is, by introducing escape clauses) and improved enforceability (by introducing independent fiscal councils, broader sanctions, and correction mechanisms), but this has happened at the cost of simplicity (Eyraud and others 2018). The need to balance these objectives and tailor them to different economic contexts also explains why different countries have adopted different fiscal frameworks and rules.

Understanding which fiscal rule "works" better is challenging. Available evidence finds that the adoption of fiscal rules correlates with lower fiscal deficits and smaller output volatility (Debrun and others 2008; Eyraud and others 2018; and IMF 2015). However, empirical analysis, which addresses the potential endogeneity problem, fails to confirm that fiscal rules lead to lower fiscal deficits (Caselli and Reynaud 2019). Furthermore, Caselli, Stoehlker, and Wingender (2020) showed the importance of going beyond average treatment effect, which masks significant heterogeneity across countries, and found that countries with large deficits tend to reduce it after adopting a fiscal rule.

The overall quality of fiscal institutions may also affect the effectiveness of the fiscal rule. Countries with higher-quality institutions may find it easier to comply with the fiscal rule (for example, because they can better project fiscal outcomes over the near and medium term). At the same time, however, the presence of good-quality institutions may make fiscal rules redundant because the government already has the credibility and capacity to implement effective fiscal policy. A paper by Bergman and others (2016) investigated whether institutional quality is a complement to or a substitute for fiscal rules in the context of European Union countries. It found that fiscal rules tend to reduce government structural primary deficit for any level of government efficiency, although with a diminishing marginal effect, and that fiscal transparency improves the effectiveness of fiscal rules (by avoiding a procyclical bias in fiscal policy). This result suggests that fiscal rules have a key role to play, especially when the quality of institutions is low, and that a strong fiscal framework tends to reinforce the credibility of fiscal policies in the short and medium term.

WHAT IS THE IMPACT OF FISCAL RULES? AN EMPIRICAL ANALYSIS

This section looks at data to empirically assess the impact of fiscal rules on fiscal policy and the cost of debt while controlling for the role of institutional quality (as a proxy of governments' commitment to the fiscal rule and therefore its credibility). To do so, an unbalanced panel of 214 countries over the period 1985–2019 is used (to exclude the year of the COVID-19 pandemic, which caused many countries to suspend their fiscal rule), built by using three main data sources: (1) the IMF World Economic Outlook database, (2) the IMF Fiscal Rules dataset (Davoodi and others 2022b), and (3) the World Bank's Worldwide Governance Indicators. Because of the challenges in identifying a causal relationship between the adoption of fiscal rules and fiscal policy outcomes, the results should be interpreted more as strong correlations than as causal linkages.

Fiscal Rules and the Cost of Debt

The empirical analysis supports the view that the adoption of fiscal rules is related to a reduction in the cost of debt and that institutional quality can reinforce the impact of fiscal rules by increasing credibility. The empirical strategy uses the following regression equation:

$$\frac{Interest}{GDP}_{it} = c + \alpha_i + \delta_t + \gamma GDPCYCL_{it} + \beta \frac{CAB}{GDP_{it}} + \phi \frac{CAB}{GDP_{it}} * \mathbb{1}(FISCRULE)$$
$$+ \theta \frac{GovDebt}{GDP}_{i(t-1)} + \varepsilon_{it}, \qquad (4.1)$$

where α_i and δ_t are the country and year fixed effects, respectively; $GDPCYCL_{it}$ is the cyclical component of GDP, computed as the residual from a regression of the log nominal GDP over a linear time trend (virtually equivalent results are obtained with a quadratic polynomial); $\dfrac{CAB}{GDP_{it}}$ is the cyclically adjusted balance as a share of GDP for country i in year t (a proxy for discretionary spending); the dummy $\mathbb{1}(FISCRULE)$ equals 1 from the year of adoption of a fiscal rule, interacted with the cyclically adjusted balance to capture the extent to which the introduction of the fiscal rule changes the response of interest rate spending to fiscal policy; and $\dfrac{GovDebt}{GDP}$ is the previous year government debt-to-GDP ratio, which accounts for the impact of the size of debt on interest payments. This regression is run both on the full sample and separately for emerging market countries, which are a closer comparison group with Morocco.

Regression results show that while an increase in cyclically adjusted fiscal deficits raises interest spending, this effect is weaker for countries adopting a fiscal rule (Table 4.1, column 1). This suggests that the introduction of a fiscal rule may anchor expectations and reduce the risk premium requested by investors. These results hold also when restricting the analysis to the subset of emerging markets (Table 4.1, column 2).

Good governance can reinforce the effect of fiscal rules and further reduce sovereign spreads. To explore the possible effect of institutional quality on fiscal rules, the econometric model presented in the previous part is augmented with an indicator of institutional quality from the World Bank's Worldwide Governance Indicators. Three indicators (effectiveness of the government in conducting policies and achieving its objectives, the regulatory framework, and the control of corruption) are aggregated to form an average measure of institutional quality and create a dummy variable $\mathbb{1}(QUALITY)$ that is 1 if at least one of the three indicators is above the 75th percentile of the distribution and zero otherwise. The following equation augments equation (4.1) with the quality dummy, estimated

TABLE 4.1.

Cost of Debt and Fiscal Rules across Countries

	Interest Spending as a Ratio to GDP	
GovDebt/GDP	0.001**	0.01***
	[0.000]	[0.002]
GDPCYCL	−1.024***	−0.953***
	[0.117]	[0.161]
CAB/GDP	−0.104***	−0.095***
	[0.011]	[0.012]
FISCRULE *CAB/GDP	0.031**	0.061***
	[0.014]	[0.018]
Constant	3.772***	3.490***
	[0.431]	[0.456]
Observations	1,542	984
Countries	All	EMs

Sources: IMF, Fiscal Rules Dataset; and IMF staff calculations.
Note: CAB/GDP = cyclically adjusted balance over GDP; EMs = emerging markets; FISCRULE = dummy for a country with a fiscal rule; GDPCYCL = cyclical GDP; GovDebt/GDP = government debt over GDP.
$*p < .10; **p < .05; ***p < .01.$

TABLE 4.2.

Fiscal Rules and Quality of Institutions

	Interest/GDP	
GovDebt/GDP	0.001***	0.010***
	[0.000]	[0.002]
GDPCYCL	−0.829***	−0.945***
	[0.122]	[0.172]
QUALITY	0.667***	0.699***
	[0.117]	[0.184]
CAB/GDP	−0.100***	−0.091***
	[0.011]	[0.013]
FISCRULE *CAB/GDP	0.031*	0.043**
	[0.017]	[0.021]
FISCRULE *CAB/GDP *QUALITY	0.050**	0.110***
	[0.020]	[0.039]
Constant	3.763***	3.608***
	[0.453]	[0.456]
Observations	1,697	984
Countries	All	EMs

Sources: IMF, Fiscal Rules Dataset; World Bank, Worldwide Governance Indicators; and IMF staff calculations.

Note: CAB/GDP = cyclically adjusted balance over GDP; EMs = emerging markets; FISCRULE = dummy for a country with a fiscal rule; GDPCYCL = cyclical GDP; GovDebt/GDP = government debt over GDP; QUALITY = dummy for high institutional quality.

*$p < .10$; **$p < .05$; ***$p < .01$.

both on its own and interacted with the fiscal rule dummy and the cyclically adjusted budget balance.

$$\frac{Interest}{GDP}_{it} = c + \alpha_i + \delta_t + \gamma GDPCYCL_{it} + \zeta \mathbb{1}(QUALITY) + \beta \frac{CAB}{GDP_{it}} + \phi \frac{CAB}{GDP_{it}}$$
$$* \mathbb{1}(FISCRULE) * \mathbb{1}(QUALITY) + \theta \frac{GovDebt}{GDP}_{i(t-1)} + \varepsilon_{it} \quad\quad (4.2)$$

The empirical results indicate that the quality of institutions reinforces the impact of the fiscal rule by helping reduce the cost of debt after a deterioration of the cyclically adjusted fiscal balance (see Table 4.2, column 1). Although a higher fiscal deficit increases the interest payment, this effect is attenuated by the presence of a fiscal rule (positive coefficient in the first interaction term), especially in the presence of high-quality institutions (positive coefficient in the second interaction term).[3] These results are confirmed when the sample is restricted to emerging market economies (Table 4.2, column 2). For an average emerging market economy like Morocco, the introduction of a fiscal rule could reduce by about half the increase in interest payment following a higher fiscal deficit and improving institutional quality could fully neutralize the increase in the interest bill.

---

[3] The positive coefficient for the "quality" variable indicates that countries with higher quality tend to have a higher interest burden, but this might be driven by the possibility that countries with good institutions tend to have a higher level of debt (indeed, the level of debt in advanced economies is higher than the level of debt in low-income and emerging market economies).

Fiscal Rules and Countercyclical Fiscal Policies

Although a lower cost of debt frees resources for an expansionary fiscal policy during downturns, in the absence of carefully designed escape clauses, fiscal rules may end up imposing tight constraints to government spending and lead to countercyclical fiscal policy stances. It is no surprise, then, that standard regressions relating GDP fluctuations to fiscal policy without classifying fiscal rules according to their degree of flexibility show that the discipline effect of fiscal rules is dominant, and that fiscal policy is more procyclical under fiscal rules (Guerquil, Mandon, and Tapsoba 2016).

Our baseline panel regression is specified as:

$$y_{it} = c + \alpha_i + \delta_t + \gamma GDPCYCL + \beta GDPCYCL * \mathbb{1}(FISCRULE) + \varepsilon_{it} \qquad (4.3)$$

where y_{it} denotes the fiscal outcomes (overall balance, primary balance, cyclically adjusted balance, all as share of GDP). The dummy $\mathbb{1}(FISCRULE)$ is interacted with the cyclical component of GDP to capture the extent to which the introduction of the fiscal rule changes the response of the fiscal variables to the business cycle.

The results confirm that both overall and primary fiscal balances tend to respond less to the business cycle after the adoption of a fiscal rule (Table 4.3, columns 1 and 2). This is consistent with countries adopting a fiscal rule increasing spending by less (or reducing it by more), relative to countries without a fiscal rule, when the economy is hit by a shock. The cyclically adjusted fiscal balance is less responsive to cyclical GDP fluctuations (Table 4.3, column 3), pointing to a more conservative discretionary policy response in countries with a fiscal rule. These results hold also when considering the subsample of emerging market economies (Table 4.3, columns 2, 4, and 6).

In general, our results corroborate the role of fiscal rules as a discipline device that avoids excessive deficits and accumulation of debt by constraining the response of government to economic shocks, thus leading to a smaller cost of debt. Adopting a fiscal rule, however, is consistent with the pursuit of countercyclical fiscal policy only in the presence of carefully designed escape clauses. Guerguil, Mandon, and Tapsoba (2016) and IMF (2022) showed that "flexible"

TABLE 4.3.

Fiscal Rules and the Cyclicality of Fiscal Policy across Countries						
	Overall Balance		**Primary Balance**		**Cyclically Adjusted Balance**	
GDPCYCL	3.684***	4.460***	3.672***	4.879***	−0.166	0.184
	[0.259]	[0.382]	[0.264]	[0.397]	[0.371]	[0.487]
FISCRULE * GDPCYCL	−3.455***	−2.613***	−3.389***	−3.438***	−3.585***	−2.523***
	[0.507]	[0.847]	[0.503]	[0.842]	[0.473]	[0.751]
Constant	−3.221***	−1.941	−0.620	0.596	−3.567***	−2.060
	[0.703]	[1.435]	[0.802]	[1.675]	[0.820]	[2.781]
Observations	5,233	2,531	4,957	2,397	2,122	1,030
Countries	All	EMs	All	EMs	All	EMs

Sources: IMF, Fiscal Rules Dataset; and IMF staff calculations.
Note: EMs = emerging markets; FISCRULE = fiscal rule; GDPCYCL = cyclical GDP.
*$p < .10$; **$p < .05$; ***$p < .01$.

fiscal rules—that is, rules that include escape clauses—and rules that target cyclically adjusted fiscal aggregates are associated with countercyclical fiscal policies. The possibility of fiscal rules creating space for countercyclical fiscal response is further explored in the model simulation conducted in the next section.

A QUANTITATIVE ANALYSIS OF A DEBT-ANCHORED FISCAL RULE IN MOROCCO

In this section, a general equilibrium model calibrated on the Moroccan economy is used to simulate the impact of a debt-anchored fiscal rule. The effect of the rule on the overall fiscal balance and the cost of debt, as well as the economic channels through which the rule operates, are explored.[4]

The model, based on Hatchondo, Martinez, and Roch (2020, 2022), permits investigation of the trade-off between flexibility and commitment in the context of a fiscal rule. It consists of a sovereign default general equilibrium model in which the government's objective is to maximize the welfare of a representative agent subject to an intertemporal budget constraint. Each period, the government decides on the amount of bonds to issue to finance its spending, as well as whether it should default on its existing stock of debt. Issuing bonds increases the cost of debt. More specifically, the government issues only long-term bonds, with a spread that depends both on the current and projected levels of debt and the probability of default (increasing with the size of debt). If the government chooses to default, it loses access to capital markets.

The model is calibrated to represent a small open economy like Morocco. For some parameters of the model, such as the risk-free interest rate, the discount factor, and the relative risk aversion coefficient, standard values from the literature are used (see Table 4.4). Other key parameters, such as the volatility and persistence of GDP, and the quarterly coupon payment, are estimated using the Moroccan data (see Table 4.4).[5] Finally, the parameters governing the costs of default are calibrated to match some empirical moments of Moroccan sovereign spread and debt ratio. The exercise uses quarterly data from 2012 to 2022. Table 4.5 shows that the model (without a fiscal rule) matches the data well. For example, in the no-fiscal-rule scenario, the model steady-state debt ratio is 61 percent of GDP, which is in line with the average central government debt ratio between 2010 and 2019.

In the absence of a credible commitment device, such as a fiscal rule, the government makes its optimal spending and borrowing decisions period by period, without considering their impact on the value of the existing stock of debt. This "time inconsistency" leads the government to overborrow. Facing a higher cost of

---

[4] We do not explicitly bring the quality of fiscal institutions in the model, but implicitly assume that the fiscal rule is credible and effectively implemented.

[5] Data for the mean and the standard deviation of the Moroccan sovereign spread come from the J.P. Morgan Emerging Market Bond Index Spread series from the first quarter of 2013 to the second quarter of 2022.

TABLE 4.4.

Calibration of Parameter Values

Parameters Estimated or Derived from Literature				Parameters Calibrated to Match Targets			
r	Risk-free interest rate	0.01	Standard	σ_u	Volatility of default cost	0.1	Std. dev. spread = 0.45%
β	Discount factor	0.97	Standard	d_0	Parameter governing the default cost	0.184	Avg. debt = 61%
ρ	Persistence of GDP process	0.83	Morocco GDP	d_1	Parameter governing the default cost	0.65	Avg. spread = 2.2%
σ_ε	Std. dev. of innovations to GDP process	1.6%	Morocco GDP				
μ	Mean log-GDP	$-0.5\sigma_\varepsilon^2$	$E(y) = 1$				
ψ	Default probability	0.083	E (exclusion duration) = 3 years				
δ	Coupon payment per period	0.0183	Debt duration = 6.5 years				
γ	Relative risk aversion coefficient	2	Standard				

Sources: J.P. Morgan Emerging Market Bond Index Spread series; and IMF staff calculations.
Note: Avg. = average; Std. dev. = standard deviation.

borrowing, during economic downturns the government finances a greater share of its debt through taxes rather than new issuances, amplifying the recessionary impact of the downturn. Hence, in the no-commitment equilibrium, the government's optimal fiscal policy tends to be procyclical.

A debt-anchored fiscal rule can reduce the time-inconsistency problem. Under such a rule, the government commits to a medium-term debt ceiling (that is, the anchor). The model implicitly assumes that the government cannot change the rule and will always comply with it; that is, the fiscal rule credibly ties the government's hands. The debt ceiling and transition path in the model are the result of an optimization exercise that maximizes households' intertemporal utility under the intertemporal budget constraint and the additional constraint represented by the fiscal rule (see Hatchondo, Martinez, and Roch 2020, 2022 for the details). The solution to this problem in our model leads to a debt-to-GDP medium-term anchor of 58.75 percent and a transition path of six years (Figure 4.4).

TABLE 4.5.

Data and Model Simulations

	Data	Model Steady State
Mean debt (percent of GDP)	61	61
Mean spread (percent)	2.2	2.23
Standard deviation spread	0.45	0.45
Ratio of consumption to income volatility	1.2	1.1

Source: IMF staff calculations.

Figure 4.4. Average Sovereign Spread and Debt with and without a Fiscal Rule

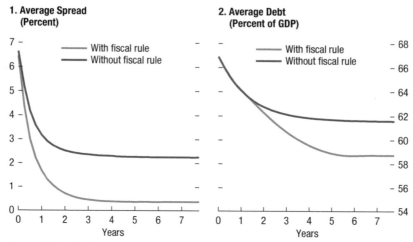

1. Average Spread
   (Percent)

2. Average Debt
   (Percent of GDP)

With fiscal rule
Without fiscal rule

Years

Source: IMF staff calculations.
Note: The figure shows the average path of the spread and the debt level from the simulation of 25,000 samples of eight years each.

The lower debt-to-GDP ratio targeted in the fiscal rule scenario (compared to the no-rule steady-state ratio of 61 percent) implies that sovereign spreads are lower and less volatile under the rule (the average spread goes from 2.23 to 0.36, whereas its volatility drops from 0.45 to 0.11) (Table 4.6). Because the cost of borrowing is less responsive to income shocks, fiscal policy becomes less procyclical, as reflected by the lower volatility of aggregate consumption relative to income. In the medium term, households are better off with the fiscal rule (their intertemporal utility increases).

The government benefits from the introduction of a credible medium-term anchor and related constraints on the debt path. The average spread under a fiscal rule is below that in the no-rule economy already from the time of the rule announcement, even if the initial level of debt is the same (Figure 4.4).

TABLE 4.6.

Model Simulations: Steady State with and without a Fiscal Rule		
	No Fiscal Rule	**With Fiscal Rule**
Mean debt (percent of GDP)	61	58.75
Mean spread (percent)	2.23	0.36
Standard deviation spread	0.45	0.11
Ratio of consumption to income volatility	1.1	1.0

Source: IMF staff calculations.

CONCLUSION

Morocco is facing a challenging economic environment. The legacy of the pandemic and the fallout from geopolitical tensions imply that fiscal policymakers face a difficult trade-off between supporting growth and structural reforms on one side and rebuilding fiscal space on the other. Morocco has recently strengthened its fiscal policy framework with the publication of a medium-term fiscal framework that provides some visibility on the authorities' fiscal plans over the next three years. Still, combining this Medium-Term Fiscal Framework with a new fiscal rule based on a medium-term debt target and an associated operational rule could further improve the transparency and credibility of fiscal policy, and improve the terms of the trade-off faced by Morocco. Our results suggest that fiscal rules are generally associated with a lower cost of public debt because they tend to generate confidence in the government's ability to maintain fiscal discipline. Even though fiscal rules seem to restrict fiscal policy's ability to react to shocks, our model simulations show that a fiscal framework based on a medium-term debt target and an operational rule facilitates debt reduction by delivering a lower cost of debt (by a factor of six) while allowing fiscal policy to react to negative shocks. While the model implicitly assumes that the fiscal rule is credible and effectively implemented, looking at past experiences of fiscal rules suggests that a key condition for their success is the presence of credible and effective fiscal institutions.

REFERENCES

Alesina, Alberto, and Guido Tabellini. 1990. "A Positive Theory of Fiscal Deficits and Government Debt." *Review of Economic Studies* 57: 403–14.

Bergman, U. Michael, Michael M. Hutchison, and Sven E. Hougaard Jensen. 2016. "Promoting Sustainable Public Finances in the European Union: The Role of Fiscal Rules and Government Efficiency." *European Journal of Political Economy* 44: 1–19.

Caselli, Francesca, and Julien Reynaud. 2019. "Do Fiscal Rules Cause Better Fiscal Balances? A New Instrumental Variable Strategy." IMF Working Paper 19/049, International Monetary Fund, Washington, DC.

Caselli, Francesca, Hamid Davoodi, Carlos Goncalves, Gee Hee Hong, Andresa Lagerborg, Paulo Medas, Anh Dinh Minh Nguyen, and Jiae Yoo. 2022. "The Return to Fiscal Rules." IMF Staff Discussion Note 22/002, International Monetary Fund, Washington, DC.

Caselli, Francesca, Daniel Stoehlker, and Philippe Wingender. 2020. "Individual Treatment Effects of Budget Balance Rules." IMF Working Paper 20/274, International Monetary Fund, Washington, DC.

Davoodi, Hamid, Paul Elger, Alexandra Fotiou, Daniel Garcia-Macia, Xuehui Han, Andresa Lagerborg, Raphael Lam, and Paulo Medas. 2022a. "Fiscal Rules and Fiscal Councils." IMF Working Paper 22/11, International Monetary Fund, Washington, DC.

Davoodi, Hamid, Paul Elger, Alexandra Fotiou, Daniel Garcia-Macia, Andresa Lagerborg, Raphael Lam, and Sharanya Pillai. 2022b. "Fiscal Rules Dataset: 1985–2021." International Monetary Fund, Washington, DC.

Debrun, Xavier, Laurent Moulin, Alessandro Turrini, Joaquim Ayuso-i-Casals, Manmohan Kumar, Allan Drazen, and Clemens Fuest. 2008. "Tied to the Mast? National Fiscal Rules in the European Union." *Economic Policy* 23 (54): 297–362.

Eyraud, Luc, Xavier Debrun, Andrew Hodge, Victor Lledó, and Catherine Pattillo. 2018. "Second-generation Fiscal Rules: Balancing Simplicity, Flexibility, and Enforceability." IMF Staff Discussion Note 18/4, International Monetary Fund, Washington, DC.

Guerguil, Martine, Pierre Mandon, and Rene Tapsoba. 2016. "Flexible Fiscal Rules and Countercyclical Fiscal Policy." IMF Working Paper 16/8, International Monetary Fund, Washington, DC.

Hatchondo, Juan Carlos, Leonardo Martinez, and Francisco Roch. 2020. "Constrained Efficient Borrowing with Sovereign Default Risk." IMF Working Paper 20/277, International Monetary Fund, Washington, DC.

Hatchondo, Juan Carlos, Leonardo Martinez, and Francisco Roch. 2022. "Fiscal Rules and the Sovereign Default Premium." *American Economic Journal: Macroeconomics* 14 (4): 244–73.

International Monetary Fund (IMF). 2015. *Fiscal Monitor: Now Is the Time. Fiscal Policies for Sustainable Growth*. International Monetary Fund, Washington, DC, April.

International Monetary Fund (IMF). 2018. *How to Select Fiscal Rules—A Primer*. Washington, DC, March.

International Monetary Fund (IMF). 2022. "The Return to Fiscal Rules." IMF Staff Discussion Note 22/002, International Monetary Fund, Washington, DC.

International Monetary Fund (IMF). 2023. "Morocco 2022 Article IV Consultation Staff Report." Country Report 23/042, International Monetary Fund, Washington, DC.

Persson, Torsten, and Lars E. O. Svensson. 1989. "Why a Stubborn Conservative would Run a Deficit: Policy with Time-inconsistent Preferences." *The Quarterly Journal of Economics* 104 (2): 325–45.

Persson, Mats, Torsten Persson, and Lars E. O. Svensson. 2006. "Time Consistency of Fiscal and Monetary Policy: A Solution." *Econometrica* 74 (1): 193–212.

PART III

Achieving a More Productive and Diversified Economy

CHAPTER 5

Raising Morocco's Potential Growth: Assessing the Impact of Structural Reforms

Hippolyte Balima, Olivier Bizimana, and Ananta Dua

INTRODUCTION

A well-known stylized fact of the Moroccan economy is the deceleration of gross domestic product (GDP) growth after the global financial crisis of 2008 compared with the previous decade (Figure 5.1). This has slowed Morocco's output convergence to Organisation for Economic Co-operation and Development (OECD) countries (Figure 5.2) and raised questions regarding whether the country's growth potential has weakened. While real GDP bounced back from the health crisis and drought-related recession in 2020, questions remain as to whether the pandemic and climate change may have further impacted Morocco's growth prospects.

Against this background, Morocco's policymakers have made raising potential output growth a priority. In the aftermath of the pandemic, several reforms were

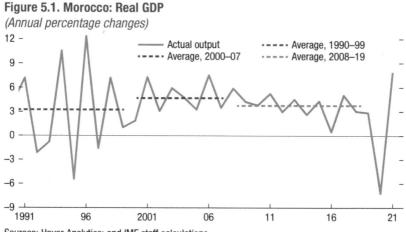

Figure 5.1. Morocco: Real GDP
(Annual percentage changes)

Sources: Haver Analytics; and IMF staff calculations.

Figure 5.2. Morocco: GDP per Capita
(International dollars at purchasing power parity)

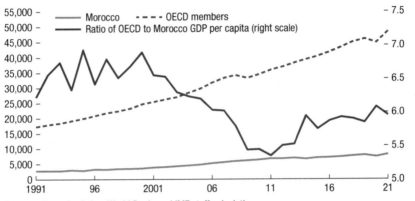

Sources: Haver Analytics; World Bank; and IMF staff calculations.
Note: OECD = Organisation for Economic Co-operation and Development.

launched, including a comprehensive reform of social protection programs, an overhaul of the health and education systems, a new strategy to deal with water scarcity, and several measures to develop the private sector and reduce the role of the state in the economy, in line with the recommendations of the new development model (NMD) report (see Chapter 2).

Although the literature suggests that well-designed structural reforms can have meaningful effects on potential output growth, there is substantial uncertainty with regard to the magnitude and timing of their impact on economic activity and welfare (Bouis and Duval 2011; Duval and Furceri 2018; October 2019 *World Economic Outlook*). The objective of this chapter is to address three main questions: (1) How has Morocco's potential output growth evolved over the past two decades and what were its main drivers? (2) To what extent has the pandemic crisis affected potential output in Morocco? and (3) What are the potential effects of structural reforms on Morocco's potential output in the medium to long term? To answer these questions, a series of standard methodologies found in the literature were used, including multivariate filtering (MVF) techniques to estimate Morocco's potential growth, its main drivers, and the impact of the pandemic on potential output. A production function approach and a general equilibrium model were then used to analyze the impact of the reforms on Morocco's potential output growth.

ESTIMATING MOROCCO'S POTENTIAL OUTPUT

In this section, Morocco's potential output was estimated using MVF.[1] This methodology defines potential output as the level of output consistent with stable (non-accelerating) inflation, and it is based on two relationships, namely (a) between

---

[1] See Alichi and others (2015) and Blagrave and others (2015) for more details on the MVF.

TABLE 5.1.

Potential Output: Definition and Sources	
Variable	**Source**
Potential Output Growth and Its Components	
Potential output growth	Estimates using multivariate filter
Capital stock	University of Groningen, PWT—capital stock level in 1990; Estimates based on the perpetual inventory method with GFCF
Depreciation rate of capital stock	University of Groningen, PWT
Working-age population	UN Department of Economic and Social Affairs
Labor force participation	International Labor Organization Estimates and Projections
Nonaccelerating inflation rate of unemployment	Estimates using multivariate filter
Other Macro Variables	
Gross domestic product (constant prices)	HCP; October 2019 *World Economic Outlook*
Inflation	HCP; October 2019 *World Economic Outlook*
Unemployment	HCP; October 2019 *World Economic Outlook*

Source: Authors.
Note: GFCF = gross fixed capital formation; HCP = Haut Commissariat au Plan; PWT = Penn World Table.

inflation and cyclical unemployment (the deviation of the unemployment rate from the level consistent with stable inflation [nonaccelerating inflation rate of unemployment, or NAIRU]) (Phillips curve), and (b) between cyclical unemployment and the output gap (Okun's law):

$$\pi_t = \pi_t^e + \delta u_t + \varepsilon_t^\pi$$

$$u_t = \tau y_t + \varepsilon_t^u$$

where π_t is inflation, y_t is the output gap, u_t is cyclical unemployment, π_t^e is inflation expectations, and ε_t^π and ε_t^u are shock, or disturbance, terms. The parameters in these equations (δ, τ), together with data on actual output growth, inflation, and unemployment, are used to derive estimates of potential output and the NAIRU, which are unobserved.[2]

The MVF model is estimated using data from 1990 to 2019 (see Table 5.1 for the sources of data). The collapse of output in 2020 and its rapid rebound in 2021 represent a structural break in the data that is likely to introduce a downward bias in the estimates of potential growth before 2020.[3] To avoid this problem, potential output before the crisis is estimated using data prior to 2020, and those estimates are then frozen.[4] Moreover, the sample was extended beyond 2021 using projections until 2023 from the October 2021 *World Economic Outlook*.

---

[2] The model also requires "expert judgement" on steady-state values and near-term forecasts of observables as well as unobservable variables (output gap, potential growth, and NAIRU). The steady-state values for GDP growth and the unemployment rate are assumed to be equal to the pre-pandemic historical average (between 2010 and 2019).

[3] Filtering methods compute the trend value of a variable using its past and future values. Estimates of the trend become more unstable toward the end of the sample due to fewer available future values (the well-known end-of-sample problem). To correct this problem, the projections from the October 2019 *World Economic Outlook* were used because they are not affected by the pandemic shock.

[4] Bodnár and others (2020) used a similar approach.

Figure 5.3. Morocco: Contributions of Components of Potential Output Growth
(Percentage points)

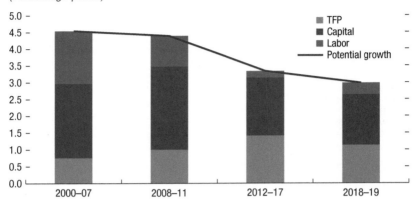

Source: IMF staff calculations.
Note: Figure shows period averages. TFP = total factor productivity.

To shed light on the drivers of potential growth in Morocco, a standard Cobb-Douglas production function was used:

$$\bar{Y}_t = \bar{A}_t K_t^{(\alpha)} \bar{L}_t^{(1-\alpha)}$$

in which $\bar{Y}_t$ is the potential output estimated with the multivariate filter; K_t is the stock of capital; $\bar{L}_t$ is potential employment; $\bar{A}_t$ is trend total factor productivity (TFP), which is treated as a residual; and α is the income share of capital. Potential employment $(\bar{L}_t)$ in turn can be expressed as a function of the estimate of NAIRU $(\bar{U}_t)$, the working-age population (W_t), and the trend labor force participation rate $(\overline{LFRP}_t)$:[5]

$$\bar{L}_t = (1 - \bar{U}_t) W_t \overline{LFRP}_t$$

Potential growth is calculated as $\Delta\ln(\bar{Y}_t) = \Delta\ln(\bar{A}_t) + \alpha\Delta\ln(K_t) + (1 - \alpha)\Delta\ln(\bar{L}_t)$

This estimate shows that, after averaging about 4.5 percent between 2000 and 2007, Morocco's potential output growth began to slow after the global financial crisis to reach about 3 percent right before the pandemic (Figure 5.3).[6] This reflects different contributions from production factors and their productivity:

- *Labor inputs:* The contribution of trend employment to potential growth declined from 1.6 percentage points between 2000 and 2007 to about 0.3

---

[5] The trend labor force is obtained by detrending (using a Hodrick-Prescott filter) the participation rate.

[6] Our results are broadly consistent with previous studies on Morocco. For example, using three different methods (Hodrick-Prescott filter, production function, and multivariate filter), Chafik (2017) found that Morocco's potential growth declined from about 4.5 percent between 2000 and 2007 to about 4 percent between 2008 and 2016.

in 2018–19, accounting for about three-quarters of the drop over that period. This performance was largely driven by slower growth of Morocco's working-age population and to a lesser extent by the decline of the trend labor force participation rate (by about 6 percentage points) (Figure 5.4). Estimates of the NAIRU declined, but from the very high level of about 13.3 percent in 2000 to about 10.2 percent in 2019 (Figure 5.4).

Figure 5.4. Morocco: Pre-Covid Potential Output Growth Estimates

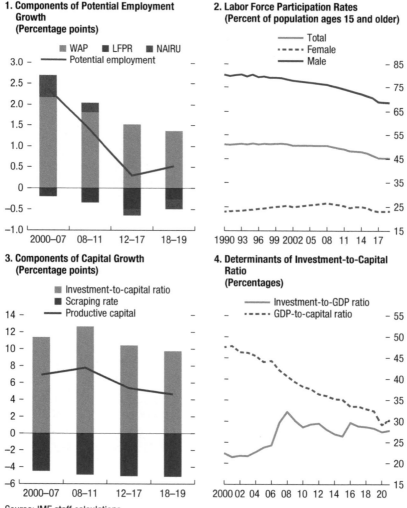

Source: IMF staff calculations.
Note: Panels 1 and 2 show period averages. LFPR = labor force participation rate;
NAIRU = nonaccelerating inflation rate of unemployment; WAP = working-age population.

- *Capital stock:* The contribution from capital accumulation fell from 2¼ percentage points in the early 2000s to about 1.5 percentage points in 2018–19. This is turn reflects an investment-to-GDP ratio that rose between 2000 and 2007 and stabilized in the following years (slightly below 30 percent) (Figure 5.4). By contrast, the growth rate of capital productivity (the ratio of GDP to capital stock) has been on a downward trend over the past two decades.

- *Total factor productivity:* The TFP contribution to potential output growth rose from 0.8 percentage points in 2000–07 to 1.1 percent in 2018–19. Being calculated as a residual, TFP can capture factors other than technical progress, such as the effects of changes in hours worked, labor quality, and capital utilization.

Potential output is estimated to have contracted by about 0.5 percent in 2020 (Figure 5.5). The combination of the pandemic and the drought caused a large fall in investment in 2020, the largest contraction since the beginning of the series. As a result, the contribution of capital accumulation to potential growth dropped from 1.5 percentage points in 2019 to 1 percentage point in 2020. Potential employment growth remained broadly unchanged at 0.5 percent in 2020 as the continued expansion in working-age population offset the slight uptick in the estimated NAIRU, while the trend labor force participation rate remained roughly unchanged. Hence, the contribution of labor to potential output growth fell slightly by 0.1 percentage point in 2020. Still, most of the decline of potential growth in 2020 is explained by the fall in TFP (the estimated contribution of TFP to potential output growth went from 1 percentage point in 2018–19 to about –2 percentage points in 2020). This may reflect the adjustment costs to work routine and supply chains of the containment measures adopted in response to the health crisis, as well as costly reallocation of resources across sectors. On the upside, the acceleration of digitalization caused by remote working

Figure 5.5. Morocco: Potential Growth and Its Drivers
(Percent)

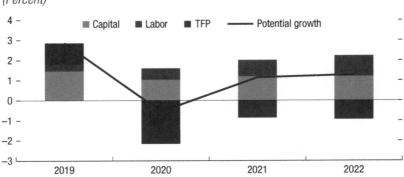

Source: IMF staff calculations.
Note: TFP = total factor productivity.

and containment measures is likely to boost TFP, although this effect may only be more visible over time.

As the economy reopened and investment picked up in 2021–22, potential output growth rose to about 1 percent, driven by capital accumulation (the contribution of capital input to potential growth accelerated by about 0.2 percentage point) and labor input (the contribution of potential employment increased in 2021–22 by about 0.5 percentage point, reflecting the recovery in the participation rate and continued expansion in working-age population). TFP continued to contract during the economic recovery, albeit at a slower pace, with a contribution of about –1 percentage point in 2021–22 (Figure 5.5).

MOROCCO'S AGENDA OF STRUCTURAL REFORMS

Morocco has launched an ambitious post–COVID-19 structural reforms agenda to boost potential output and make growth more inclusive in the medium term. Key areas where Morocco has initiated or unveiled deep reforms include:[7]

- *Social protection and health sector:* The reform, which started in 2020, aims at extending health care coverage to all Moroccans and improving the efficiency and targeting of the country's social safety nets. A series of decrees has been approved in 2021 and 2022 to include self-employed individuals (about 11 million Moroccans) into a new mandatory insurance health care scheme, while those previously benefiting from free health care will be given the option of using both public and private health care starting from 2023. A complete overhaul of the health care system also began in 2022, with the objective of improving efficiency and quality of the supply of health care.[8] The reform of Morocco's social protection system also envisages the extension of conditional cash transfers (family allowances), pensions (to self-employed people), and unemployment insurance, as well as the introduction of a unified social registry to better target Morocco's social programs.[9]

- *Education:* The 2019 Education Act aimed at starting universal preschool education; enhancing teachers' formation and assessment; redesigning curricula at all levels, including by prioritizing STEM (science, technology,

---

[7] The government's reform agenda includes other areas, such as reforms of the taxation and pension systems, the liberalization of the electricity market, and a new strategy to address water scarcity. Because these reforms are still at an early stage, we do not consider them in the chapter.

[8] The supply of health care will be reorganized around new regional health care centers under the direction of a new national high-health authority. The reform also foresees the building of new hospitals, the recruiting of additional medical personnel with remuneration linked to productivity, the introduction of protocols that favor family doctors and local practices, and greater use of digitalization to facilitate exchange of patient information.

[9] All Moroccan households wishing to apply for social programs will need to register under the unified social registry. Each household will be assigned a "standard of living" score based on self-declared and verified information on socioeconomic status, and its eligibility for social programs will depend on the scores being below certain thresholds.

engineering, and math) and early reading at primary levels; and reducing regional disparities in education. In 2022, a new four-year roadmap was unveiled that aims at (1) reducing by one-third the drop-out rate in primary education, (2) increasing by one-third the number of students with basic skills at the end of primary school, and (3) doubling the number of students who benefit from extracurricular activities. Achieving these objectives will require more investment in physical capital (school infrastructure) and human capital (with an overhaul of the recruiting, training, and payment of teachers).

- *Product market:* The ongoing reform of the state-owned enterprise (SOE) sector introduces a national agency responsible for the valorization, strategic management, and monitoring of Moroccan SOEs. The reform aims at (1) eliminating the SOEs whose mission is deemed no longer essential, (2) merging the SOEs that operate in the same sector to exploit potential synergies, and (3) corporatizing all SOEs with commercial activities to strengthen their governance. Together with the operationalization of the Mohammed VI Fund, the implementation of a new charter of investment, and continued strengthening of competition and consumer protection legislative frameworks, these reforms are expected to foster market neutrality between public and private sector firms and to provide an important contribution to private sector development.

- *Governance:* Morocco has also accelerated reforms that should improve the quality of governance. This includes progress in the fight against corruption, with the National Authority for Probity, Prevention, and the Fight Against Corruption (INPPLC) now endowed with the necessary means and legal framework to implement the national anticorruption strategy, with the appointment of the INPPLC's secretary general and members of its board of directors in late 2022. This legal framework is expected to improve the effectiveness of anticorruption measures. Efforts are also ongoing, including those to strengthen the country's penal procedural code, reinforce its whistleblower legislation, and introduce more preventive measures in the fight against corruption.

- *Gender gaps:* At 21 percent in 2021, the rate of participation by Moroccan women in the labor force lags other countries at a similar income level. Several recent initiatives should promote gender equality. Among these, increasing preschool enrollment rate from the current 70 percent to 100 percent by 2028 should help the participation of women in the labor market. In particular, through regulation issued in 2022, Bank Al-Maghrib required credit institutions, to (1) consider gender in defining their strategic orientations, (2) integrate gender into their financing and investment strategies, including through issuing gender bonds, and (3) design banking products and services specifically for women, especially entrepreneurs. In addition, the new development model has laid out proposals to substantially increase women's participation in the economy and society. These include measures to foster women's participation by strengthening social protections for working women during pregnancy and maternity leave, developing infrastructure to facilitate their working life (public daycare and preschool facilities, childcare facilities for large corporations), working-hour flexibility, a tax deduction for domestic workers, as well as a law on wage parity and a tax incentive for virtuous companies in terms of gender policy.

Previous studies on the macroeconomic impacts of structural reforms generally found that structural reforms boost output in the medium term, although the potential payoffs and transmission channels vary depending on the type of reforms, their complementarity and sequencing, as well as country-specific conditions (Blanchard and Giavazzi 2003; IMF 2015; October 2019 *World Economic Outlook*). For instance, the October 2019 *World Economic Outlook* showed that for the average emerging market and developing economy, major reforms across several areas—including trade, domestic and external finance, product and labor markets, and governance—can lead to a sizable increase in GDP in the medium term (October 2019 *World Economic Outlook*).

Research indicates that social protection and health supply policies can contribute to social stability and protect and enhance productivity and human capital, particularly among poor households, and thus positively impact potential growth (Mathers and Slater 2014; OECD 2019). Enhancing human capital will boost productivity and support long-term growth prospects, although the payoffs of education reforms typically materialize in the longer term (Benos and Zotou 2014; Dabla-Norris and others 2013). The impact of product and labor market reforms has received greater attention, especially for advanced economies. Studies found that product and labor market deregulation reduces and redistributes rents (through the effects on entry costs, the degree of competition, and the bargaining power of workers), and therefore boosts aggregate labor productivity and employment over the long term (Barnes and others 2013; Bouis and Duval 2011; Duval and Furceri 2018; April 2016 *World Economic Outlook*). In the case of Morocco, well-designed labor market and product market reforms could substantially increase output and employment in the medium term (see Sarr, Benlamine, and Munkacsi 2019). Several studies suggest that long-term growth in emerging markets and developing economies stands to benefit significantly from governance reforms (Mo 2001; October 2019 *World Economic Outlook*). In particular, reforms of the legal system and property rights help promote private sector development and investment (Dabla-Norris and others 2013; IMF 2015). The empirical literature also found evidence of complementarity between governance and other reforms. In particular, the impact of reforms, especially product market deregulation, tend to be larger in countries where the quality of governance is stronger, which suggests that policymakers should prioritize policies that strengthen governance (October 2019 *World Economic Outlook*). Finally, gender gaps in entrepreneurship and in female workers' pay have significant negative effects on aggregate productivity, whereas gender gaps in labor force participation reduce income per capita (see Teignier and Cuberes 2014).

ESTIMATING THE IMPACT OF STRUCTURAL REFORMS ON POTENTIAL OUTPUT: A PRODUCTION FUNCTION APPROACH

To quantify the impact of reforms on Morocco's output, a standard production function augmented with human capital was first used:

$$Y = A \, K^{1-\beta} \, (HL)^{\beta}$$

where Y is GDP, A is TFP, K is the capital stock, HL is the effective labor input, and β is the share of labor income (taken from the Penn World Table database). The effective labor input is the interaction of an indicator of the quality of human capital H and the number of workers L (from ILOSTAT). In particular:

- H measures the unit of human capital, defined using the World Bank's human capital index.
- The number of workers is defined as $L = w * p * e$, where w is the working-age population (aged 15 and older), p is the labor force participation rate, and e is the employment rate (all from ILOSTAT).

Assume that the implementation of the *education, social protection, and health care reforms* will affect medium-term output through the indicator of human capital H (because they will increase the average years of education and the human capital index, respectively); *product market and governance reforms* are assumed to directly impact TFP A; and finally, *reforms to boost women's participation in the labor market* affect output directly through an increase in p, the labor force participation rate.

In order to estimate the impact of the reforms, structural indicators were first identified in the areas where Morocco has initiated reforms, and then Morocco's distance from the average OECD country on each of these indicators was quantified using the latest available data points for the different indicators.[10] Then, the marginal impact on output from Morocco's closing its gap on these indicators was estimated using the production function estimated for Morocco. In particular,

- *Human capital:* A 1 percent improvement on this indicator is assumed to improve output by about 0.4 percent (which is the share of labor in the production function). Morocco's score on the human capital index is about 50 percent lower than the OECD average (Figure 5.6).[11] Hence, if Morocco was able to close half of the gap in H with the OECD average in 15 years, output would improve by about 1.3 percent at the end of that period.
- *Product market:* The World Economic Forum indicator of the degree of competition in product markets was used. Based on this indicator, Morocco

---

[10] Figure 5.8 defines the data source for each structural indicator.

[11] Using alternative indicators of education (primary or lower-secondary completion rates, adult literacy rate) or health (life expectancy, mortality rates, universal health service coverage) broadly shows similar gaps with the OECD average (see Annex Figures 5.1.1 and 5.1.2).

Figure 5.6. Morocco: Structural Indicators Gaps

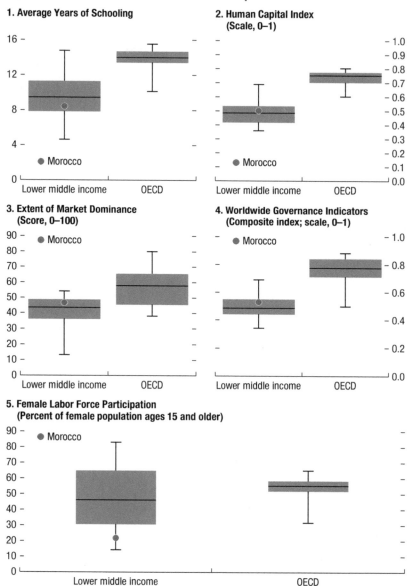

1. Average Years of Schooling

2. Human Capital Index
(Scale, 0–1)

3. Extent of Market Dominance
(Score, 0–100)

4. Worldwide Governance Indicators
(Composite index; scale, 0–1)

5. Female Labor Force Participation
(Percent of female population ages 15 and older)

Sources: Institute for Health Metrics and Evaluation; World Bank, World Development Indicators and Worldwide Governance Indicators; World Economic Forum, Global Competitiveness Index 4; and IMF staff calculations.
Note: OECD = Organisation for Economic Co-operation and Development.

is about 20 percent below the OECD average.[12] Chapter 3 of the October 2019 *World Economic Outlook*, "Reigniting Growth in Low-income and Emerging Market Economies: What Role Can Structural Reforms Play?" estimated time-varying elasticities of the impact of product market and governance reforms on output. These elasticities imply that a 1-unit increase in the indicator of product market improves output by about 0.9 percent in the medium to long term. Hence, if Morocco was able to close half of the gap with the OECD average in 15 years, output would improve by about 0.1 percent at the end of that period.

- *Governance:* A composite indicator of the quality of governance was used as in the October 2019 *World Economic Outlook*, built as as a simple average of the six indices of the World Bank's Worldwide Governance Indicator (control of corruption, government effectiveness, political stability, regulatory quality, rule of law, and voice and accountability). The composite indicator of the quality of governance suggests that Morocco's score is about 65 percent below the OECD average, with main gaps in voice and accountability, regulatory framework, and control of corruption. The *World Economic Outlook* elasticity used implies that a unit increase in the indicator of governance improves output by about 2 percent in the medium to long term. Hence, if Morocco was able to close half of the gap with the OECD average in 15 years, output would improve by about 0.3 percent at the end of that period.

- *Female participation in the labor force:* Morocco's female labor force participation (FLFP) (from ILOSTAT) is only two-fifths the average OECD level.[13] If Morocco were able to double its FLFP in 15 years, the direct impact on output would be about 2.8 percent.

To illustrate the large uncertainty around estimates, three different scenarios were observed:

- *A median-success reform scenario* assumes that the reforms of social protection, health, education, product market, and governance would close half of the distance between Morocco and the OECD average over a period of 15 years. For the FLFP, this scenario assumes that it would increase to about 34 percent (from about 22 percent in 2021) over 15 years. As a result, it was found that real GDP would increase by 4.4 percent by 2036 on a cumulative basis (the sum of the effects on output from the first column of Table 5.2).

- *In a low-success reform scenario*, Morocco's reforms of social protection, health, education, product market, and governance would close only 10 percent of the gap with the OECD average over a period of 15 years. In addition, FLFP

---

[12] Using alternative indicators of product market reforms (degree of competition in services, extent of state ownership of assets) shows similar gaps with the OECD (see Annex Figure 5.1.4).

[13] Indicators of labor market policies also show some gaps relative to OECD average (Annex Figure 5.1.3).

TABLE 5.2.

Impact of Structural Reforms on Output after 15 Years
(Percent)

	Median Success	Low Success	High Success
Social protection and health	0.057	0.011	0.137
Education	1.228	0.246	2.948
Product market	0.045	0.018	0.107
Governance	0.302	0.060	0.724
Gender gap	2.776	0.555	6.662

Source: Authors' calculations.

would increase to only 27 percent over this period. In this case, the level of output would increase by 0.9 percent by 2036 on a cumulative basis (Table 5.2, second column).

- *In a high-success reform scenario*, the structural reforms of social protection, health, education, product market, and governance would close 80 percent of Morocco's gap over 10 years—that is, Morocco's score in these indicators would be 20 percent above the OECD average after 15 years. FLFP would increase to about 40 percent over this period. In this case, output could increase cumulatively by 10.6 percent over 15 years (Table 5.2, third column).

ESTIMATING THE IMPACT OF STRUCTURAL REFORMS ON POTENTIAL OUTPUT: A GENERAL EQUILIBRIUM MODEL APPROACH

In this section, IMF's Flexible System of Global Models (FSGM) was used to simulate the dynamic macroeconomic effects of structural reforms on Morocco's potential output and fiscal position. The FSGM is an annual, multiregion, general equilibrium model of the global economy combining both microfunded and reduced formulations of various economic sectors (see Andrle and others 2015 for more details).[14] In the model, total consumption consists of spending both from households that can save and from those who can only consume out of current income. Firms produce goods and services using labor and their holdings of private capital. Potential output is based on Cobb-Douglas production function with trend TFP, the steady-state labor force, NAIRU, and capital stock. The effects of structural reforms on potential output are captured through their impact on the factor inputs and TFP. The government budget constraint ensures a stable nonexplosive public debt-to-GDP ratio in the long term, while in the short-term fiscal policy accommodates the

---

[14] This analysis uses the Middle East and Central Asia Department Model, a module of the FSGM, which contains individual blocks for 12 countries—including Morocco and seven other countries from the Middle East and Central Asia—and 10 regions (including four Middle East and Central Asia subregions)—and the rest of the world.

impact of the business cycle.[15] Lump-sum transfers are assumed to adjust over time to ensure that long-term debt remains sustainable.[16] Monetary policy is determined by a reaction function that links interest rates to expected inflation in the medium term.

Using the FSGM to assess the macroeconomic effects of structural reforms has several benefits. First, it allows quantification of output gains and potential costs both in the short term and medium to long term once the reforms are expected to have paid off. Second, it sheds light on the transmission channels through which the reforms affect the economy. Third, it permits analysis of the impact of the reforms in isolation and simultaneously. Fourth, it allows the assessment of the fiscal implication of the reforms.

The fiscal impact of the reforms depends on how they are financed. In these simulations, two options are considered:

- *Budget-neutral reforms* (option 1). The fiscal costs of the reforms are fully offset by a decrease in other public expenditures.[17] In particular, the simulations assume that the additional spending associated to the reforms is offset by a reduction in lump-sum transfers that keeps the structural deficit unchanged.

- *Debt financing* (option 2). The budgetary cost of the reforms is fully financed with additional public debt. Under this scenario, the structural deficit increases with the additional discretionary spending, while lump-sum transfers adjust to cover the increased debt-service costs from the higher debt. Following Kumar and Baldacci (2010), it is assumed that each unit increase in the public debt to GDP ratio causes an increase of the sovereign risk premium of 3 basis points.[18]

The reforms simulated in the model are designed to match those estimated using the production function framework in the second section. A significant difference with the previous approach is that the reforms of social protection, health, education, product market, and governance are all modeled as a shock to TFP—that is, the estimated impact of these reforms on potential output from Table 5.2 is now used to calibrate an exogenous shock to TFP in the model. This is because the production function in FSGM does not explicitly include human capital (the

---

[15] We refer to the government's long-term fiscal balance target as the "structural balance."

[16] In principle, any expenditure or tax instrument in FSGM can be used for this purpose. We chose lump-sum transfers for their nondistortionary effect.

[17] In the model simulations, the reforms of education, social protection, and health are assumed to increase government spending in line with the estimates contained in the 2023 budget. In particular, the social protection and health care reform is projected to cost about 2.5 percent of GDP per year at steady state, while the reform of the education system about 0.3 percent of GDP annually (IMF 2023). Product market and governance reforms, as well as policies to reduce the gender gap in the labor market, are assumed to be implemented at no direct fiscal costs.

[18] The assumption of 3 basis points is based on Kumar and Baldacci (2010), who find that appropriate risk premium elasticities would be in the range of 3–5 basis points for a panel of advanced and emerging market economies.

positive impact of human capital accumulation is implicitly included in the exogeneous component of trend TFP). For example, in the median scenario, the impact of governance reform is modeled as a TFP shock of 0.3 percent over 15 years—that is, the estimated increase in TFP and output from the production function in Table 5.2. Similarly, the education reform is assumed to lead to an increase in TFP of 1.2 percent over 15 years. The overall package of reforms, excluding the gender gap, is assumed to boost TFP by about 1.6 percent after 15 years. The total labor force participation rates are assumed to increase by about 6 percentage points in the median reform scenario, whereas the upper bound and lower bound assume an increase of about 1 percentage point and 14 percentage points, respectively.

Model Simulation Results

The simulation results show that the effects of structural reforms are sizable in the medium and long term in all scenarios:

- *The reforms of social protection, health care, education, product market, and governance have significant impact on long-term output.* These reforms are mapped into an exogenous permanent shock in TFP that ranges from about 4 percent to 0.3 percent in the high- and low-success scenarios, respectively (Figure 5.7). The resulting rise in the marginal productivity of capital and labor stimulates private investment and raises labor demand, which lifts consumption in the long term (Figure 5.8). In the budget-neutral scenario, cumulative increases of real output over a 15-year period range from 2.5 to 24 percent (and about 10 percent in the median-success scenario) (Figure 5.8 and Annex Figure 5.2.1). These larger output gains compared with the production function approach mainly reflect the spillovers (dynamic impact) of higher productivity on capital accumulation and labor in the model. In addition, the simulations incorporate the fiscal gains from reforms in the medium term.

- *The reduction of the gender gaps yields the largest payoffs in the medium to long term* (Figure 5.9). The increase in FLFP is associated with cumulative output gains over the next 15 years that are twice as large as those produced by the other reforms. These sizable gains reflect the large structural gaps relative to the average OECD country in the labor force participation rate, and hence the significant increase required to reduce it.

- *In the long term, reforms are less effective in the debt-financing scenario* (Figure 5.7 and Annex Figure 5.2.2). In the short term, higher multiplier effects from the increase in public spending to finance social protection and education reforms boost private consumption and therefore output. But in the long term, the increase in the government's borrowing costs from the higher level of debt crowds out private investment and depresses the capital stock, partially offsetting the output gains from higher productivity (Figure 5.7). Cumulative real GDP gains over the following 15 years are estimated in a range between 0.7 percent and 22 percent (about 8¾ percent in the median-success scenario) (Figure 5.8).

Figure 5.7. Morocco: Effects of Reforms on Output

1. Real GDP: Effects of Reforms—Budget Neutral
(Percentage difference from baseline)

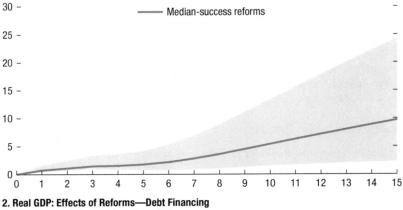

2. Real GDP: Effects of Reforms—Debt Financing
(Percentage difference from baseline)

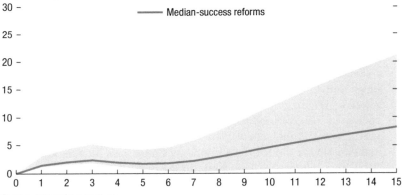

Source: Authors' calculations.
Note: The dark blue lines represent the median reform scenario. The upper and lower shaded areas denote the high- and low-success reform scenarios, respectively. The horizontal axes represent the number of years following the reform initiation.

Figure 5.8. Morocco: Effects of Reforms—Median Success

■ Reforms (deficit financed)   ■ Reforms (budget neutral)

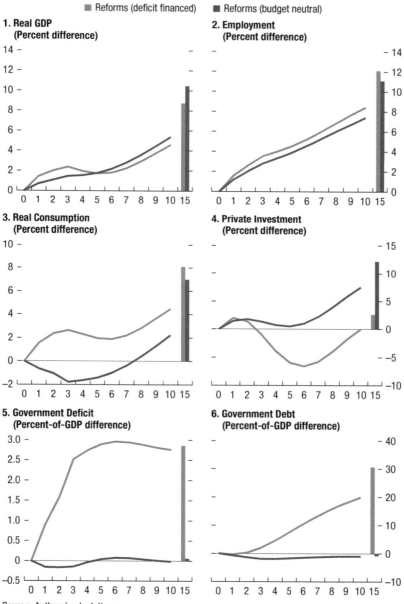

Source: Authors' calculations.
Note: The horizontal axes represent the number of years following the reform initiation.

Figure 5.9. Morocco: Macroeconomic Effects of Reforms—Median Success (Budget Neutral)

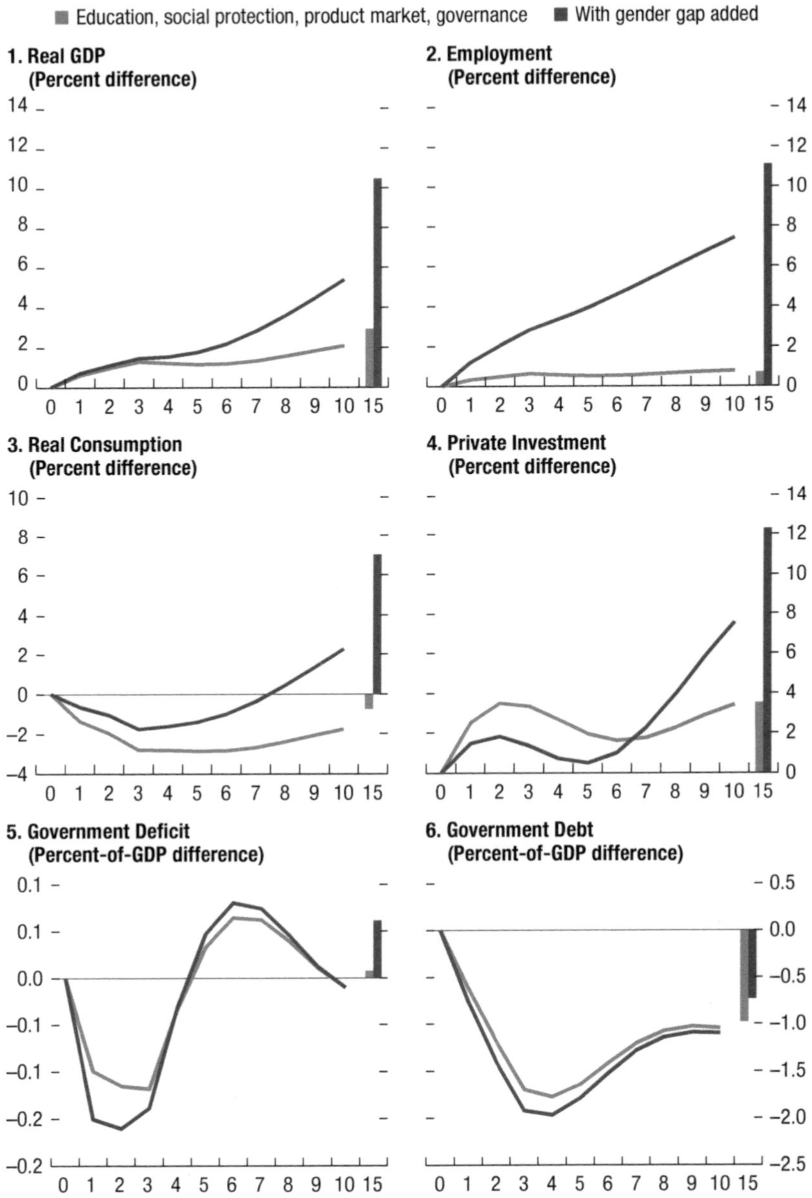

■ Education, social protection, product market, governance   ■ With gender gap added

1. Real GDP
(Percent difference)

2. Employment
(Percent difference)

3. Real Consumption
(Percent difference)

4. Private Investment
(Percent difference)

5. Government Deficit
(Percent-of-GDP difference)

6. Government Debt
(Percent-of-GDP difference)

Source: Authors' calculations.
Note: The horizontal axes represent the number of years following the reform initiation.

CONCLUSION

The downward trend in Morocco's growth prospects over the last two decades, together with the likely scarring from the pandemic recession, raises concerns about the continued convergence toward higher-income status. In this chapter, the IMF's MVF was used to estimate potential output in Morocco and the impact of the pandemic shock on its drivers. It was found that the downward secular trend in potential growth observed since the global financial crisis was primarily driven by the decline of labor force participation and higher NAIRU, whereas the pandemic shock affected the supply side of the economy through several channels and thus could lead to long-lasting effects on the level of potential output.

The announced plan of structural reforms can do much to reverse these trends. This production function approach suggests that if in the next 15 years these reforms were to reduce by half the current gap relative to the average OECD country, Morocco's real output could increase by about 7 percent at the end of this period. These model simulations confirm that there are large output gains to be reaped from the implementation of the reform package: if neutral on the fiscal budget, these reforms could improve output by 10 percent under the same assumptions about their effectiveness. Given the relatively larger starting gap in FLFP, reforms that would reduce the gender gap in Morocco's labor market appear to be particularly critical to improving potential growth (in these model simulations, they account for about three-fifths of the overall output gain in the long term).

ANNEX 5.1. STRUCTURAL REFORM GAPS

Annex Figure 5.1.1. Education

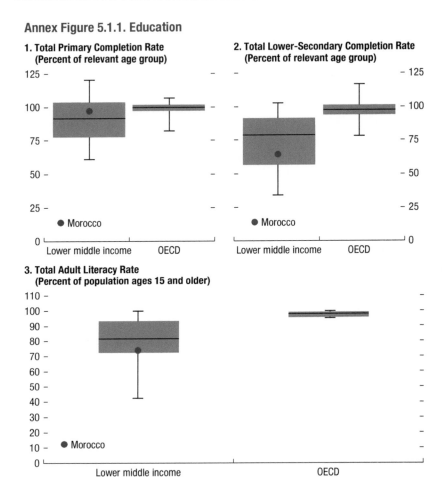

Sources: World Bank, World Development Indicators; and IMF staff calculations.
Note: OECD = Organisation for Economic Co-operation and Development.

Annex Figure 5.1.2. Health

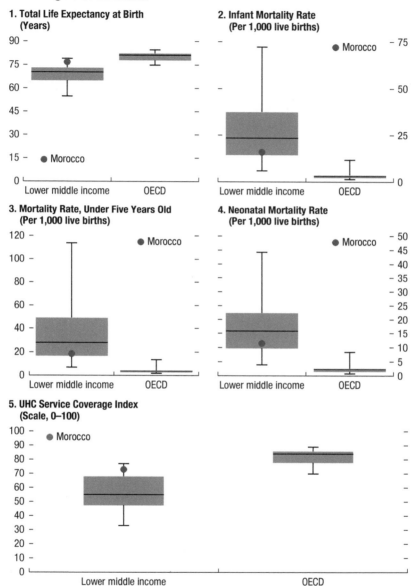

1. Total Life Expectancy at Birth
   (Years)

2. Infant Mortality Rate
   (Per 1,000 live births)

3. Mortality Rate, Under Five Years Old
   (Per 1,000 live births)

4. Neonatal Mortality Rate
   (Per 1,000 live births)

5. UHC Service Coverage Index
   (Scale, 0–100)

Sources: World Bank, World Development Indicators; and IMF staff calculations.
Note: OECD = Organisation for Economic Co-operation and Development; UHC = universal health coverage.

Annex Figure 5.1.3. Labor Market Indicators

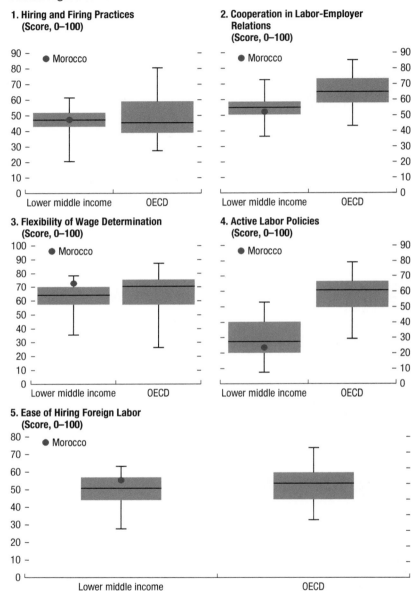

Sources: World Economic Forum, Global Competitiveness Index 4; and IMF staff calculations.
Note: OECD = Organisation for Economic Co-operation and Development.

Annex Figure 5.1.4. Product Market Indicators

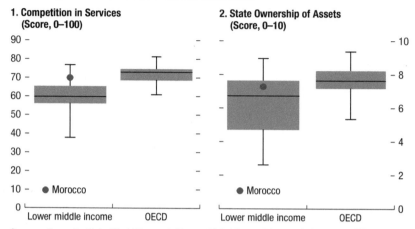

1. Competition in Services
(Score, 0–100)

2. State Ownership of Assets
(Score, 0–10)

Sources: Fraser Institute; World Economic Forum, Global Competitiveness Index 4; and IMF staff calculations.

ANNEX 5.2. ILLUSTRATIVE REFORM SCENARIOS

Annex Figure 5.2.1. Morocco: Effects of Reforms—Budget Neutral

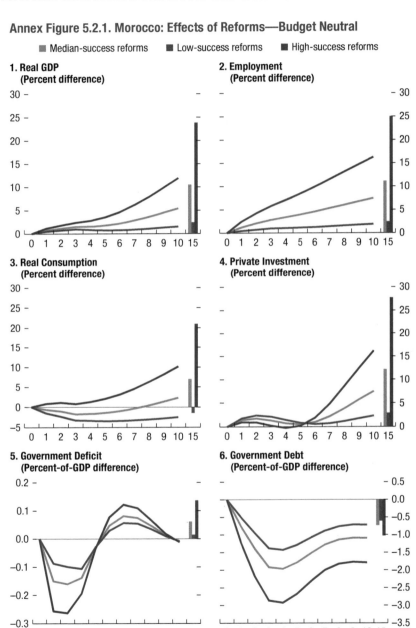

Source: Authors' calculations.
Note: The horizontal axes represent the number of years following the reform initiation.

Annex Figure 5.2.2. Morocco: Effects of Reforms—Deficit Financed

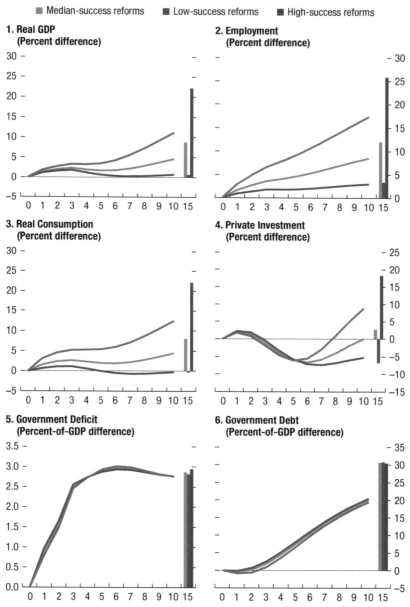

Source: Authors' calculations.
Note: The horizontal axes represent the number of years following the reform initiation.

REFERENCES

Alichi, Ali, Olivier Bizimana, Silvia Domit, Emilio Fernández-Corugedo, Douglas Laxton, Kadir Tanyeri, Hou Wang, and Fan Zhang. 2015. "Multivariate Filter Estimation of Potential Output for the Euro Area and the United States." IMF Working Paper 15/253, International Monetary Fund, Washington, DC.

Andrle, Michal, Patrick Blagrave, Pedro Espaillat, Keiko Honjo, Benjamin L. Hunt, Mika Kortelainen, René Lalonde, Douglas Laxton, Eleonora Mavroeidi, Dirk Muir, Susanna Mursula, and Stephen Snudden. 2015. "The Flexible System of Global Models—FSGM." IMF Working Paper 15/64, International Monetary Fund, Washington, DC.

Barnes, Sebastian, Romain Bouis, Philippe Briard, Sean Dougherty, and Mehmet Eris. 2013. "The GDP Impact of Reform: A Simple Simulation Framework." OECD Economics Department Working Paper 834, Organisation for Economic Co-operation and Development, Paris.

Benos, Nikos, and Stefania Zotou. 2014. "Education and Economic Growth: A Meta-Regression Analysis." *World Development* 64: 669–89.

Blagrave, Patrick, Roberto Garcia-Saltos, Douglas Laxton, and Fan Zhang. 2015. "A Simple Multivariate Filter for Estimating Potential Output." IMF Working Paper 15/79, International Monetary Fund, Washington, DC.

Blanchard, Olivier, and Francesco Giavazzi. 2003. "Macroeconomic Effects of Regulation and Deregulation in Goods and Labor Markets." *Quarterly Journal of Economics* 118 (3): 879–907.

Bodnár, Katalin, Julien Le Roux, Paloma Lopez-Garcia, and Bela Szörfi. 2020. "The Impact of COVID-19 on Potential Output in the Euro Area." *ECB Economic Bulletin* (7).

Bouis, Romain, and Romain Duval. 2011. "Raising Potential Growth After the Crisis: A Quantitative Assessment of the Potential Gains from Various Structural Reforms in the OECD Area and Beyond." OECD Economics Department Working Paper 835, Organisation for Economic Co-operation and Development, Paris. https://research.stlouisfed.org/publications/economic-synopses/2020/05/20/is-the-covid-19-pandemic-a-supply-or-a-demand-shock.

Chafik, Omar. 2017. "Estimation de la Croissance Potentielle de l'Economie Marocaine." BAM Document de Travail 2, Bank Al-Maghrib, September.

Dabla-Norris, Era, Giang Ho, Kalpana Kochhar, Annette J. Kyobe, and Robert Tchaidze. 2013. "Anchoring Growth: The Importance of Productivity-enhancing Reforms in Emerging Market and Developing Economies." IMF Staff Discussion Note 13/08, International Monetary Fund, Washington, DC.

Duval, Romain, and Davide Furceri. 2018. "The Effects of Labor and Product Market Reforms: The Role of Macroeconomic Conditions and Policies." *IMF Economic Review* 66 (1): 31–69.

International Monetary Fund (IMF). 2015. "Structural Reforms and Macroeconomic Performance: Initial Considerations for the Fund." Staff Report, Washington, DC, November.

International Monetary Fund (IMF). 2023. "Morocco: 2022 Article IV Consultation Staff Report." Washington, DC, January.

Kumar, Manmohan S., and Emanuele Baldacci. 2010. "Fiscal Deficits, Public Debt, and Sovereign Bond Yields." IMF Working Paper 10/184, International Monetary Fund, Washington, DC.

Mathers, Nicholas, and Rachel Slater. 2014. "Social Protection and Growth: Research Synthesis." Department of Foreign Affairs and Trade, Commonwealth of Australia, Canberra.

Mo, Pak Hung. 2001. "Corruption and Economic Growth." *Journal of Comparative Economics* 29 (1): 66–79.

Organisation for Economic Co-operation and Development (OECD). 2019. "Can Social Protection Be an Engine for Inclusive Growth?" Development Centre Studies, Paris.

Sarr, Babacar, Mokhtar Benlamine, and Zsuzsa Munkacsi. 2019. "Macroeconomic Effects of Labor and Product Market Reforms in Morocco." IMF Working Paper 19/222, International Monetary Fund, Washington, DC.

Teignier, Marc, and David Cuberes. 2014. "Aggregate Costs of Gender Gaps in the Labor Market: A Quantitative Estimate." UB Economics Working Paper 14/308, University of Barcelona.

CHAPTER 6

Drivers of Manufacturing Employment in Morocco

Abdelaaziz Ait Ali and Oumayma Bourhriba

INTRODUCTION

Morocco has seen the share of manufacturing in total output and employment decline since the turn of the millennium, together with a worsening in the manufacturing employment trend since the global financial crisis of 2008 (Figure 6.1). Morocco is not alone in experiencing these developments (Dasgupta and Singh 2006; Rodrik 2015). In advanced countries, many consider these trends "normal" given the low income-elasticity of manufacturing products. Moreover, if labor productivity advances more rapidly in manufacturing than in services, the manufacturing share of employment, as well as the relative price of manufactures, would be expected to decline (Baumol 1967; Rowthorn and Ramaswamy 1997).

Figure 6.1. Manufacturing Indicators in Morocco, 2000–20
(Percent, right scale is productivity index 2000 = 100)

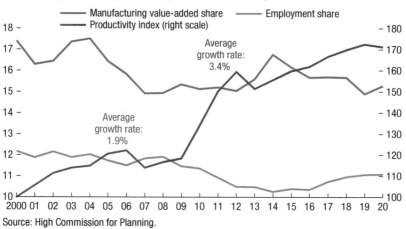

Source: High Commission for Planning.

However, in Morocco as in many other developing countries, the contraction of manufacturing raises the specter of "premature deindustrialization"—namely, the concern that manufacturing will not enable Morocco to climb the development ladder as had been the case of early industrializers (such as Great Britain and France over the course of the nineteenth century) and some more recent industrializers in East Asia. Morocco's high rates of youth unemployment, and underemployment, especially of women, accentuate these concerns.

Against this background, this chapter aims to provide a better understanding of the causes of the recent decline in manufacturing employment in Morocco. The debate over deindustrialization in Morocco gained momentum following the global financial crisis because manufacturing employment had been increasing before (by 1.6 percent a year on average between 2000 and 2008), maintaining its share in total employment. Our analysis thus focuses especially on the comparison between the years before and after the global financial crisis.

We employ a simple accounting framework to show that most of the deceleration in manufacturing employment since the global financial crisis can be attributed to a lower final domestic demand for manufactures in Morocco, only partially offset by increasing intermediate demand. The acceleration of labor productivity in manufacturing also contributed to lower employment in the sector. By contrast, Morocco's opening to international trade should not be seen as a major cause of lower manufacturing employment in recent years, because Morocco's trade deficit in manufacturing products did not deteriorate after the global financial crisis.

Although manufacturing continues to be a vital part of the Moroccan economy, and opportunities clearly exist to expand it, Morocco will not be able to rely solely on manufacturing to "pull" labor out of agriculture. Instead, this will require a broad approach to the challenge of diversifying the sources of employment, drawing on opportunities across all sectors of the Moroccan economy.

THE IMPORTANCE OF MANUFACTURING AS A SOURCE OF EMPLOYMENT AND GROWTH

Nicholas Kaldor was among the first to introduce three "growth laws" expressing the benefits of the manufacturing sector for the entire economy. First, the demand of manufactures tends to expand more rapidly than the demand for other goods. Second, manufacturing is a source of increased productivity within the sector, reflecting the potential for automation, learning, returns to scale, and so forth. Third, manufacturing raises overall productivity by absorbing unused or low-productivity resources from other sectors (Thirlwall 1983).

In the same vein, Dani Rodrik has argued that light labor-intensive manufacturing creates higher productivity jobs than agriculture and can be a crucial source of foreign exchange. He provides evidence that manufacturing productivity tends to catch up to international levels even when many of the other conditions required for broader economic development are barely met, and he argues that the most successful countries have all relied on rapid industrialization (Rodrik 2015).[1]

Although recognizing that the arguments of Kaldor and Rodrik are broadly supported by available evidence, others have proposed a more nuanced view based on postwar period trends (Dadush 2015). Although all countries rely on manufacturing to some extent, and a few (such as South Korea) have achieved spectacular growth based partly on penetration of world manufacturing markets, many countries have enjoyed less rapid but respectable growth without relying mainly on manufacturing. Dadush (2015) showed that 39 economies (including Chile, Egypt, and Morocco) have been able to double their per capita income over the last 20–30 years and achieved large improvement in other development indicators without exhibiting a comparative advantage in manufactures or relying principally on manufacturing. India is a country that has been especially successful in developing a vibrant export sector mainly based on information technology services, even though manufacturing also played an important role in driving growth (Chakravarty and Mitra 2009).

In a recent review of global manufacturing employment trends, Ait Ali and Dadush (2019) observed that global manufacturing value added has grown rapidly since 2000, at least matching world gross domestic product (GDP) growth, reflecting mainly rising demand for manufactures especially in developing countries. However, manufacturing employment increased at only a slow pace, both before and after the global financial crisis. Manufacturing provided only about 10 percent of the new jobs needed to compensate for losses of jobs in agriculture and the growth of the active population. The vast majority of net job creation in manufacturing was in China, whereas most countries—both developing and developed—saw manufacturing employment fall as a share of total employment, and several, including nearly all advanced countries, saw an absolute decline (with services accounting for the greatest share of employment growth even in the rapid industrializers in East Asia).

Although policymakers must care deeply about the evolution of the manufacturing sector, they must also be realistic about the sector's potential to create jobs, given its relatively small size, its falling share of output relative to services in most countries, and the pressure to automate, which results in high labor productivity growth (Dadush 2015; IMF 2022). By the same token, many service sectors are increasingly capable not only of generating a large number of jobs but also of exhibiting some of the desirable features of manufactures. Manufactures exports contain a high share of imported and domestic services (Cezar and others 2017) and, when exports are measured in terms of value added, it turns out that cross-border exports of services are now larger than exports of manufactures (WTO 2019). An efficient service sector is an essential companion to a competitive manufacturing sector, and the value added of many firms classified as belonging to the manufacturing sectors consists mainly of intangible activities that are, in fact, services.

---

[1] Rodrik's most recent positions are more nuanced. He calls for more broader "industrial policy" that aims to foster all sectors of the economy. He considered that "employment de-industrialization is virtually inevitable in middle-income and advanced economies alike" (Aiginger and Rodrik 2020).

A FEW STYLIZED FACTS ON THE EVOLUTION OF MANUFACTURING IN MOROCCO

Expressed in current prices, the contribution of Morocco's manufacturing sector to overall value added fell between 2000 and 2009 but has since reversed slightly (Figure 6.2). Expressed in constant prices, the decline continued, although at a slower pace. The relative price of manufactures increased after the global financial crisis, possibly reflecting a shift toward higher value added and capital-intensive manufacturing sectors (such as automotive), in the context of increased trade liberalization and export orientation of Morocco's manufacturing sector.

The decline of the manufacturing share of value added (from 16.3 percent in 2000 to 13.8 percent in 2020) is in line with the trend observed across lower-middle-income countries and is less sharp than that observed in high-income countries (Figure 6.3). By contrast, upper-middle-income countries, which include China and several Asian developing nations, saw their manufacturing share stable at relatively high levels (around 22 percent on average), whereas low-income countries experienced the greatest increase although remaining at relatively low levels (around 10 percent in 2020 from 8 percent in 2000, on average).

Meanwhile, employment in Morocco's manufacturing sector, which is the focus of this chapter, declined from 12.2 percent to 11 percent of total employment over the 2000–19 period, with an especially sharp decline between 2008 and 2019 (Figure 6.4). Employment in manufacturing as a share of total

Figure 6.2. Change in Manufacturing Share in Total Value Added and Employment in Morocco
(Percentage point)

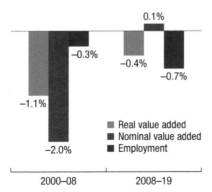

Source: High Commission for Planning.

Figure 6.3. Change in Manufacturing Value-Added Share in GDP, 2000–20
(Percentage point)

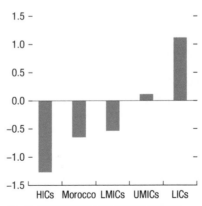

Source: United Nations Conference on Trade and Development.
Note: HICs = high-income countries;
LICs = low-income countries;
LMICs = lower-middle-income countries;
UMICs = upper-middle-income countries.

Figure 6.4. Real Value Added and Employment Growth Contribution per Sector in Manufacturing, 2007–18
(Percent)

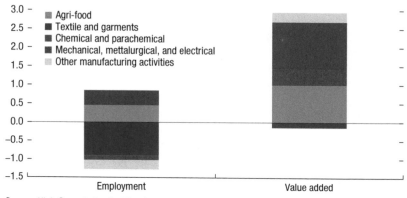

Source: High Commission for Planning.

employment fell by more in the second period than the first, despite the sector's improved relative performance, reflecting increased labor productivity.

This was partly due to a change in mix from labor-intensive manufactures (such as textiles and garments) to capital-intensive manufactures (such as the mechanical sector). Output in the textile and garments sector shrank by over 15 percent in 2009 and never recovered. Meanwhile, the mechanical industry, notably the automotive industry, grew on average by 5 percent a year between 2008 and 2018, above the 3.3 percent average of manufacturing as a whole. The rise of the mechanical, metallurgical, and electrical sectors, and especially the automotive industry, was facilitated by various forms of government support to foreign investment in the sector. Conversely, the textile and garments industry suffered from the end of the quotas set by the European Union on Asian textile exports, especially from China, as the multifiber agreement was phased out.

Labor productivity gains in the manufacturing sector accelerated from 1.9 percent to 3.4 percent per year, with particularly strong growth up to 2015. A 2016 study by the High Commission for Planning estimated that the employment elasticity has been near zero for the industry sector, compared to 0.86 for construction and 0.7 for retail trade.

WHAT CAUSED THE DECLINE IN MANUFACTURING EMPLOYMENT?

In this chapter, we look at the role played by demand, trade, and productivity factors in explaining the change in employment in Morocco before and after the global financial crisis. Several studies have focused on the role of manufacturing in economic growth and job creation. Gregory, Zissimos, and Greenhalgh (2001) used a multisectoral model to assess how trade patterns, technological change, and the growth of final demand contributed to the evolving skill structure of employment in the UK. Kletzer (2002) and Tuhin (2015) used an econometric model of labor demand to estimate the relationship among employment changes, trade flows (imports and exports), and domestic demand. Dieppe (2021) used a SVAR (structural vector auto-regression) approach to estimate the impact of technology-driven productivity changes and demand shocks on employment.[2]

In this chapter we propose a simple accounting framework based on Bivens (2004). The analysis is based on two simplifying assumptions: (1) current production equals current demand, and (2) higher demand leads proportionally to an increase in the number of employees, not just the number of hours. We extended the approach to split the domestic demand factor into intermediate and final demand while considering the role of productivity.

We start from two identities. The first is the relation among employment, value added, and productivity:

$$\Delta L_m \equiv \Delta VA_m - \Delta P_m \tag{6.1}$$

where VA_m, L_m, and P_m denote value added, labor, and productivity in the manufacturing sector, respectively. The second equation is derived from the equality of total resources (value added, sale of intermediate goods to other sectors, and imports) and total uses (final domestic demand, purchases of intermediate goods from other sectors, and exports) in the manufacturing sector as defined in supply and use tables. In this equation, the manufacturing value added is represented in terms of the other resources and uses variables:

$$VA_m \equiv DFD_m + NID_m + (X_m - M_m) \tag{6.2}$$

where M_m, DFD_m, X_m, and NID_m denote imports, final domestic demand, exports, and net intermediate demand of manufacturing goods, respectively. The left-hand side of this identity denotes total supply of manufacturing products that are either produced domestically or imported. The right-hand side captures uses of manufacturing goods, absorbed by domestic demand and exports. The net intermediate demand term reflects the sale of intermediate goods to other sectors, less the purchases of such goods from other sectors.

By substituting equation (6.2) into equation (6.1), we obtain:

$$\Delta L_m \equiv \Delta(DFD_m + (X_m - M_m) + NID_m) - \Delta P_m \tag{6.3}$$

The manufacturing employment change is accounted for by the changes in final domestic demand, net trade balance, net intermediate demand, and productivity. This equation is a purely descriptive identity—that is, it is always true and does not imply causality in any direction. It is nevertheless useful in quantifying the main factors associated with changes in manufacturing employment.

---

[2] Their model includes the log level of labor productivity, the log of employment per capita, consumption as a share of GDP, investment as a share of GDP, consumer price inflation, and monetary policy interest rates.

This exercise is intended to identify the factors that have contributed most to the changes in manufacturing employment. Intuitively, employment in the manufacturing sector is positively correlated to domestic and foreign demand, but it is negatively correlated to productivity and imports.

- *Domestic demand.* A rise in domestic demand (final and intermediate) for manufacturing products would boost manufacturing employment unless satisfied by more imports; hence, the magnitude of the impact depends on the size of the domestic market relative to imports.

- *Productivity.* Although higher productivity could be associated with lower employment, because fewer workers are required to produce the same amount of output, the ultimate effect depends on technological changes, the prices of competing goods and services, and the price elasticity of demand (Nordhaus 2005). Higher productivity could lead to lower costs and prices of manufacturing goods and thus a higher demand, which could in return enhance employment. Dieppe (2021) found that in emerging market and developing economies as well as in advanced economies, employment falls after technology-driven productivity improvements.

- *Trade.* The impact of international trade on manufacturing employment is also ambiguous because it ultimately depends on whether domestic firms are able to face international competition (Abraham and Brock 2003; Kletzer 2002). If import competition were to cause a decline in manufacturing employment, the labor displaced could be eventually reabsorbed in non-manufacturing sectors, although there is no clear evidence that this has happened. For instance, Menezes-Filho and Muendler (2011) found that labor displaced by trade liberalization in Brazil since 1990 was not fully absorbed by firms with comparative advantage. At any rate, the dynamics between trade and employment are likely to change over time: although trade may reduce employment and/or entail a reallocation of labor within sectors in the short term, over the long term, growth in international trade could boost economic growth, increase wages, and spur employment (Hoekman and Winters 2005; Newfarmer and Sztajerowska 2012). Opening to trade would increase developed countries' demand for unskilled labor-intensive goods and developing countries' demand for skilled labor-intensive goods (Ghose 2000; Kletzer 2002; Revenga 1992). Still, opening to trade has produced concerns in both directions, with developed countries fearing that jobs would be exported to low-wage countries, and developing countries concerned about their lack of competitiveness in relation to countries producing high-technology goods (McMillan and Verduzco 2011).

To quantify the terms in equation (6.3), we use the supply and use tables for Morocco, available annually since 1998. This quantification poses four issues. First, uses are expressed in purchasing prices (that include margins and taxes), whereas total supply is available in basic prices. To express uses in basic prices as well, we allocate margins and indirect taxes across users (sectors) based on their relative shares of total uses (Guilhoto and Sesso Filho 2005). The underlying assumption is that margin coefficients and tax rates on products are the same for all users.

The second issue relates to converting all variables into constant prices. To do so, we have used the consumer price index (CPI) for domestic final demand and the PPI (production prices index) for intermediate consumption. For exports and imports, we used import and export price indexes provided by the Morocco Ministry of Finance (Bettah and Zniber 2019). Doing so yields a small difference between uses and supply (0.7 percent on average per year), which has been reallocated across each component of total uses, based on their weight.

The third issue is that some manufacturing products (less than 3 percent) are produced in the non-manufacturing sector (for example, processed food products originated in the agricultural sector). Similarly, a few products from firms in the manufacturing sector are not classified as manufacturing goods. We included all manufacturing products in the analysis, whatever their source, and excluded non-manufacturing output.

The fourth issue concerns the base year. The available supply and use tables have two different base years (1998 and 2007); hence, the growth rates of manufacturing uses and supply will be overestimated. The High Commission for Planning has a time series of national accounts from 1998 to 2021, with value added by sector adjusted for the change of base years. We thus "adjust" the manufacturing value added from the supply and use tables in 2007 and 2008 (when the base year changes) by applying the growth rates from the valued added series in High Commission for Planning national accounts. The ratio between this adjusted manufacturing value added and the original value added from supply and use tables is applied to all other variables of equation (6.3).

The results of our accounting exercise, reported in Table 6.1, confirm that 2008 represents a turning point for Morocco's manufacturing sector because the following period coincides with structural changes that have profoundly altered the employment structure and prospects of the sector. In particular

- *Before the global financial crisis, job creation in the manufacturing sector reflected the rapid growth of domestic demand, only partially offset by a higher trade deficit.* Domestic demand for manufacturing goods (final and intermediate) grew at 4.4 percent per year in real terms between 2000 and 2008 and was the sole contributor to the growth of employment in the manufacturing sector. This was a period of rapid economic growth in Morocco, supported by expansive monetary and fiscal policies. The increased openness of the Moroccan economy (that coincided with lower tariff rates as the EU–Morocco Free Trade Area provisions were implemented) coupled with a stable real exchange rate

TABLE 6.1.

Contribution to Manufacturing Employment Change
(Percentage points, unless otherwise specified)

Periods	Domestic Final Demand	Net Intermediate Demand	Net International Trade	Productivity	Average Employment Growth Rate (percent)
2000–08	11.3	−0.9	−8.3	−2.0	2.0
2008–19	4.6	1.5	−3.0	−3.5	−0.8

Sources: High Commission for Planning data; and authors' calculations.

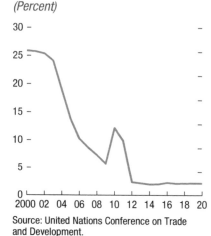

Figure 6.5. Effectively Applied Tariffs over Morocco's Manufacturing Imports, 2000–20
(Percent)

Source: United Nations Conference on Trade and Development.

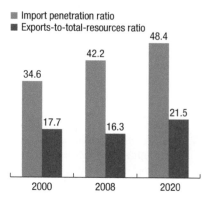

Figure 6.6. Manufacturing Imports Penetration and Exports to Total Resources Ratios, Constant Prices
(Percent)

Source: High Commission for Planning.

facilitated the penetration of foreign products and widened the manufacturing trade deficit. Effectively applied tariffs on manufactured goods declined from 25.9 percent in 2000 to 7.4 percent in 2008 (Figure 6.5); import penetration increased from 34.8 percent of total domestic demand in 2000 to 42.2 percent in 2008 (Figure 6.6); and the ratio of exports to total resources dropped by 1.5 percentage point. When the contribution to employment was negative, international trade did not prevent a strong expansion of the domestic production of manufacturing goods.[3] Labor productivity increased at a moderate rate and offered a moderately small contribution to the change in manufacturing employment in this period.

- *After the global financial crisis, subdued growth of domestic demand and accelerating labor productivity gains are the main drivers of the decline in manufacturing employment.* Although economic growth in Morocco held up well during 2008–09, the country did not escape the global demand slowdown and was eventually forced to tighten fiscal policy to maintain both internal and external balances. The trade deficit continued to be a drag on employment growth in manufacturing, although far less than before the global financial crisis. Labor productivity growth surged to nearly 4 percent per year until 2015 but has since

---

[3] The largest deterioration in the trade deficit was with the European Union, Morocco's largest trading partner, and China (see Annex Table 6.1.1), and this reflected increased imports of machinery, especially transport equipment. By contrast, Morocco's trade balance in manufactures improved compared with Brazil and many African and Asian economies, most often because of increased exports of fertilizers. Although many countries saw a similar trend, the deterioration in Morocco's trade deficit was among the largest relative to the size of its economy (see Annex Table 6.1.2).

TABLE 6.2.

Destination of Foreign Direct Investments by Sector (Percent)		
	2010	**2019**
Non-automotive manufacturing industries	11.7	17.8
Automobile industry	1.9	19.0
Accommodation and catering	11.4	6.9
Financial and insurance activities	16.9	11.1
Real estate activities	20.7	20.5
Other services	33.1	16.5
Other activities	4.3	8.2

Source: Office des changes.

moderated. Reflecting the insertion in global value chains and increased importance of the mechanical sector, especially automotive, manufacturing became more integrated with the rest of the Moroccan economy, moving upstream of the value chain and increasing its role as a provider of intermediate inputs.

These results suggest that contrary to the prevailing perception, trade has played a lesser role in accounting for job losses in Morocco's manufacturing sector in recent years. Import penetration increased only slightly in the years after the global financial crisis, whereas the export ratio increased.[4] The free trade agreement with Turkey, which entered into force in 2006, led to increased imports from Turkey but had little effect on Moroccan exports. In contrast, the trade balance in manufactures with Europe and North America improved, mainly due to exports of automobiles and fertilizers.

The acceleration of labor productivity since the global financial crisis, which has come hand in hand with the steadily increasing openness of the Moroccan economy, helps explain the manufacturing sector's job-poor growth. This process frequently involves pressure to automate and hire more skilled labor and, as firms serve an international clientele that demands high and predictable quality, on-time delivery, and so forth, they are forced to modernize. At the same time, the attractiveness of the Moroccan economy to manufacturing companies appears to have increased in the last decade, as the inflow of foreign direct investments to manufacturing has grown and outstripped that directed at tourism and real estate. Between 2010 and 2019, the share of the manufacturing sector in total foreign direct investments reached 36.8 percent, driven mainly by the automobile sector (Table 6.2).

The improvement in manufacturing productivity in Morocco is also striking in international comparison. Indeed, in the first period (2000–08), Morocco's manufacturing productivity growth was below the median in a sample of 137 countries. In the second period (2008–19), however, Morocco's productivity was above 97 percent of economies (Figure 6.7).

To assess the extent to which reallocation within the manufacturing sector has contributed to productivity growth, we distinguish between "within" sector

---

[4] The average applied tariff in manufactures continued to drop, reaching 2.2 percent in 2020, whereas the manufacturing trade deficit with China continued to increase, especially in road vehicles, machinery, and garments and textiles (Table 6.1).

Figure 6.7. Productivity Growth Distribution across the World
(Percent)

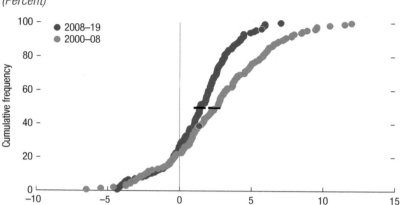

Sources: International Labour Organization, World Economic and Social Outlook database; United Nations Conference on Trade and Development; and United Nations Statistics Division.
Note: The black lines and red dots represent the medians and Morocco, respectively. Initially, the sample included 166 countries. A box-and-whisker plot was used to exclude the outliers within the sample. An outlier is identified as being larger than the third quartile by at least 1.5 times the interquartile range (third quarter to first quarter) or smaller than first quartile by at least 1.5 times the interquartile range.

productivity improvement and that due to moving from low to high productivity sectors, or "between" sectors (McMillan and Rodrik 2011). Most of the "within" productivity increase is explained by improvements in the mechanical, metallurgical, and electrical sectors, followed by chemical industry. The reallocation of labor from textiles and garments and toward the agri-food sector is mainly behind the "between" component of the productivity increase (Figure 6.8).

Figure 6.8. Decomposition of Productivity Growth in the Manufacturing Sector
(Percentage points)

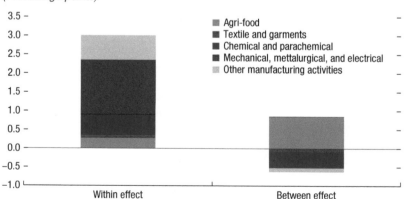

Source: High Commission for Planning.

CONCLUSION

This chapter analyzed the potential causes of the decline of manufacturing employment in Morocco. The findings are indicative rather than conclusive. For example, the chapter does not delve deeply into the underlying causes of the rapid labor productivity increase in manufacturing, which—even though it means fewer jobs in manufacturing—is an encouraging phenomenon. Nor does it analyze the deeper causes of the decline in Morocco's manufacturing trade balance after the process of trade liberalization. This process can be expected to have important growth-enhancing effects in the long term, especially in the context of continued reforms to improve the investment climate. Insofar as the higher trade deficit in manufactures is the mirror image of inflows of foreign direct investment destined to long-term investment in Morocco, it could represent a promising development. We leave these important questions to future research.

With these caveats in mind, the analysis suggests that Morocco is unlikely to be able to rely only on manufacturing to increase its job-creation capacity and reduce the share of its labor force still in the agricultural sector (about 35 percent of total employment). Demand for manufactures in Morocco is likely to continue to grow in coming years but only at a moderate pace, and there is no indication that labor productivity growth in manufacturing is about to slow sharply—nor would that be desirable.

Importantly, the chapter suggests that the trade deficit in manufacturing is often overstated as a cause of poor job creation in Morocco's manufacturing sector. But that also implies that even a sizable shift in the manufacturing trade balance is unlikely to materially change the prospect for employment growth in the foreseeable future (Lawrence 2020). Even if the COVID-19 pandemic has led to calls for a smaller reliance on foreign supply and more import-substitution policies, such policies are unlikely to change employment trends in Morocco on a sustained basis. The Moroccan economy is too small to support a competitive manufacturing sector mainly through domestic demand.

Relying on the manufacturing sector to expand employment also needs to confront challenging global trends (Ait Ali & Dadush 2019). Nearly all high-income countries saw jobs in manufacturing decline in absolute terms since the global financial crisis, whereas only a handful of middle-income countries have experienced substantial job creation in the manufacturing sector. Although trade is often seen as the culprit, sluggish job creation in manufacturing at the global level cannot be due to trade. Instead, large labor productivity gains are likely to be more of a factor.

That said, the importance of a vibrant manufacturing sector in Morocco remains evident. The analysis underscores the need for policies that enable the manufacturing sector to remain internationally competitive. Fostering competitiveness in the sector goes hand in hand with enabling automation and technology, which often means more sparing use of labor, especially unskilled labor.

The analysis also points to the centrality of policies that enhance the expansion of employment in services. In Morocco, traded and labor-intensive services such as tourism appear to be especially promising. Labor-intensive activities, such as construction and retailing, that earn no foreign exchange, may not be at the top of any list of priority sectors, but they can be a very important part of a job-creation strategy that rests on multiple pillars. In this regard, Morocco is fortunate in being able to rely on diverse sources of foreign exchange, ranging from migrant remittances to tourism and phosphates. To provide more jobs, Moroccan policies should pay attention to those sectors that employ large numbers of people and where employment is expanding as a result of the ongoing structural transformation of the Moroccan economy. Such a strategy is not a substitute for, but is fully consistent with, continued efforts to enhance the competitiveness of Morocco's manufacturing sector.

ANNEX 6.1.

ANNEX TABLE 6.1.1.

Morocco's Manufacturing Trade Balance per Economic Partner
(Billions of US dollars, unless otherwise specified)

	Country	2000	2008	Change between 2000 and 2008 (percent)[1]	Country	2008	2019	Change between 2008 and 2019 (percent)
Top 10 most-widening deficits	Italy	331	−1,911	17.3	China	−2,029	−4,120	41.4
	China	153	−2,029	16.9	Turkey	−873	−1,733	17.1
	France	621	−1,338	15.1	Portugal	−342	−829	9.7
	Spain	541	−1,104	12.7	Germany	−1,307	−1,604	5.9
	Germany	189	−1,307	11.6	Romania	−160	−439	5.5
	Turkey	7	−873	6.8	India	669	397	5.4
	Japan	108	−687	6.2	United Kingdom	70	−183	5.0
	United States	19	−621	4.9	Czech Republic	−84	−277	3.8
	Sweden	187	−375	4.3	Vietnam	−26	−191	3.3
	Korea	77	−453	4.1	Hungary	−70	−217	2.9
Top 10 most-increasing surpluses or most-shrinking deficits	Mexico	−11	34	1.6	Netherlands	−7	62	3.0
	Bangladesh	0	55	2.0	Ukraine	3	178	3.4
	Senegal	−10	49	2.1	Finland	41	−98	3.8
	Singapore	−41	38	2.8	Canada	187	−178	4.0
	Iran	−38	58	3.4	Sweden	41	45	5.3
	New Zealand	−27	83	3.9	United States	73	−109	6.7
	United Kingdom	−111	70	6.5	Japan	108	−249	9.4
	Pakistan	−3	426	15.4	Italy	331	−1,241	16.0
	Brazil	−27	715	26.6	Spain	621	−366	22.3
	India	−320	669	35.5	France	541	−88	26.1

Source: United Nations Conference on Trade and Development.

[1] Represents the share of the change of trade balance between 2008 and 2000 with each partner in the total deterioration of trade balance with the 10 countries between 2008 and 2000.

ANNEX TABLE 6.1.2.

Change in Manufacturing Trade Balance per Country
(Billions of US dollars, unless otherwise specified)

	Country	Change between 2000 and 2008	Change between 2000 and 2008 (percent of GDP)	Country	Change between 2008 and 2019	Change between 2008 and 2019 (percent of GDP)
	United States	−156,604	−1.1	United States	−514,905	−2.5
	Russian Federation	−134,616	−8.0	Canada	−48,180	−2.9
	United Arab Emirates	−77,955	−24.4	Brazil	−37,416	−1.9
Top 10 most-widening deficits	United Kingdom	−71,599	−2.4	France	−19,689	−1.0
	Australia	−70,636	−6.7	Australia	−18,218	−0.7
	Canada	−63,839	−4.1	Ukraine	−15,269	−1.8
	Spain	−46,593	−2.9	Iraq	−12,470	−8.1
	Saudi Arabia	−37,520	−7.2	Chile	−12,172	−5.0
	Brazil	−31,876	−1.9	Colombia	−11,414	−2.7
	Greece	−29,765	−8.4	Egypt	−10,022	−3.3
	Morocco	**−9,480**	**−10.2**	**Morocco**	**−1,142**	**−1.0**
	Barbados	3	0.1	United Kingdom	9,184	0.3
	Palau	13	6.5	Oman	10,185	13.3
	Palestine	53	0.7	Romania	10,780	4.3
	St. Lucia	127	8.8	Russian Federation	16,548	1.0
Top 10 most-shrinking deficits	Belize	142	10.5	India	17,126	0.6
	Eswatini	253	7.7	Iran	20,342	3.1
	Zimbabwe	558	8.8	Greece	26,465	12.9
	Luxembourg	689	1.2	Venezuela	27,670	18.4
	Turkey	1,968	0.3	Spain	46,546	3.3
	Israel	4,480	2.1	United Arab Emirates	53,765	12.9
				Japan	−165,663	−3.2
				Germany	−36,400	−0.9
Countries with shrinking surpluses	Philippines	−4,430	−2.4	Belgium	−26,139	−4.9
	Malaysia	−4,173	−1.8	Finland	−16,397	−6.1
				Sweden	−12,411	−2.3
				Austria	−10,661	−2.4
	Singapore	17,944	9.3	Italy	9,399	0.5
	Ireland	24,299	8.9	Netherlands	9,754	1.1
	Switzerland, Liechtenstein	27,090	4.7	Czech Republic	13,176	5.2
	Netherlands	35,453	3.7	Switzerland, Liechtenstein	13,813	1.9
Top 10 most-improving surpluses	Taiwan Province of China	48,508	11.7	Taiwan Province of China	14,551	2.4
	Italy	52,046	2.2	Singapore	16,123	4.3
	Korea	76,425	7.3	Ireland	22,205	5.6
	Japan	114,678	2.2	Malaysia	23,325	6.4
	Germany	274,732	7.4	Korea	37,375	2.3
	China	548,712	11.9	China	487,817	3.4

Source: United Nations Conference on Trade and Development.

REFERENCES

Abraham, Filip, and Ellen Brock. 2003. "Sectoral Employment Effects of Trade and Productivity in Europe." *Applied Economics* 35 (2): 223–38.

Aiginger, Karl, and Dani Rodrik. 2020. "Rebirth of Industrial Policy and an Agenda for the Twenty-First Century." *Journal of Industry, Competition and Trade* 20 189–207.

Ait Ali, Abdelaziz, and Uri Dadush. 2019. "Manufacturing Employment, International Trade and China." Policy Center for the New South Research Paper 19/04, Policy Center for the New South, Morocco.

Baumol, William J. 1967. "Macroeconomics of Unbalanced Growth: The Anatomy of Urban Crisis." *American Economic Review* 57 (3): 415–26.

Bettah, Mounia, and Leila Zniber. 2019. "Solde des Echanges Éxtérieurs: Contribution des Facteurs Structurels et Cycliques." Department of Economic Studies and Financial Forecast, Ministry of Finance Policy Brief 11.

Bivens, Josh. 2004. "Shifting Blame for Manufacturing Job Loss: Effect of Rising Trade Deficit Shouldn't Be Ignored." Economic Policy Institute Briefing Paper 149, Economic Policy Institute, Washington, DC.

Cezar, Rafael, A. Duguet, Guillaume Gaulier, and Vincent Vicard. 2017. "Competition for Global Value Added." Banque de France Working Paper 628.

Chakravarty, Sangeeta, and Arup Mitra. 2009. "Is Industry Still the Engine of Growth? An Econometric Study of the Organized Sector Employment in India." *Journal of Policy Modeling* 31 (1): 22–35.

Dadush, Uri. 2015. "Is Manufacturing Still a Key to Growth?" Policy Center for the New South Policy Paper 15/07.

Dadush, Uri, and Yana Myachenkova. 2018. "Assessing the EU–North Africa Trade Agreements." Bruegel and Policy Center for the New South Policy Paper 18/11.

Dasgupta, Sukti, and Ajit Singh. 2006. "Manufacturing, Services and Premature De-Industrialisation in Developing Countries: A Kaldorian Empirical Analysis." Centre for Business Research, University of Cambridge Working Paper 327.

Dieppe, Alistair, ed. 2021. *Global Productivity: Trends, Drivers, and Policies.* World Bank.

Ghose, Ajit K. 2000. "Trade Liberalization and Manufacturing Employment." ILO Working Paper 2000/3, International Labour Organization, Geneva.

Gregory, Mary, Ben Zissimos, and Christine Greenhalgh. 2001. "Jobs for the Skilled: How Technology, Trade and Domestic Demand Changed the Structure of UK Employment, 1979–90." *Oxford Economic Papers* 53 (1): 20–46.

Guilhoto, Joaquim J. M., and Umberto A. Sesso Filho. 2005. "Estimação da Matriz Insumo-Produto a Partir de Dados Preliminares das Contas Nacionais." *Economia Aplicada* 9 (2): 277–99.

High Commission for Planning (HCP). 2016. "Study on the Return to Physical Capital in Morocco." High Commission for Planning, Rabat.

Hoekman, Bernard, and L. Alan Winters. 2005. "Trade and Employment: Stylized Facts and Research Findings." World Bank Policy Research Working Paper 3676, World Bank, Washington, DC.

Kletzer, Lori G. 2002. *Imports, Exports, and Jobs: What Does Trade Mean for Employment and Job Loss?* Kalamazoo, MI: W.E. Upjohn Institute for Employment Research.

Lawrence, Robert Z. 2020. "Trade Surplus or Deficit? Neither Matters for Changes in Manufacturing Employment Shares." PIIE Working Paper 20-15, Peterson Institute for International Economics, Washington, DC.

McMillan, Margaret S., and Dani Rodrik. 2011. "Globalization, Structural Change and Productivity Growth." NBER Working Paper 17143, National Bureau of Economic Research, Cambridge, MA.

McMillan, Margaret S., and Iñigo Verduzco. 2011. "New Evidence on Trade and Employment: An Overview." In *Trade and Employment: From Myths to Facts,* edited by Marion Jansen, Ralf Peters, and José Manuel Salazar-Xirinachs. Geneva: International Labour Organization, 23–60.

Menezes-Filho, Naercio A., and Marc-Andreas Muendler. 2011. "Labor Reallocation in Response to Trade Reforms." NBER Working Paper 17372, National Bureau of Economic Research, Cambridge, MA.

Newfarmer, Richard, and Monika Sztajerowska. 2012. "Trade and Employment in a Fast-Changing World." In *Policy Priorities for International Trade and Jobs*, edited by Douglas Lippold. Paris: Organisation for Economic Co-operation and Development, 7-73.

Nordhaus, William. 2005. "The Sources of the Productivity Rebound and the Manufacturing Employment Puzzle." NBER Working Paper 11354, National Bureau Economic Research, Cambridge, MA.

Revenga, Ana L. 1992. "Exporting Jobs? The Impact of Import Competition on Employment and Wages in U.S. Manufacturing." *The Quarterly Journal of Economics* 107 (1): 255–84.

Rodrik, Dani. 2015. "Premature Deindustrialization." Institute for Advanced Study Working Paper 107, Institute for Advanced Study, Princeton.

Rowthorn, Robert, and Ramana Ramaswamy. 1997. "Deindustrialization: Its Causes and Implications." In *Economic Issues 10*. Washington, DC: International Monetary Fund.

Thirlwall, A. P. 1983. "A Plain Man's Guide to Kaldor's Growth Laws." *Journal of Post Keynesian Economics* 5 (3): 345–58.

Tuhin, R. 2015. "Impact of Trade on International Employment: Evidence from Australian Manufacturing Industries." Department of Industry, Science and Resources, Australian Government Research Paper 2/2015, Canberra.

World Trade Organization (WTO). 2019. *World Trade Report 2019: The Future of Services Trade*. Geneva.

CHAPTER 7

Climate Change and Development in Morocco

Moëz Cherif, Javier Díaz-Cassou, and Carole Megevand

INTRODUCTION

Morocco is broadly recognized as a climate hotspot. Average temperatures have increased by 0.2°C per decade since the 1960s (Figure 7.1), a trend that exceeds the global average by about 11 percent (Driouech and others 2020). Precipitation levels have followed an overall downward trajectory, resulting in a drastic reduction in the per capita availability of renewable internal freshwater resources (Figure 7.2). Changes in temperatures and amounts of precipitation are expected to amplify in the coming decades, with potentially major impacts on the water cycle, posing a threat to the agricultural sector and other economic activities, and justifying the inclusion of the adaptation agenda at the core of Morocco's policy priorities.

With a particularly generous endowment in renewable energy sources, Morocco is well placed to reap the benefits that could come from the global decarbonization agenda. The country has one of the highest rates of solar insolation worldwide, with about 3,000 hours per year of sunshine (and up to 3,600 hours in the desert). The average wind speed is 5.3 meters per second in more than 90 percent of the country's territory. Fully exploiting this large renewable energy potential could have several advantages for the Moroccan economy. First, decarbonizing the energy mix would reduce Morocco's reliance on imported fuels, helping shield the economy from the impacts of external shocks.[1] Moreover, developing the country's green hydrogen potential could turn Morocco into an exporter of energy. Second, reducing Morocco's industrial exports' carbon intensity would yield a critical comparative advantage in those markets that are embracing a green transition, most notably the European Union. Third, the energy transition could bring net job creation on a substantial scale.

This chapter is based on the World Bank's 2022 *Country Climate and Development Report* (CCDR) on Morocco (World Bank 2022). CCDRs are new core diagnostic reports that integrate climate change and development considerations. They will help countries prioritize the most effective actions that can reduce greenhouse gas emissions and boost adaptation while delivering on broader development goals.

[1] Between 2010 and 2020, energy accounted for 19.4 percent of total imports.

Figure 7.1. Temperature
(Degrees Celsius)

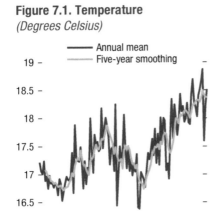

Source: World Bank, Climate Change
Knowledge Portal (2021).

**Figure 7.2. Renewable Internal
Freshwater Resources per Capita**
(Cubic meters)

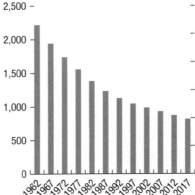

Source: World Bank, Climate Change
Knowledge Portal (2021).

Morocco already has a relatively ambitious climate policy, but important challenges lie ahead. On the adaptation front, the cornerstone of the country's strategy has historically been the deployment of infrastructure projects (dams, water basin interconnections, and irrigation). However, despite the tenfold increase in total water storage capacity that has taken place since the 1960s, the actual volume of water stored has been on a declining trend for most of the past decade, and underground water resources are being unsustainably overexploited. On the mitigation front, Morocco has developed various flagship solar and wind projects, earning the country the reputation of an emerging "climate champion." However, these efforts have been offset by a growing use of coal for power generation, and Morocco's power sector remains among the most carbon intensive in the world. Ahead of the 2021 UN Climate Change Conference (COP26), Morocco revised its nationally determined contribution with an enhanced mitigation target aimed at achieving a 45.5 percent reduction of greenhouse gas emissions by 2030 compared to a business-as-usual scenario.

This chapter focuses on the intersection between climate action and economic development in Morocco. It begins with a discussion on adaptation, focused on the impacts of droughts, water scarcity, and climate-related natural disasters (floods). Then, it moves on to the mitigation front, with a quantification of the investments that would be required to decarbonize key sectors of the Moroccan economy, a description of the potential advantages from adopting such pathway, and a discussion on some of the reforms that would be needed to enable the private sector to lead that effort. Finally, the third section discusses the structural, fiscal, and financial policies that would facilitate the transition toward a resilient and low-carbon economy in Morocco.

Figure 7.3. Morocco's Water Inflows
(Billions of cubic meters per year)

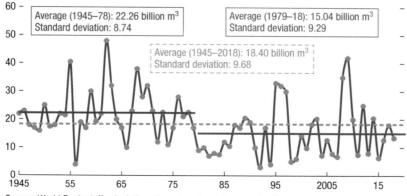

Source: World Bank staff calculations, based on the National Water Plan.
Note: m³ = cubic meters.

THE WATER CHALLENGES

Water scarcity has intensified markedly over recent decades. Surface water inflows have declined by more than 30 percent between 1945–1978 and 1979–2018, from 22 billion cubic meters (m³) to 15 billion m³ (Figure 7.3). This has turned Morocco into one of the most water-stressed countries of the world while increasing pressures on underground water beyond sustainable levels, especially in dry years.[2]

Despite the development of a more resilient irrigated agriculture, droughts still constitute a major source of macroeconomic volatility. The modernization of irrigation systems and the public support to investment in on-farm equipment have allowed Morocco to increase areas under drip irrigation by 3.5 times between 2008 and 2018, fueling a 92 percent increase in agricultural value added during that period. However, rainfed areas still cover 80 percent of agricultural lands, with highly variable crop yields that are closely correlated with precipitation levels.[3] Although the primary sector of the economy only represents 13 percent of gross domestic product (GDP), rainfall shocks explain close to 37 percent of the variability of Morocco's total output over the medium term.[4] This trend has been particularly apparent in recent years because a severe drought amplified the recession induced by the pandemic, whereas a relatively rainy year contributed to

---

[2] Groundwater withdrawals amount to about 5 billion m³ per year, which exceeds by an estimated 1.1 billion m³ the level of renewable groundwater sources.

[3] The coefficient of yield variation for key cereals such as wheat reached 0.34 between 2000 and 2020 in Morocco, versus 0.23 in Tunisia, 0.18 in Algeria and Spain, 0.11 in France, and 0.06 in Turkey (calculations based on FAOSTAT data).

[4] As obtained from the forecast error variance decomposition of a structural vector autoregression used to trace out the impulse reaction function of real GDP to rainfall shocks in Morocco (Díaz-Cassou and others 2022).

Figure 7.4. GTAP-BIO Simulation of Water Rationing Scenarios
(Percentage change from baseline)

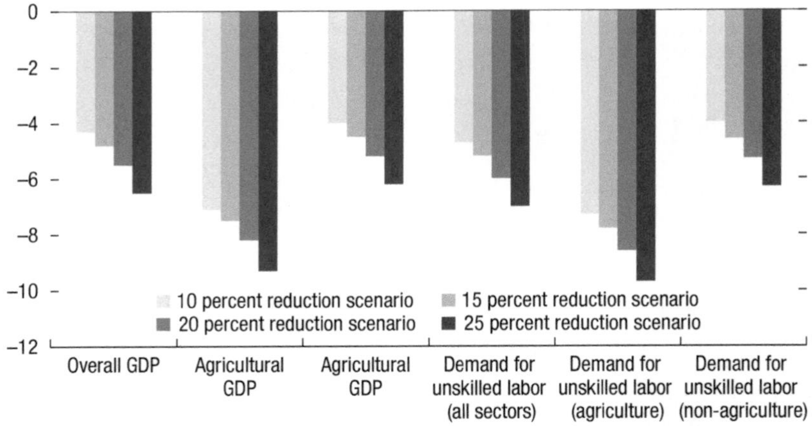

Source: World Bank, Global Trade Analysis Project (GTAP)-BIO-Water modeling exercise.
Note: The four simulated scenarios correspond to reductions in water supply from 10 to 25 percent in 5 percent increments across all sectors of the Moroccan economy. These scenarios also assume that climate change will induce agricultural yields (a 15 percent drop for rainfed crops and a 5 percent increase for irrigated crops).

boosting the post-Covid economic rebound that took place in 2021, followed by yet another drought that caused an abrupt deceleration in 2022. Droughts do also have impacts on the balance of payments because Morocco's reliance on imported food items increases in dry years (primarily cereals), and on public finances because the government provides emergency support to farmers.

Beyond the short-term impact of droughts, a continuation of recent trends could have major economic impacts over the medium and the long term. The World Bank's 2022 *Country Climate and Development Report* (CCDR) uses a computable general equilibrium model (the Global Trade Analysis Project [GTAP]-BIO-Water model) to simulate the potential impacts of various water-rationing scenarios. Factoring in the changes in agricultural yields that are expected to result from climate change in Morocco (Ouraich 2010), a 25 percent reduction in water supply (broadly, a continuation of current trends) could reduce GDP by 6.5 percent by the middle of the twenty-first century (Figure 7.4).[5] This would have major impacts also on the labor market, reducing the demand for unskilled workers by up to 7 percent (9.7 percent in the agricultural sector).[6] The effects

---

[5] This is relative to a baseline projection with no rationing.

[6] As a result, climate change could intensify migratory flows between rural areas and urban centers. According to the modeling exercise conducted in the World Bank's Groundswell 2.0 report (Clement and others 2021), in a pessimistic climate scenario, the number of climate migrants could reach 1.9 million individuals in Morocco, which is more than 5 percent of the population. Internal climate migrants tend to relocate to urban areas that are more vulnerable to climate-related natural disasters, such as floods, to which coastal cities are particularly prone.

would also be felt on the trade balance, increasing net imports of food by up to $891 million, potentially threatening Morocco's food security.

Morocco's response to water scarcity has traditionally been based on the deployment of hydraulic infrastructure on a massive scale. Between the late 1960s and 2020, Morocco built 126 dams, increasing its total storage capacity from 2 to 19.1 billion m³. In addition, the country has developed 15 water basin interconnections of about 785 kilometers to secure municipal water supply and irrigation needs. Complementarily, Morocco has invested in the modernization of irrigation systems while subsidizing the adoption of on-farm equipment, resulting in a pronounced improvement of water productivity in the agricultural sector.

The National Water Plan (PNE) 2020–50 is an ambitious infrastructure strategy to be implemented in the coming decades with the goal of closing the actual and the projected gap between demand and supply.[7] On the supply side, it foresees investment in conventional water resources mobilization (dams and interconnections) but also in nonconventional technologies (desalination and wastewater use). On the demand side, it includes actions to reduce water losses in transport and distribution, with additional efforts to increase water efficiency in the agricultural sector through the continued modernization of irrigation systems.

The plan is estimated to require an overall investment of about $41 billion over the 2020–50 period, which under current policies would be mostly shouldered by the public sector. Given Morocco's limited fiscal space, an important policy question is whether there are other more economically beneficial alternative uses for a portion of the public resources expected to be committed to the PNE, such as reducing debt or undertaking alternative investments. To address this question, the 2022 CCDR uses the World Bank's Macro-Fiscal Model (MFMod) to simulate the impact of the PNE.[8] The results suggest that a partial implementation of the plan always yields worse macroeconomic outcomes than its full implementation (see Table 7.1). Despite the large volume of resources required, full completion of the PNE remains the preferable policy choice.[9]

However, in the context of climate change, engineering solutions alone are unlikely to solve Morocco's water challenge unless they are complemented by more ambitious demand management policies. Deploying new hydraulic infrastructure projects continues to be essential to cope with water scarcity, but it may

---

[7] This gap is currently estimated at 1.8 billion m³ per year at the national level and is projected to reach 7 billion m³ per year by 2050 in the absence of new infrastructure (about 35 percent of demand).

[8] For this purpose, a standalone World Bank MFMod with a climate module was developed for the Moroccan economy. The modeling exercise incorporates the agricultural output losses simulated by the GTAP-BIO model discussed previously. However, a difference between the GTAP-BIO model and the MFMod simulations is that in the latter, water is rationed only for the agricultural sector and not to all sectors of the economy.

[9] This result is consistent with a recent IMF publication, which estimates that investing in climate infrastructure to improve the resilience of the Moroccan economy against the recurrence of droughts would be more beneficial than an equivalent investment in standard infrastructure (IMF 2022).

TABLE 7.1.

Macroeconomic Impact of the National Water Plan's Partial Implementation
(Percentage deviation from baseline)

	GDP			Consumption			Investment			Debt		
	2030	2040	2050	2030	2040	2050	2030	2040	2050	2030	2040	2050
S1 Debt	−0.04	−0.19	−0.48	−0.07	−0.28	−0.56	−0.49	−0.54	−0.73	−2.46	−3.48	−2.90
S1 Investment	0.01	−0.09	−0.38	0.01	−0.12	−0.40	0.04	−1.44	−0.64	0.12	0.16	0.16
S2 Debt	−0.12	−0.55	−1.32	−0.20	−0.78	−1.51	−1.28	−0.19	−1.99	−6.14	−8.67	−7.25
S2 Investment	0.00	−0.31	−1.07	0.00	−0.39	−1.14	0.05	−0.60	−1.79	0.30	0.42	0.43

Source: Authors' calculations using intermediate results of the World Bank's Global Trade Analysis Project (GTAP)-BIO model and the Macro-Fiscal Model.

Note: The baseline corresponds to the full implementation of the National Water Plan (PNE). S1 = scenario 1; S2 = scenario 2.

• S1 Debt: Reduction in PNE investments on additional water mobilization infrastructure corresponding to a 10 percent reduction in water supply for irrigation; freed resources used for debt reduction (fiscal consolidation).

• S1 Investment: Reduction in PNE investments on additional water mobilization infrastructure corresponding to a 10 percent reduction in water supply for irrigation; freed resources used for alternative productive investment.

• S2 Debt: Reduction in PNE investments on additional water mobilization infrastructure corresponding to a 25 percent reduction in water supply for irrigation; freed resources used for debt reduction (fiscal consolidation).

• S2 Investment: Reduction in PNE investments on additional water mobilization infrastructure corresponding to a 25 percent reduction in water supply for irrigation; freed resources used for alternative productive investment.

no longer be a sufficient condition if existing climate projections materialize. Indeed, despite the tenfold increase in water storage capacity that has been achieved since the 1960s, the actual water volume in reservoirs has trended downward over most of the past decade, reaching critically low levels in 2022. Moreover, although the adoption of modern on-farm irrigation equipment has increased water productivity, it has not systematically led to a reduction in the consumption of irrigation water at the aggregate level, but rather the opposite. This phenomenon is often referred to as the Jevons paradox: when unconstrained in their water use through prices or quantities, farmers equipped with new irrigation techniques tend to intensify production or shift toward crops with higher added value that consume more water. In other words, more efficient irrigation systems tend to increase pressures on water resources unless accompanied by a strong demand management policy.

Such a policy may need to include a revision of current water tariffs, particularly for irrigated agriculture. These tariffs have been kept artificially low in Morocco and are not aligned either with recovery costs or with the scarcity value of the resource.[10] Increasing the water use fee for private irrigators and ensuring that the use of groundwater resources is appropriately controlled and priced could help relieve pressure on water resources while providing additional resources for water basin agencies to better maintain existing infrastructure and enforce water regulations. This could be combined with a system of tradable quotas, providing the flexibility needed to ensure optimal water allocation among users. The Moroccan authorities are beginning to take steps in that direction, recognizing that the underpricing of water for irrigated agriculture is no longer sustainable.

In addition to droughts, Morocco is exposed to other climate-related natural hazards. Due to its geographic position, high rainfall variability, and topography, Morocco is particularly prone to floods: 20 major events have been recorded between 2000 and 2021, causing average direct losses estimated at $450 million per year.[11] The MFMod was used to generate a probability distribution of GDP outcomes based on historical data on the occurrence of floods in Morocco (Figure 7.5). According to this simulation, in the absence of risk-reduction

---

[10] Water pricing in irrigated agriculture is divided into (a) service provision (or irrigation) fees, and (b) water use fee. The former is aimed at covering the operation, maintenance, and amortization costs of collective irrigation systems. The latter is designed to contribute to operating and maintenance costs of dams and other hydraulic assets and should reflect the scarcity value of water. However, it is currently set at a very low level (DH0.02/m³) and only a very small portion of users pay it. As a result, the total amount of fees collected from irrigation users is very low (between DH26 million and DH40 million per year), which has left river basin agencies chronically underfunded to conduct their mandate. It has also led to an inefficiently low volume of resources devoted to the maintenance of infrastructure and upstream watersheds, contributing to the siltation problem that affects Morocco's reservoirs.

[11] Sea-level rise constitutes another long-term threat, especially for low-lying areas, that contributes to exacerbating the risk of floods. More than 65 percent of the population and 90 percent of industry is concentrated along the coastline. Hallegatte and others (2013) estimated that a 40-centimeter sea-level rise would result in mean annual losses of up to $1,256 million in the city of Casablanca alone. Up to 24 percent of the Tangier Bay would also be at risk of flooding (Snoussi and others 2009).

Figure 7.5. GDP Responses to Flood Damages without Policies, Representative Causal Pathway 4.5 Climate Projection
(Percent deviation from baseline)

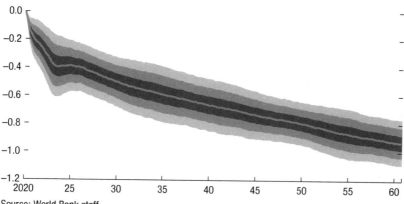

Source: World Bank staff.
Note: The baseline under the two climatic scenarios is no flooding. The figure captures only the impacts of damages to physical capital and not the ancillary impacts on economic activity that could be caused by floods. The blue line represents the median result; the shaded red areas show the 10th to 90th percentiles.

investments and policies, the projected median impact of floods would gradually increase from 0.2 percent of GDP in 2025 to more than 0.5 percent of GDP by the 2030s, and almost 1 percent by 2050. This illustrates the potential impact of floods for the long-term performance of the economy and justifies the adoption of an appropriate disaster risk management and disaster risk financing (DRF) framework.

Morocco has already developed a sophisticated disaster risk management and DRF architecture. A central element of the country's strategy has been the transition from a focus on disaster response to a preparedness approach that prioritizes investment in both structural and nonstructural disaster risk reduction. A national flood protection plan based on the deployment of risk reduction investment was implemented between 2003 and 2017 and renewed in 2016 with a 2035 horizon. The Natural Disaster Resilience Fund, initially created to finance post-disaster reconstruction, was turned into an innovative mechanism to co-finance investment in disaster risk reduction and preparedness at the local level. In addition, Morocco has deployed a sophisticated dual catastrophic risk insurance regime with (1) a private pillar guaranteeing floods coverage for insured households through additional mandatory premiums received and managed by insurance companies, and (2) a public pillar providing basic compensation for uninsured households through the Solidarity Fund against Catastrophic Events.

However, the scale of risk reduction investments remains suboptimally low to cope with average hazards. Disaster risk management investments reduce the damages caused by future floods but require payments that need to be mobilized based on forecasts, and these payments carry an implicit cost for the economy. Converging toward an optimal level of risk reduction implies weighing the benefits of lower future damages against the cost of financing upfront payments either through taking on additional debt or reallocating other productive investments to flood prevention. Using the MFMod, the 2022 CCDR conducted a series of macrosimulations to capture this trade-off and compare the impact of various investment pathways. These results are summarized in Figure 7.6, which shows that the net present value of risk reduction investments is maximized when annual investment reaches 15–20 percent of the annual average loss caused by droughts, the equivalent of $60–$90 million per year. Although this is largely the investments programmed under the updated national flood protection plan (2016–35), only about one-fourth of the investments that had been programmed under the previous flood protection plan were executed, implying that the actual volume of resources devoted to risk reduction has remained below the estimated optimal level.

Scaling up existing disaster risk financing instruments would increase resilience against extreme natural hazards. Although Morocco already has a sophisticated DRF system, its scale remains limited: its combined private and public pillars can only provide 5–10 percent of the direct economic damages associated with average catastrophic scenarios and about 25 percent of losses on covered assets in extreme events. The 2022 CCDR conducted a scenario-based

Figure 7.6. GDP Gains and Losses by Level of Disaster Risk Management Investment

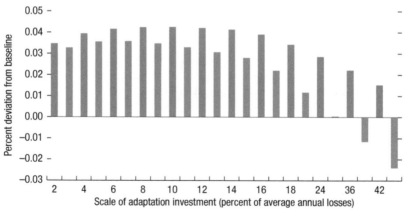

Source: World Bank staff.
Note: The figure shows the difference between the net present value of GDP under different scenarios regarding the scale of risk reduction investment (measured as percentage of annual average losses) and a baseline scenario with no investment in flood protection. The size of the impacts depends on how Morocco finances risk reduction investments (debt versus substitution of other investment): positive net impacts are higher when financed by debt (blue bar) than when financed by investment substitution (gray bar).

cost–benefit analysis to compare systems with different coverage levels.[12] It concludes that the net cost of scaling up current DRF systems is moderate when no disasters materialize or when disasters are of an average magnitude. However, the net benefits of such schemes increase exponentially when the severity of the event increases, which could well be the case in the context of climate change.[13]

DECARBONIZATION AS A STRATEGIC OPPORTUNITY FOR THE MOROCCAN ECONOMY

Morocco's greenhouse gas emissions are comparatively small. The country's total annual greenhouse gas emissions doubled between 2000 and 2019 (from 44.6 to 91.2 million tons of CO_2-equivalent). However, Morocco only contributes to 0.2 percent of global emissions, and the carbon intensity of its economy is still 9.2 percent lower than that of the world and 30 percent below the MENA region. Moreover, since the early 2010s, Morocco has entered a relative decoupling trend in which real GDP grows faster than greenhouse gas emissions, implying that the carbon intensity of the GDP has begun to decline.

Despite Morocco's plentiful renewable energy potential, its reliance on coal for power generation has expanded over time. The energy sector accounted for 65.1 percent of total gross greenhouse gas emissions in 2018.[14] The power sector dominates energy-related emissions, with 36.1 percent of total, followed by the transport sector (29 percent). In this context, Morocco's mitigation policies have understandably focused on the decarbonization of the power-generating sector, with the development of various flagship solar and wind projects that have brought the share of renewable energy to about 20 percent of the power genera-tion energy mix in 2021. However, three new coal power plants were commis-sioned in the 2010s, bringing the total coal-fired power-generating capacity above 4 gigawatts (39 percent of total power generation in 2021). As a result, the carbon intensity of the power sector has continued to increase (see Figure 7.7), placing Morocco's power sector among the most carbon intensive in the world, with about 600 tons of CO_2 emitted per gigawatt-hour in 2020.

---

[12] The "benefits" associated with each of these scenarios are the direct losses covered by public DRF instruments as well as the risks transferred to the insurance market, to which a multiplying factor is applied depending on the severity of the event. The multiplying factor is derived from the reality that the quick injection of preplanned financial flows after such events will limit the spillover effects and the transmission of the shock to other sectors or economic agents, whereas a delayed response will generate additional costs. The "costs" are the estimated pricing of DRF instruments, including opportunity costs.

[13] The most ambitious insurance system simulated in this exercise would yield a net cost of close to $6 million in years with no hazard, which would reach $257 million under a one in a 100-year event, and as much as $1,066 million in a one in 250-year event.

[14] The other sectors that emit the most are agriculture (22.1 percent), industrial processes (6 percent), and waste management (5.4 percent).

Figure 7.7. Power Sector Emissions and Carbon Intensity

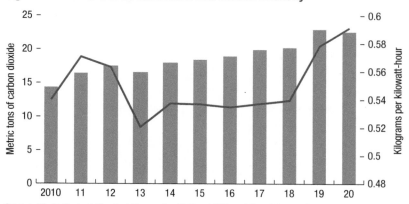

Source: World Bank staff calculations using National Office of Electricity and Drinking Water data.
Note: The red line represents the carbon intensity of the power sector and the blue bars represent power sector emissions.

The 2022 CCDR builds a decarbonization scenario based on the deployment of renewable energies and the electrification of key end-use sectors of the Moroccan economy by 2050. To do so, it relied on the World Bank's Energy Planning Model, a tool that minimizes the costs of expanding and operating a power system while meeting specific environmental constraints. The report compared two scenarios: (a) a least-cost scenario in which power generation capacity is expanded with no constraint on CO_2 emissions, and (b) a scenario that imposes a 95 percent decarbonization of power generation combined with additional capacity expansion to allow for the penetration of e-mobility, the electrification in the industrial sector, and the production of green hydrogen. Importantly, the materialization of the latter scenario could put Morocco on a trajectory of net-zero greenhouse gas emissions by the 2050s if combined with other actions on reforestation, agriculture, waste management, and energy efficiency, all of which are already contemplated in the nationally determined contribution.

The decarbonization scenario would require a massive increase in the installed capacity of the power sector (Figure 7.8). As various end-user sectors are electrified, total supply would have to exceed that of the baseline scenario by 165 percent (182 terawatt-hours).[15] This would require a fivefold increase in installed capacity (from 30 gigawatts in the baseline scenario to 147 gigawatts), partly due to the lower-capacity utilization factor of renewable energy plants relative to coal power plants used in the baseline scenario. Most of the decarbonization effort would initially come from wind (onshore and offshore), whereas solar would pick up in the 2030s. Natural gas would be needed as a bridge fuel in the transition to decarbonization,

---

[15] This additional supply would be distributed as follows: 46 terawatt-hours for transport, 28 terawatt-hours for industry, and 107 terawatt-hours for green hydrogen (including the use of electricity for water desalination for electrolyzers' input).

Figure 7.8. Power Generation by Type of Plant
(Terawatt-hours)

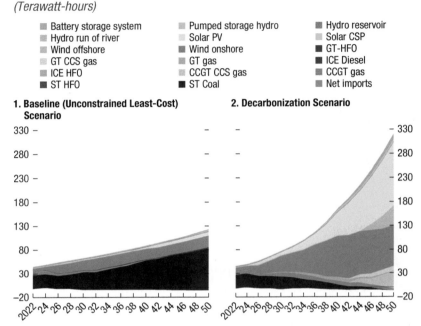

Source: World Bank staff calculations using the Energy Planning Model.
Note: CCGT = combined cycle gas turbine; CCS = carbon capture and storage; CSP = concentrated solar power; GT = gas turbine; HFO = heavy fuel oil; ICE = internal combustion engine; PV = photovoltaic; ST= steam turbine.

both as a less carbon-intensive alternative to coal and as a source of flexibility for the power system. The load factor of coal plants would be gradually reduced, but the retirement of coal plants (predominantly private) would mostly occur after 2044.

Decarbonizing the economy would require large investments, particularly toward the end of the projection period. Relative to the unconstrained least-cost scenario, decarbonization would require additional investment of $46.3 billion over the 2022–50 period (from 6.7 billion over 2022–30 to $13.8 billion over 2030–40 and $25.8 billion during 2040–50, all in net present value terms). This trend reflects the increasing marginal abatement cost of carbon that is expected to materialize in coming decades, as the country moves ahead with cheaper technologies first and then is forced to adopt more expensive ones, such as gas-fired thermal generation with carbon capture and sequestration and battery storage. This trend is also reflected in the projected evolution of the average cost of electricity generation, which is expected to decline until about 2040 but to enter an upward trend afterward (Figure 7.9).

Given the scale of the investments required to engage in the ambitious decarbonization pathway described above, assessing its potential impacts on the Moroccan economy is critical. As was done with the water sector, the MFMod is used in the 2022 CCDR to assess the broad macroeconomic effects of projected

Figure 7.9. Average Electricity Generation Costs
(US dollars per megawatt-hour)

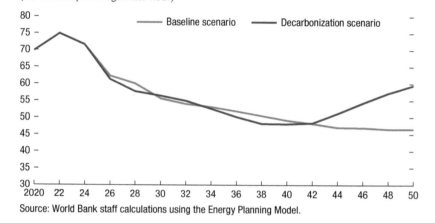

Source: World Bank staff calculations using the Energy Planning Model.

mitigation investments. A central assumption was that the bulk of the required investments (85 percent) is undertaken by the private sector, with the public sector only investing to extend the transmission lines and the distribution grid. In this scenario, decarbonization would yield a modest improvement of real GDP compared to the baseline scenario and would help reduce the debt-to-GDP ratio by 2.5 percentage points by 2030 (Figure 7.10).

Decarbonization would reduce fuel imports by $10 billion (in net present value terms) between 2022 and 2040, reducing Morocco's exposure to international commodity shocks. Moreover, it would increase Morocco's external position and comparative advantages through a series of channels. First, Morocco could potentially become an energy exporter should the green

Figure 7.10. Macro-fiscal Impacts of Decarbonization Investments
(Percentage deviation from baseline)

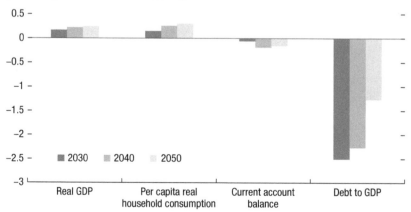

Source: World Bank staff calculations using the Micro-Fiscal Model.

Figure 7.11. Intensity of Carbon Dioxide Emissions Embedded in Gross Exports
(Tons of emissions per million US dollars)

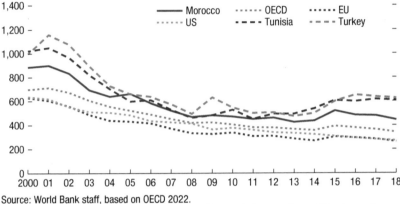

Source: World Bank staff, based on OECD 2022.
Note: EU = European Union; OECD = Organisation of Economic Co-operation and Development.

hydrogen agenda in which it is embarking succeed. Second, developing a low-carbon manufacturing base would allow Morocco to partially circumvent carbon border adjustment mechanisms, such as the one that is being introduced by the European Union.[16] Third, decarbonizing its export sectors would allow Morocco to reap the benefits of changing consumer preferences toward low-carbon products. The intensity of CO_2 emissions embedded in Morocco's exports is already lower than that of competing countries, such as Tunisia and Turkey. However, it is still 70 percent higher than that of the European Union, 65 percent above that of the US, and 31 percent higher than the average for Organisation for Economic Co-operation and Development (OECD) members in 2018 (Figure 7.11).

Finally, the energy transition could create jobs on a substantial scale. The 2022 CCDR used the Clean Energy Employment Assessment Tool to estimate the economy-wide job creation until 2030 that could be associated with the energy transition investment under the decarbonization scenario described above. This exercise focused on four subsectors: the deployment of utility-scale solar, distributed solar,

---

[16] The carbon border adjustment mechanism (CBAM), announced by the European Union to take effect in 2024 and covering emissions from chemicals, metals, and electricity, is likely to have a limited impact on Morocco, with levies estimated at less than 0.1 percent of GDP by 2026. However, the gradual expansion of the CBAM to cover other sectors could produce larger effect on a few sectors of the Moroccan economy, most notably the chemical industry (with about 75 percent of the world's phosphate reserves, Morocco is the fifth-largest exporter of fertilizers). According to the 2022 CCDR, under an expanded CBAM, chemical exports to the European Union (mostly fertilizers) could fall by 2–3 percent. To cope with that challenge, the state-owned phosphate enterprise OCP has already adopted an ambition plan to lower its carbon emissions and reach carbon neutrality by 2040.

utility-scale wind, and an increase in energy efficiency.[17] According to this assessment, the energy transition could add about 28,000 net jobs across the economy per year, about 9 percent of the 300,000 annual jobs shortfall currently estimated in Morocco (World Bank 2021). It is worth noting that this estimate should be interpreted as a lower bound given that it does not account for potential new jobs that could be generated by other clean energy technologies, such as energy storage, or by end-user sectors, such as industry and e-mobility.

For the benefits of the decarbonization scenario to materialize, the private sector would need to play a leading role. As mentioned, the macrosimulations presented previously assume that close to 85 percent of the investments required for this scenario to materialize are undertaken by the private sector. This is a realistic objective, but it would require a radical shift in current institutional and market arrangements. A first step could be to allow for third-party access to the transmission and distribution networks at regulated tariffs so that private investors in renewable energy can sell directly to eligible customers without discrimination, and eventually create open wholesale and balancing markets that will make investment in renewable energy more market driven. The National Office of Electricity and Drinking Water (ONEE), the vertically integrated public utility, would need to be unbundled into generation, transmission, and distribution to avoid conflicts of interest, with priority given to the creation of a transmission system operator to manage network access for both public and private actors fairly. The electricity regulator would also have to be strengthened so that it could enforce the unbundling of ONEE, calculate fair access tariffs for the transmission and distribution networks, and set full cost-recovery tariffs for end users. The legal and regulatory framework of the electricity market would also need to be enhanced in preparation for alignment with the European Union electricity market structure. A clear roadmap for such a transition, combined with early implementation of the appropriate policy and legal framework, would contribute to lowering the risk for private sector investors, thus reducing the investment costs.

A conducive market environment also needs to be put in place for Morocco to realize its green hydrogen potential. The deployment of the green hydrogen market will require large investments in production and transport infrastructure, mostly financed by the private sector. To facilitate such an investment, the government would need to finalize its gas policy and regulatory framework and extend it to green hydrogen; prepare an implementation plan for the green hydrogen strategy

---

[17] The Clean Energy Employment Assessment Tool tracks the flow of expenditures associated to investments in these four technologies and considers four channels that impact jobs: (1) the *Investment Impact* from the spending needed to set up the projects; (2) the *Investment Shift Impact*, the opposite of the Investment Impact, whereby spending on clean energy technologies subtracts resources from future conventional (fossil fuel) energy projects; (3) the *Substitution Impact* from the saving that consumers can achieve through higher energy efficiency or the introduction of clean energy, as well as the spending on operation and maintenance (O&M) throughout the project's lifetime; and (4) the *Revenue Impact*, the opposite of the Substitution Impact (the additional spending related to the green transition). Once these effects are computed, the Clean Energy Employment Assessment Tool calculates their impact on jobs by applying employment multipliers derived from an input–output framework.

(including the needed transport infrastructure); develop cooperative partnerships with potential importers of Moroccan green hydrogen; and prepare certifications, norms, and standards. The nascent nature of this market and the high uncertainty that still surrounds this technology imply that an active use of financial de-risking instruments may be needed to attract private investment.

TOWARD A "WHOLE-OF-ECONOMY" APPROACH TO CLIMATE CHANGE

Implementing the adaptation and mitigation strategies discussed in the previous sections would require investment of about $77.7 billion (net present value terms) between 2022 and 2050, corresponding to an average of 3.5 percent of GDP per year during the entire period (Figure 7.12). Importantly, adaptation investment should be frontloaded because addressing the risk of severe GDP losses from water scarcity and floods should be the utmost priority for the authorities. Mitigation investment tends to increase toward the end of the projection period, also reflecting the rising marginal abatement cost of carbon from 2040 onward, as discussed above.

A whole-of-economy approach will be needed both to mobilize the resources required to finance this investment effort and to create an enabling environment for climate action to deliver transformative change. As discussed previously, climate change adaptation and mitigation require the implementation of key policies in sectors such as energy, water, agriculture, and disaster risk management. However, to bring about the necessary investments and maximize the effectiveness of these sectoral policies, more general institutional reforms also have a critical role to play.

Figure 7.12. Total Investments for a Low-Carbon and Resilient Morocco

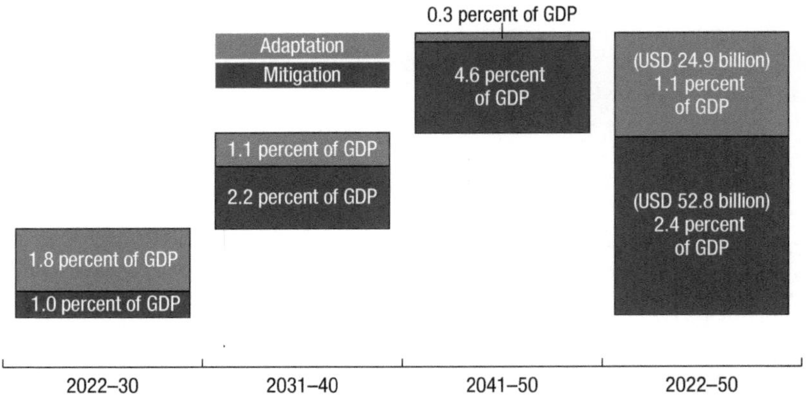

0.3 percent of GDP

| Adaptation |
| Mitigation |

4.6 percent of GDP

(USD 24.9 billion)
1.1 percent of GDP

1.1 percent of GDP

2.2 percent of GDP

(USD 52.8 billion)
2.4 percent of GDP

1.8 percent of GDP

1.0 percent of GDP

| 2022–30 | 2031–40 | 2041–50 | 2022–50 |

Source: World Bank staff.
Note: Total amount is presented in net present value terms (2022 real US dollars). The figure uses a 6 percent discount rate. Percentage of GDP is calculated as the net present value of investments divided by the present value of baseline GDP.

Policies to Maximize Private Climate Investment

The New Development Model sets a clear roadmap for unleashing the potential of the Moroccan private sector. It calls for leveling the playing field for market players, limiting the protection that certain public and private market operators still enjoy, and sanctioning anticompetitive practices. Some important steps have already been taken in this direction, including the reactivation of the Competition Council in 2018 and the launch of ambitious state-owned enterprise reform that could streamline the role of the public sector in the economy, thus strengthening private sector development and competitiveness. However, multiple regulatory constraints that still protect incumbents in key sectors—including those central to climate change mitigation and adaptation—remain to be addressed. Importantly, these bottlenecks are not only constraining the potential growth of the Moroccan economy, but they are also slowing the impulse that the private sector could give to the climate agenda.

Scaling up private investment in renewable energy is central to decarbonizing the Moroccan economy, but the private sector can also play an important role on the adaptation side. In the water sector, the authorities intend to use public–private partnership schemes to leverage private sector financing and technical and managerial skills in the desalination program. Although some public–private partnership projects are already underway, this trend could be accelerated if a clear roadmap for attracting private financing would be developed. Also, given the centrality of the energy and water sectors in the resilient and low-carbon pathway, the reform of ONEE should be prioritized to create an enabling environment that allows private operators to enter and grow in the commercial segments of the water and electricity sectors.

Greening small and medium enterprises can be challenging and may require tailored government support. Although some small and medium enterprises can lead on the climate innovation agenda, a majority of them may find it difficult to adapt to the policies and regulations that will be adopted in Morocco and elsewhere to sustain the green transition. Moreover, small and medium enterprises often have less access to information on such regulations and more broadly on the benefits of greening their practices. They may also have less leeway with which to absorb the higher cost of environmentally friendly technologies (OECD and ASEAN Secretariat 2021). Overall, these market failures could justify well-tailored government interventions, in the absence of which the green transition could create additional entry barriers and thus lead to higher market concentration.

Since 2016, Bank Al-Maghrib (BAM), the Moroccan Capital Market Authority, and the Ministry of Economy and Finance have built foundations geared toward greening the financial system. The most relevant achievements have been the development of a broad roadmap to align financial institutions and capital markets with sustainable development goals, the introduction of disclosure and reporting standards, and the adoption of key reforms to stimulate the creation of a corporate green bond market. However, a national strategy on climate finance is still being prepared.

One of the key barriers that still hamper the development of a sustainable financial market is the lack of a national "green taxonomy" of the economic activities that should be considered environmentally sustainable. Such taxonomies are being adopted in an increasing number of jurisdictions as an important tool to help issuers and investors identify green financial assets and projects. Moroccan authorities are aware of this gap and are scaling up their efforts to build the required institutional and market capacity to accelerate progress in this area.

The green bond market is still incipient. Between 2016 and 2018, Moroccan Capital Market Authority produced guidelines describing the principles and actions needed to issue a green bond, including the use of proceeds and the evaluation and selection of eligible projects. However, as of 2020 only five green bonds (for a total outstanding value of about $400 million) have been issued in Morocco by banks, corporate entities, and state-owned enterprises, whereas no sovereign green bond has yet been issued. This may indicate the presence of obstacles in the mobilization of capital for these products (demand side) and/or in making projects bankable (supply side).

Blended finance instruments could be further used to raise capital for climate action. Few public financial institutions have a formal green mandate, although certain entities (such as Crédit Agricole, CDG Capital, and the Fonds d'Equipement Communal) have taken steps to green their practices. In addition, Tawilcom (the former Central Guarantee Fund) has launched various programs to provide guarantees and co-financing specifically targeted at climate-sensitive sectors, including Green Invest and the Green Value Chain initiatives. The recently created Mohammed VI Strategic Investment Fund should also help de-risk and crowd in commercial green investments.[18]

An Environmental Tax Reform

Even if the participation of the private sector is maximized, a substantial part of the investment effort will inevitably have to be led by the public sector. However, following the COVID-19 pandemic, Morocco faces a constrained fiscal space, and the country will probably need a fiscal consolidation process that may increase competition for scarce public resources. As suggested by the experience of other countries, an environmental tax reform could mobilize a substantial amount of resources, thus contributing to fiscal sustainability while promoting behavioral changes aligned with climate objectives.

Despite recent progress, Morocco still has substantial implicit "brown" subsidies stemming from the underpricing of fuels. The successful reform implemented between 2013 and 2015 eliminated most explicit fuel subsidies, the only

---

[18] The Mohammed VI Strategic Investment Fund was established to complement the government of Morocco's COVID-19 recovery package. It aims to provide equity and quasi-equity instruments to strengthen the solvency of companies and contribute to the rebounding of investments in priority areas for economic growth (infrastructure, innovation, enterprises). The target size has been set at DH45 billion, of which DH15 billion is provided by the state; DH30 billion is to be raised from domestic and foreign public and private investors.

exception being the butane gas subsidy. However, Morocco still foregoes a substantial amount of public revenues that could be collected from fuel imports and consumption due to various exemptions and reduced rates.[19] Moreover, the current tax regime is still far from internalizing the environmental and health externalities associated with fossil fuels. As such, the International Monetary Fund (IMF) estimates that fuel subsidies still surpass 5 percent of GDP even after the elimination of most of the explicit subsidies (IMF 2021).

An environmental tax reform could be implemented in three stages. The first stage could target the removal of the last remaining explicit price subsidy in Morocco (for butane gas). The second stage would be to reduce and eventually eliminate "brown" tax expenditures. And the third stage could be the introduction of a carbon tax on producers, designed to being compatible with the carbon border adjustment mechanism announced by the European Union.

An environmental tax reform along those lines could generate an important flow of fiscal revenues. With other conditions remaining the same, the removal of butane gas subsidies would generate savings amounting to 0.9 percent of GDP (the average for 2015–20), the elimination of current tax expenditures could raise additional revenues for an amount of at least 0.3 percent of GDP, and the introduction of a carbon tax of \$20 per ton of CO_2-equivalent would raise fiscal revenues by close to 1 percent of GDP in the short term. This first static approximation, however, does not factor in the behavioral and economic adjustments that higher environmental taxes would trigger. As economic agents adjust to the new relative prices induced by the reform, this would gradually erode the base of environmental taxes and progressively reduce the revenues collected by the state.

The 2022 CCDR estimates that the macroeconomic impact of this tax reform would be negative only in the short term and turn positive in the longer term. According to the macrosimulations conducted with the MFMod, both the elimination of the butane gas subsidy and the introduction of a carbon tax would result in GDP losses around the time of the reform, but the output response would turn positive by 2030 (scenarios 1 and 2, respectively, in Figure 7.13). In addition, these reforms would be an effective tool for creating fiscal space: the elimination of the butane gas subsidy would reduce the debt-to-GDP ratio relative to baseline by 2.5 percentage points by 2030, whereas the introduction of a carbon tax would reduce it by 6.5 percentage points. The model simulations also show that a VAT reform that generates the same amount of fiscal revenues would have a weaker positive impact on output over the long term (scenario 3).

---

[19] Fuels are subject to two main taxes in Morocco: an excise tax collected upstream, the Internal Consumption Tax (ICT); and a value-added tax (VAT) on consumption. ICT rates vary significantly across fuels, whereas a reduced VAT rate of 10 percent is applied on all fuels (the normal rate is 20 percent). Importantly, some strategic sectors benefit from VAT and ICT exemptions on fuels (firms in water and electricity generation, ships refueling in high waters, planes in transit, and fishing boats). According to the Ministry of Finance, the reduced VAT rate on fuel alone had a cost of 0.34 percent of GDP on average between 2018 and 2021.

Figure 7.13. Environmental Tax Reform Macrosimulations
(Percentage deviation from baseline)

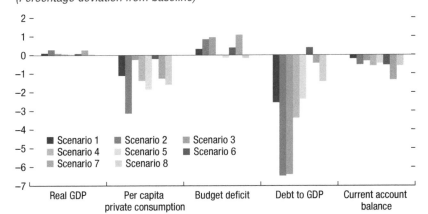

Source: World Bank Country Climate and Development Report, 2022.
Note: Baseline is the full deployment of the ambitious decarbonization strategy (all investments by the private sector, except for transmission and distribution of capital expenditures and operating expenses) and of the National Water Plan (investments fully shouldered by public sector). Public-debt-financed risk reduction adaptation investments amounting to 15 percent of annual average losses.
Scenario 1: Elimination of the butane gas subsidy without compensatory transfers to households.
Scenario 2: Elimination of the butane gas subsidy and introduction of a carbon tax ($20 per ton of carbon dioxide) without compensatory transfer to households.
Scenario 3: No environmental reform; tax reform generating revenues equivalent to scenario 4.
Scenario 4: 10 percent of the National Water Plan deployed through the private sector, with an increase in water tariffs sufficient to cover those investments' capital expenditures plus 15 percent.
Scenario 5: 20 percent increase in the value-added price of water, applied on the price deflator for the water sector obtained from the national accounts.
Scenario 6: Butane gas subsidy reform (scenario 1), with proceeds channeled toward low-income households through a cash transfer.
Scenario 7: Butane gas subsidy reform and introduction of a carbon tax (scenario 2), with all proceeds from the subsidy reform and 20 percent of revenues collected from the carbon tax channeled toward low-income households through a cash transfer.
Scenario 8: 20 percent increase in the value-added price of water (scenario 5), with 20 percent of revenues collected channeled toward low-income households through a cash transfer.

Increasing water tariffs could also have significant fiscal impacts. To illustrate these effects, two water policy scenarios were included in the macrosimulations. In the first (scenario 4), water tariffs are raised to a level that enables private operators to cover about 10 percent of the investments in water mobilization contemplated in the PNE. In the second (scenario 5), the value-added price of water is increased by 20 percent, and the additional resources that this generates are used to reduce debt. Both scenarios would reduce the debt-to-GDP ratio (by 3.4 percent and 2.4 percent, respectively, by 2030) without hurting economic growth over the long term (after a relatively mild short-term negative response, by 2030 real GDP would surpass the baseline in both scenarios).

The price increases from the environmental tax reforms and higher water tariffs could hurt private consumption, particularly by poorer households. A few simulations were run to assess whether this impact could be offset by using part of the additional fiscal revenues to fund compensatory mechanisms (scenarios 6, 7, and 8 in Figure 7.13). The result is that instituting a compensatory transfer scheme would reduce adverse effects on private consumption, but it would not prevent them entirely. Additional work would be required to assess how a targeted compensatory scheme would impact poorer households.

Public Financial Management

In a fiscally constrained environment, the public financial management system can offer tools to optimize the use of scarce public resources for climate action. Public financial management is increasingly used worldwide to increase the efficiency and effectiveness of public climate spending, which could also be applied in Morocco (Coalition of Finance Ministers for Climate Action 2022).

Adopting a climate-sensitive budget would be helpful in translating climate ambitions into budgeting and in tracking related public expenditure. Morocco has transitioned to program budgeting since 2015, with line ministries producing three-year programs with objective performance indicators and costs in line with their sectoral priorities and strategies. However, there is no tool in place to ensure that the country's climate ambitions, as described in the nationally determined contribution, are fully reflected in these programs. Morocco could thus benefit from the experience of those national and subnational governments around the world that have adopted climate budget tagging—a budgeting tool that allows the estimation, monitoring, and tracking of climate-relevant expenditures.

Morocco's public procurement processes have yet to be adapted to the climate change challenge. At close to 20 percent of GDP, Morocco's public procurement is significantly above the 12 percent global average. The decree on public procurement embeds a provision on sustainable/green public procurement, but it still must be turned into actions so that the state can exploit its sizeable purchasing power to foster climate change mitigation and adaptation measures. Mainstreaming climate considerations into the procurement process, and reporting in relevant sectors, would offer strong leverage in bringing new solutions to the market.

Policies to Secure Financial Stability

There is growing international awareness of the potential impacts of climate change on financial stability. Climate-related risks can be broadly grouped into two categories: (1) *physical risks*, financial risks stemming from the gradual and abrupt impacts of climate change (primarily droughts and floods in the case of Morocco); and (2) *transition risks*, the financial risks that can result from the transition to a low-carbon economy, for example due to changes in climate policy, technology, or market sentiment:

- *Physical risks.* Beyond their direct impacts on crop producers and livestock farmers, droughts can also have an indirect impact on supply chain linkages, most notably in the food processing industry. Floods can disrupt key infrastructure, generating revenue losses mainly for transport, tourism, and agriculture sectors. These shocks can curb corporate and household wealth and incomes, reducing the capacity to service debt and thus causing a rise in the stock of nonperforming loans. In addition, the socioeconomic and macroeconomic impact of weather-related hazards can indirectly affect banks, for example as the increase in interest rates following the deterioration of the fiscal position reduce the market value of public bonds held by banks. The vulnerability assessment conducted jointly by the Central Bank of Morocco (BAM) and the World Bank estimates that about 35 percent of Moroccan bank assets is exposed to physical risks (CCDR 2022) (with loans to the agriculture, agro-industrial, and food processing sectors accounting for one-third and loans to tourism sector and household mortgages accounting for the rest). The materialization of a severe drought scenarios could result in a systemwide increase in nonperforming loans by between 2.1 and 3.3 percentage points by 2050 and in a decline in the capital adequacy ratio by between 1.0 and 1.6 percentage points.[20] The flood scenarios considered would result in a systemwide increase in nonperforming loans ranging from 1.2 to 1.7 percentage points, and a decline in the capital adequacy ratio ranging from 0.4 to 0.6 percentage points.[21]

- *Transition risks.* The transition to a green economy can affect financial institutions primarily through losses in their credit and investment portfolios. Especially if they are unanticipated by the market, changes in policy, technology, and consumer preferences linked with the decarbonization effort could increase nonperforming loans by reducing the profitability and debt-servicing capacity of firms. Banks' investment portfolios can also be affected through a lower value of bank holdings of affected firms' assets. These transition risks could be further amplified through macroeconomic

---

[20] These scenarios include a three-year historical drought, a drought occurring in 2030 and 2050 under a Representative Causal Pathway (RCP) 4.5 climatic scenario, and a drought occurring in 2030 and 2050 under an RCP 8.5 climatic scenario. The assessment incorporates a macro modeling exercise to simulate the impact of the simulated catastrophic scenarios on capital stock and jobs. The underlying assumption is that the destruction of capital stock in the agricultural sector results in a proportional share of agricultural loans turning nonperforming, and that the job losses associated with each scenario would result in a proportional share of consumer and mortgage loans turning nonperforming.

[21] These scenarios include a fluvial and a pluvial flood occurring in 2030 and 2050, under a Representative Causal Pathway (RCP) 4.5 and an RCP 8.5 climatic scenario. Recognizing that the impact of floods tends to be concentrated geographically, the assessment of floods was conducted at the municipal level for each individual bank, and then aggregated for the entire system.

feedback loops (not captured in the vulnerability assessment). The 2022 CCDR estimates the overall credit exposure to industries that are defined as "highly" or "moderately transition-sensitive" at 11 and 13.3 percent of total loans, respectively.[22]

A solid regulatory and supervisory framework could help mitigate those risks.[23] BAM has been a frontrunner in Africa and has already identified climate risk management as a key priority, working to fully integrate climate risks into its supervisory practice, and is working to fully integrate climate risks into its supervisory practice.[24] Indeed, a directive has already been issued on the management of climate and environmental financial risks. However, the micro-prudential framework continues to be constrained by the limited availability of data and information needed to monitor and track financial risk exposures.

CONCLUSION

Climate change constitutes an important risk for the Moroccan economy and society, and the adaptation agenda should be placed at the forefront of the country's priorities. An intensification of water scarcity trends together with more frequent and damaging droughts would result in major GDP losses with disproportionate impacts on rural and urban vulnerable households. To confront this challenge, Morocco should continue to deploy water storage and mobilization infrastructure. However, engineering solutions alone will not suffice to relieve pressure from water resources, and a solid demand management system ought to be put in place. Raising water tariffs could constitute a powerful tool to rationalize the use of the resource, and to reinforce the

---

[22] Highly transition-sensitive sectors are defined as those that have an emission intensity above 300 tons of CO_2 per million dollars produced, whereas moderately transition-sensitive sectors are those with an emission intensity between 100 and 300 tons of CO_2 per million US dollars.

[23] The introduction of a carbon tax could also increase corporate loans' credit risk, as higher carbon prices could directly reduce firms' earning potential (proportional to their level of emissions). The 2022 CCRD shows that a carbon tax of $25/tons of CO_2 (tCO_2) and $75/$tCO_2$ would increase the total share of firms at risk of debt distress (those that have an interest coverage ratio less than 1) by 1.1 percentage points and 3.2 percentage points, respectively. The introduction of a $25/$tCO_2$ carbon tax would cause 1.9 percent of total corporate loans (0.7 percent of banking sector assets) to be at increased credit risk, a share that would reach 8.4 percent (3.1 percent of banking sector assets) in the $75/$tCO_2$ scenario.

[24] BAM joined the Network of Central Banks and Supervisors for Greening the Financial System in 2018 to share and build knowledge on climate risk integration in supervision and central bank operations. An internal unit dedicated to climate risk and green finance was established in 2019. BAM's 2020 annual report has included as one of its key goals the integration of climate change adaptation and mitigation into its mission. During the 2021 UN Climate Change Conference (COP26) in November 2021, BAM also announced a series of ambitious plans to address climate risks, including issuing guidelines to the banking sector regarding stress tests and reporting on climate risks, conducting climate risk assessments, and capacity building.

financial solidity of the sector, which would allow river basin agencies to play a more active water policing role.

Blessed with vast amounts of renewable energy sources, Morocco is particularly well-placed to reap the benefits of the global decarbonization agenda. Transitioning toward a green electricity generation matrix and electrifying key sectors of the economy could allow Morocco to (1) reduce its reliance on imported energy and exposure to international price shocks; (2) bolster comparative advantage for the country's exports, potentially turning Morocco into an exporter of green energy; and (3) boost job creation in the industry and services that benefit from the decarbonization process.

A significant investment plan is needed (particularly form the private sector) for a resilient and low-carbon Morocco to emerge while increasing the efficiency and effectiveness of climate action. The 2022 CCDR estimates that investments of about 3.5 percent of GDP on average between 2022 and 2050 are needed for that outcome to materialize. Adaptation investments would be prevalent in the short term, whereas mitigation investments would be higher toward the end of the time horizon.

The deployment of such an investment plan would be more likely to succeed if the Ministry of Economy and Finance and BAM manage to articulate a whole-of-economy approach to climate change, which would include (1) structural reforms to unlock the potential of the private sector to lead the green transition, (2) an environmental tax reform to internalize the externalities associated with high-carbon products and activities and alter behaviors in a climate-oriented way while contributing to increase the government's public revenues and thus to finance the transition, (3) the adoption of public financial management tools to optimize the public sector's climate action, and (4) streamlining climate risks into supervisory micro-prudential policies.

REFERENCES

Clement, Viviane, Kanta Kumari Rigaud, Alex de Sherbinin, Bryan Jones, Susana Adamo, Jacob Schewe, Nian Sadiq, and Elham Shabahat. 2021. "Groundswell Part 2: Acting on Internal Climate Migration." World Bank, Washington, DC.

Coalition of Finance Ministers for Climate Action. 2022. "Ministries of Finance and Nationally Determined Contributions: Raising Ambitions and Accelerating Climate Action." Coalition of Finance Ministers for Climate Action, Washington, DC.

Díaz Cassou, Javier, Amina Iraqi, Carole Megevand, and Federica Marzo. 2022. *Morocco Economic Update: The Recovery Is Running Dry* (English). Washington, DC: World Bank Group.

Driouech, Fatima, Hafid Stafi, Abdou Khouakhi, Sara Moutia, Wafae Badi, Khalid ElRhaz, and Abdelghani Chehbouni. 2020. "Recent Observed Country-wide Climate Trends in Morocco." *International Journal of Climatology* 41 (S1).

Hallegatte, Stephane, Colin Green, Robert J. Nicholls, and Jan Corfee-Morlot. 2013. "Future Flood Losses in Major Coastal Cities." *Nature Climate Change* 3: 802–06.

International Monetary Fund (IMF). 2021. "Still Not Getting Energy Prices Right: A Global and Country Update of Fossil Fuel Subsidies." IMF Working Paper 21/236, International Monetary Fund, Washington, DC.

International Monetary Fund (IMF). 2022. "Feeling the Heat: Adapting to Climate Change in the Middle East and Central Asia." IMF Departmental Paper 22/008, International Monetary Fund, Washington, DC.

Organisation for Economic Co-operation and Development (OECD) and Association of Southeast Asian Nations (ASEAN) Secretariat. 2021. *Facilitating the Green Transition for ASEAN SMEs: A Toolkit for Policymakers*. OECD Publishing, Paris/Economic Research Institute for ASEAN and East Asia, Jakarta.

Ouraich, Ismail. 2010. "Climate Change Impact on Moroccan Agricultural Sector." Summary of World Bank and FAO Report, Department of Agricultural Economics, Purdue University, West Lafayette, IN.

Snoussi, Maria, Tachfine Ouchani, Abdou Khouakhi, and Isabelle Niang-Diop. 2009. "Impacts of Sea-Level Rise on the Moroccan Coastal Zone: Quantifying Coastal Erosion and Flooding in the Tangier Bay." *Geomorphology* 107 (1–2): 32–40.

World Bank. 2021. *Morocco's Jobs Landscape: Identifying Constraints to an Inclusive Labor Market*. Washington, DC: World Bank.

World Bank. 2022. "Morocco: Country Climate and Development Report." Washington, DC: World Bank. https://www.worldbank.org/en/country/morocco/publication/morocco-country -climate-and-development-report.

PART IV

Promoting Inclusion

What Explains Youth Unemployment in Morocco? A Look at Moroccans Not in Education, Employment, or Training

Federica Alfani, Fabio Clementi, Michele Fabiani, Vasco Molini, and Enzo Valentini

INTRODUCTION

This chapter analyzes the evolution of Moroccan NEETs, an acronym for young people (between the ages of 15 and 29 years, or 15 and 24 years, depending on the definition) who are not in employment, education, or training.

Appearing for the first time in the mid-1990s, the acronym was formulated to capture the social situation of a growing category of the population: youth who do not build human capital through work, education, or training. Part of the reason the term was formulated is that development experts began to recognize that the conventional metrics and predictors of success—such as employment, academic education, and/or vocational training—no longer sufficiently captured the multidimensional nature of the challenges faced by many young people during their school years or during their transition from school to the labor market, nor the resulting long-term fragility that marks their lives.

According to the most recent national census of 2014 (RGPH 2014), there were about 6 million Moroccans between the ages of 15 and 24. Morocco is currently in a development window that demographers call a "demographic bonus." This means that the proportion of working-age people in the total population is high compared to the share of the population who are either younger or older than the productive age bracket (15–64 years old).

Lopez-Acevedo and others (2021) estimated that Morocco's demographic bonus will end in 2040, when the progressive aging of the population, combined with increased life expectancy, begins to raise the share of the population aged 65 and older. With such a high proportion of people in the productive age

This chapter is based on Alfani and others (2020). © World Bank. http://hdl.handle.net/10986/33747 License: CC BY 3.0 IGO range, and a low proportion of dependents, a demographic bonus therefore presents a country—for a limited number of decades—with a one-time opportunity for accelerated economic growth.

The current age distribution of Morocco's population represents an opportunity, but it also presents the major challenge of harnessing that human capital and putting it to the best use (Lopez-Acevedo and others 2021). Until now, the Moroccan labor market has not been able to absorb all of its new entrants in an optimal way. Calculations based on subsequent rounds of the Moroccan Labor Force Survey indicate that of approximately 390,000 new entrants in the national workforce every year, barely a third manage to find employment in the formal or informal sector.

Because of the importance of this age group, the NEET phenomenon has increasingly gained attention in both developed and developing countries. In Morocco, by contrast, labor market analysis (see, for example, Verme, Gadiry, and Guennouni 2016; Verme and others 2016) has tended to focus on understanding what determines unemployment or inactivity within the entire population, with no specific focus on those between 15 and 24 years old. The work presented in this chapter aims at filling this gap by providing a comprehensive analysis of the characteristics and dynamics of NEETs in Morocco over the last decade.

Examining NEET profiles is a relatively straightforward exercise if longitudinal or panel data are available that allow the construction of transition matrices (that trace movements in and out of the NEET condition). The Moroccan Labor Force Surveys has a panel component (50 percent of the overall sample) but it rotates every 2 years, making it impossible to construct a transition matrix over a longer period than that. To overcome this data limitation, these transition matrices for individuals between 15 and 24 were estimated over a 9-year period (2010–18).

The chapter is organized as follows. After describing the profile of NEETs, drawing comparisons in different countries around the world, the third section present a literature review of studies on the NEET phenomenon. The fourth section presents data and the methodology of the analysis on Morocco, and the fifth section displays the results. The final section draws the main conclusions.

PROFILING THE NEETS AROUND THE WORLD: WHO ARE THEY, AND WHAT ARE THEIR LIFE CONDITIONS?

In 2019, the Organisation for Economic Co-operation and Development (OECD) released the latest update of its own perspective on NEETs. The OECD defines NEETs as people aged between 15 and 29 who are neither enrolled in a formal educational or training program, nor in paid employment (defined as at least 1 hour per week), during the relevant survey reference period. As Table 8.1 shows, in 2018 the average NEET rate for the 15–29-year-old population across OECD countries is about 13 percent, ranging from 6.1 percent in Iceland to 26.5 percent in Turkey. Southern European countries, Mexico, and Turkey exhibit the highest NEET rates, whereas northern and central European countries show the lowest rates. In almost all OECD countries, NEET rates are higher for women than for men; the OECD average rate for young women is almost 4 percentage

TABLE 8.1.

NEET Rates for 15–29-Year-Olds in OECD Countries
(Percent)

Country	2006	2011	2018	Country	2006	2011	2018
Iceland	5.1	9.8	6.1	Estonia	11.4	15.2	12.7
Netherlands	6.2	6.9	7.0	Poland	17.4	15.5	12.7
Malta	13.6	12.1	7.3	United States	12.9	15.9	12.7
Switzerland	10.0	21.9	8.1	Belgium	13.9	13.9	12.8
Luxembourg	8.6	7.2	8.4	OECD average	14.3	15.9	13.2
Norway	7.9	8.5	8.7	Israel	30.0	27.6	13.3
Sweden	10.5	9.1	8.9	Hungary	17.0	18.5	13.5
Germany	13.6	11.0	9.2	Cyprus	11.9	14.8	14.9
Slovenia	10.8	10.7	9.7	Slovak Republic	19.1	19.1	15.1
Japan	12.0	11.7	9.8	Croatia	15.8	19.1	15.6
Czech Republic	14.1	12.7	10	France	15.2	16.4	16.1
New Zealand	12.0	14.3	10.2	Romania	16.5	19.5	17.0
Lithuania	NA	18.0	10.5	Bulgaria	23.9	24.7	18.1
Australia	11.4	11.5	10.8	Chile	NA	21.8	18.4
Denmark	6.2	11.0	10.8	Spain	15.9	24.3	19.1
Austria	12.0	10.3	11.1	Mexico	23.2	24.0	20.9
Latvia	14.4	19.6	11.2	Greece	16.7	21.6	21.5
Portugal	12.4	15.3	11.6	Colombia	NA	20.1	22.7
Ireland	10.4	21.9	11.7	Costa Rica	NA	20.1	23.1
Canada	12.0	13.4	11.9	Italy	20.1	23.2	23.9
Finland	10.4	11.8	11.9	Brazil	NA	19.3	24.9
United Kingdom	15.1	15.5	12.6	Turkey	42.6	34.6	26.5

Source: OECD (2018).

Note: For 2011, data for Switzerland refer to 2009, those for Lithuania to 2010, and those for Colombia and Costa Rica to 2013. For 2018, data for Japan refer to 2014 and those for Chile to 2017. The Organisation for Economic Co-operation and Development (OECD) average excludes Chile and Korea. NA = not available; NEET = not in employment, education, or training.

points higher than the rate for young men. In Mexico and Turkey, rates for females are about 25 percentage points higher than rates for males. By contrast, Austria, Belgium, Canada, Luxembourg, Portugal, and Switzerland show a NEET rate higher for males than for females, although the difference is negligible.

As shown in Figure 8.1, NEET rates are generally higher for young people in their 20s than for those in their teens. In the OECD countries, on average about 18 percent of those aged between 25 and 29 years old are NEET compared to less than 6 percent of 15–19-year-olds. This difference may be the result of the expansion of upper secondary education in many OECD countries. Furthermore, NEETs are less likely to live with their parents than non-NEETs—about 50 percent of NEETs live with their parents compared to about 75 percent of non-NEETs.

Caring for children and/or living with a partner can also make a substantial difference. About 26 percent of NEETs, but only 9 percent of non-NEETs, live with a partner and one or more children—an almost 3:1 ratio. The reason is likely that parenthood compels young people to devote their time and energy to childcare rather than to education or working outside the home. Parenthood *with no partner* makes even more of a difference. Single (nonpartnered) young women account for just 1 percent of non-NEETs compared to 5 percent of NEETs—a 5:1 ratio versus 3:1. Caring for children, especially all by oneself, often forces a young person to stay at home instead of attending school or working outside the home (OECD 2016).

Figure 8.1. NEET Rate by Age Group and Gender, 2019
(Percent)

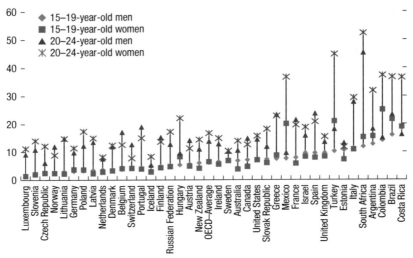

Source: Organisation for Economic Co-operation and Development, Youth Not in Employment, Education or Training (NEET) indicator.

International Labour Organization (ILO) data allow the view to be extended to other regions of the world. The ILO (2015) defines youth as "all persons between the ages of 15 and 24 (included)" and employees as "all persons of working age who during a specified brief period, such as one week or one day, were in the following categories: *a*) paid employment (whether at work or with a job, but not at work); or *b*) self-employment (whether at work or with an enterprise, but not at work)." People are defined as being in training if engaged "in a non-academic learning activity through which they acquire specific skills intended for vocational or technical jobs." Finally, vocational and technical training includes only programs that are solely school based.

As Table 8.2 shows, nearly 22 percent of youth worldwide are NEET, about 77 percent of whom are women. This underscores the observation that deeply ingrained social norms drive the unequal labor market outcomes between men and women.[1]

Figure 8.2 narrows the focus to Morocco and other countries in the Middle East and North Africa regions. The Middle East and North Africa (MENA) region, in particular the North African part, seems to perform worse than many other regions both in the developed and developing world. In 2017, Morocco was the worst performer among MENA countries that were not in a situation of conflict or state fragility (Iraq, West Bank and Gaza, and Yemen). Its NEET rate was 2 percentage points above that of Egypt and 4 and 5 percentage points higher than that of Tunisia and Algeria, respectively.

---

[1] ILO (2017) analyzes in depth the drivers of gender disparities in educational attainment and labor market outcomes, and the constraints that influence these disparities.

TABLE 8.2.

NEET Rates for 15–24-Year-Olds, by Region
(Percent)

Region	NEET Rates (latest years)			Female Share
	Total	Male	Female	
World	**21.8**	**9.8**	**34.4**	**76.9**
Developing countries	12.1	8.0	16.0	66.1
Emerging economies	25.2	9.6	41.8	80.3
Developed countries	13.1	11.3	14.9	55.7
Northern Africa	26.1	16.7	36.0	67.6
Sub-Saharan Africa	15.5	11.2	19.0	61.4
Latin America and the Caribbean	19.4	11.9	27.0	68.6
North America	16.3	14.1	18.6	55.8
Arab states	18.2	9.9	27.1	71.8
Eastern Asia	3.7	2.8	4.7	61.8
Southeastern Asia and Pacific	18.0	13.4	22.6	61.5
Southern Asia	28.6	5.8	53.3	89.5
Northern, southern, and western Europe	12.3	12.2	12.4	49.2
Eastern Europe	15.6	13.8	17.4	54.5
Central and western Asia	23.4	14.8	32.1	67.5

Source: International Labour Organization (2017).

Note: The table shows the not in employment, education, or training (NEET) rate in different regions of the world, using youth-population-weighted averaging. The number of countries with available data is as follows: world (98); developing countries (12); emerging economies (46); developed countries (40); northern Africa (3); sub-Saharan Africa (16); Latin America and the Caribbean (16); North America (2); Arab states (5); eastern Asia (4); southeastern Asia and the Pacific (8); southern Asia (6); northern, southern, and western Europe (27); eastern Europe (7); and central and western Asia (4). The most recent year is 2015, with 67 observations. There are 15 observations for 2014 and 16 observations for 2009–13.

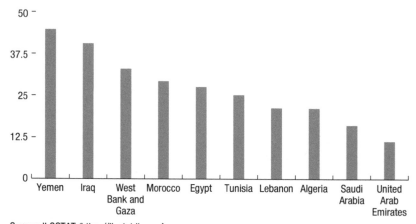

Figure 8.2. NEET Rates in the MENA Region
(Percent)

Source: ILOSTAT (https://ilostat.ilo.org/).
Note: MENA = Middle East and North Africa; NEET = not in employment, education, or training.

RESEARCH FINDINGS ON THE STATUS OF NEETS WORLDWIDE

A few studies have focused on a quantitative investigation of the condition and dynamics of NEETs for specific countries around the world. Employing longitudinal data, Ranzani and Rosati (2013) presented evidence concerning the extent, characteristics, and evolution of the NEET phenomenon in Mexico over a 10-year period. In addition, they investigated the existence and extent of state dependence by disentangling unobserved heterogeneity from genuine state dependence. For example, they found that, compared to other NEETs, females and lower-educated youths are more likely to remain in this status than be employed.

Bilgen Susanli (2016) examined the phenomenon of NEET in Turkey, drawing on data from the Household Labor Force Surveys over the 2004–13 period. The analysis indicated that gender and educational attainment are key factors in explaining the probability of being in a NEET condition. A greater number of household members that are in employment is associated with a lower likelihood of NEET. Transition matrix analysis revealed that NEET status remains highly persistent despite the substantial fall over the sample period. In South Africa, Akinyemi and Mushunje (2017), investigating the determinants of rural youth participation in agricultural activities, showed that 21 percent of youth are NEET and 77 percent of them are in the 20–24 age bracket. Variables such as age, government funding, and parent participation in farming increase the likelihood of young people's participation in agricultural activities. By contrast, being married, having young children, and receiving social grants reduce the likelihood.

Cabral (2018), focusing on Senegal, showed that about 40 percent of young people are NEET. In his analysis, the key factors affecting the probability of being NEET are the existence of a physical and mental disability, age and gender of the person, education, occupational and marital status of the household head, as well as household income.

Research by Abayasekara and Gunasekara (2019) using 2016 Labour Force Survey data revealed some of the risk factors that predispose young people to become NEET in Sri Lanka. Using binomial and multinomial logistic regression models, the results indicate that the risk factors center on being female, belonging to an ethnic and religious minority, being in the 20–24 age group, having very low or very high levels of education, being English-illiterate, belonging to a low-income household or to a male-headed household, having young children, and living in a more remote area. The authors also offer important policy recommendations for how to reduce Sri Lanka's NEET rate and include more youth in education and in the labor force.

Looking at developed countries, Quintano, Mazzocchi, and Rocca (2018) analyzed the determinants of the NEET condition in Italy through a step-by-step procedure. They first determined the main characteristics of NEET, then focused on specific homogeneous clusters of NEETs, assessing the role played by various observed personal characteristics in determining the probability of being in a NEET position. Using a bivariate selection probit model based on the propensity to look for a job against the condition of being inactive, the authors then assessed the role played by unobserved factors. The results confirmed the crucial role of education, as well as the importance of economic and social disparities between men and women in the Italian territorial districts.

ASSESSING NEETS IN MOROCCO: DATA AND DESCRIPTIVE STATISTICS

In this chapter, the Enquête Nationale sur l'Emploi, a nationally representative labor force survey conducted by the Moroccan Haut-Commissariat au Plan, is used. Its main objective is identifying the volume of active population as well as the main demographic, cultural, and socioprofessional characteristics of workers. The data set may also be used to measure the Moroccan population's access to basic social services.

The survey has been conducted every year since 1999 using a comprehensive questionnaire covering both urban and rural areas. The sampling frame follows a two-stage stratification strategy in the country's urban and rural areas and regions, which in 2013 were consolidated into 12 from an original 16. On average, every year the sample comprises about 80,000 households, out of which 60,000 reside in urban areas and 20,000 in rural areas. The survey also contains a rotating panel component that can be used to examine the persistence and dynamics of labor market status. This rotating panel component, however, is available only for about half of the sample for two adjacent years—specifically, 2010–11 through 2017–18. In this chapter, the analysis focuses on the period ranging from 2010 to 2018.[2]

Table 8.3 presents descriptive statistics of control variables for 2010 and 2018. In 2018, about 28 percent of young Moroccans (about 2 million people) could be classified as NEET, with only a slight decline from 2010 (32.4 percent). The percentage of youth who have secondary education or are pursuing any type of education beyond high school increased over time. In particular, enrollment in secondary education moved from 23 to 30 percent between 2010 and 2018, with tertiary education rising from 6.7 percent in 2010 to 13.8 percent in 2018.

Figure 8.3 shows that the NEET rates are much higher for women. Whereas the age distribution of male NEETs did not change substantially between 2007 and 2018, a significantly smaller share of younger (aged 15–20) women were in a NEET position in 2018 (19 percent of girls aged 15 were NEET in 2018 compared to more than 30 percent in 2007). The rapid increase in enrollment rates of young women in secondary and tertiary education explains this marked difference. However, when women approach the age at which they would normally be entering the labor market—their early 20s—this positive improvement has all but been erased: the NEET rate for women aged 23–24 is virtually the same in 2018 as in 2007, more than twice as high than for men (70 percent compared to 22 percent). Figure 8.4 shows that, in 2018, about 10 percent of women aged 24 were in school, and fewer than 20 percent were working, compared to about 20 and 60 percent for men, respectively.

---

[2] The year 2016 was excluded from the sample because in the available data set a set of variables regarding family background was not available that could be used subsequently in the econometric analysis. In any case, in 2016 the NEET rate was 29 percent, very similar to both previous and subsequent years.

TABLE 8.3.

Descriptive Statistics for Selected Control Variables

Variable	2010			2018		
	Mean	Min	Max	Mean	Min	Max
NEET (1 = yes)	32.4	0	1	28.4	0	1
Household member is female (1 = yes)	49.7	0	1	49.5	0	1
Household member is 20–24 years old (1 = yes)	55.7	0	1	54.2	0	1
Household member is single	87.8	0	1	88.3	0	1
Household member is married	11.8	0	1	11.2	0	1
Household member is widower/divorced	0.4	0	1	0.4	0	1
Household living in rural area	46.2	0	1	40.3	0	1
Household living in most developed regions	68.7	0	1	50.5	0	1
No education	12.5	0	1	5.1	0	1
Koranic school	1.3	0	1	0.7	0	1
Primary school	56.2	0	1	50.6	0	1
Secondary school	23.2	0	1	29.7	0	1
Tertiary education	6.7	0	1	13.8	0	1
Asset index (normalized)	37.4	0	1	43.6	0	1
Household living in rural accommodation (1 = yes)	35.8	0	1	26.9	0	1
Household living in villa (1 = yes)	1.3	0	1	1.3	0	1
Household living in apartment (1 = yes)	7.3	0	1	10.3	0	1
Household living in traditional house (1 = yes)	3.3	0	1	2.6	0	1
Household living in modern house (1 = yes)	47.3	0	1	55.5	0	1
Household living in shanty (1 = yes)	5.0	0	1	3.4	0	1

Source: Authors' elaboration based on the Enquête Nationale sur l'Emploi.
Note: Figure is based on 48,024 observations in 2010 and 55,280 in 2018. Max = maximum; Min = minimum; NEET = not in employment, education, or training.

Figure 8.3. Moroccan Population Members Who Are NEET: Males and Females by Age
(Percent)

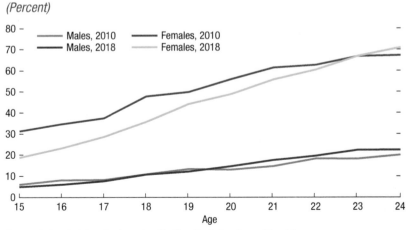

Source: Authors' elaboration based on the Enquête Nationale sur l'Emploi.
Note: NEET = not in employment, education, or training.

Figure 8.4. School-to-Work Transition for Population Aged 15–24 Years, 2018
(Percent)

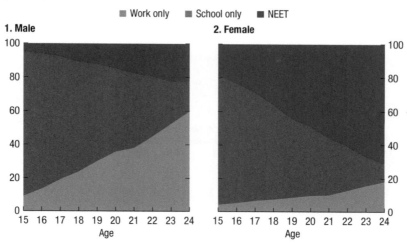

Source: Authors' elaboration based on the Enquête Nationale sur l'Emploi.
Note: NEET = not in employment, education, or training.

Both Figures 8.3 and 8.4 portray a situation for Morocco not dissimilar from other MENA region countries, where the share of employed youth is higher among young men than young women, and the share of NEET is higher for young women. Interestingly, both in Morocco and in the rest of the region (Doss and others 2018), when the NEET information is crossed with marital status, married women—either with or without children—represented a significant percentage of female NEETs. When this married group is removed from the NEET calculation, the share of female NEETs (for example, those who are neither married nor have children) becomes comparable to the share of NEET men.

WHAT AFFECTS THE PROBABILITY OF BEING NEET IN MOROCCO?

This question was answered estimating a logit model for the NEET binary dependent variable (NEET = 1, non-NEET = 0).[3] The results (Figure 8.5) suggest the following:

- The likelihood of being NEET increases with *age,* suggesting a complex transition from school to the labor market that tends to result in unemployment as the person gets older.

- The *area of residence* matters; people living either in big towns or in rural areas are less likely to become NEET than those living in medium-sized towns. In big towns, there are many more chances to continue studying or

---

[3] See Annex 8.1 for more details.

Figure 8.5. Results of Logit Regression

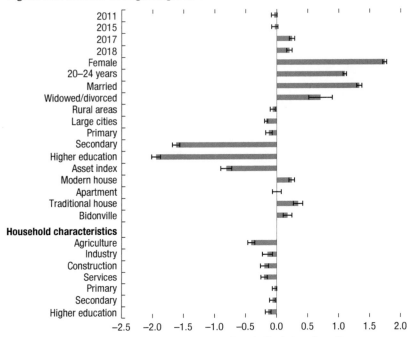

Source: Authors' calculations using International Labour Organization Labour Force Surveys, 2010–18.
Note: Dependent variable is the not in employment, education, or training (NEET) binary variable (NEET = 1, non-NEET = 0). Number of observations = 194,609; Wald χ^2 = 33,419.46 (p-value = 0.00); pseudo R^2 = 0.2741.

to find a job, whereas in rural areas young people are often involved, depending on the season, in family-based farming activities.

- The effect of *education* is as expected: all other things being equal, higher levels of education are associated with a lower probability of being NEET. This effect is particularly pronounced in the case of higher (tertiary) education.

- As expected, *household well-being* also matters substantially. The Asset Index (constructed by aggregating various household assets) is negatively associated with the probability of having a NEET in the household. The wealthier the household, the higher the chances are that young members will continue on to higher education or find a job. Coming from less-affluent families, on the other hand, can in practice virtually preclude the possibility of continuing to study beyond a certain level, or it may affect access to the jobs market.

- Finally, the *education level of the household head* and their *sector of activity* both significantly impact the probability of having NEETs in the family, In particular, whenever the family (and household head) is active in the agriculture sector, young members tend also to be active in that sector.

Figure 8.6. Results of Logit Regression by Gender

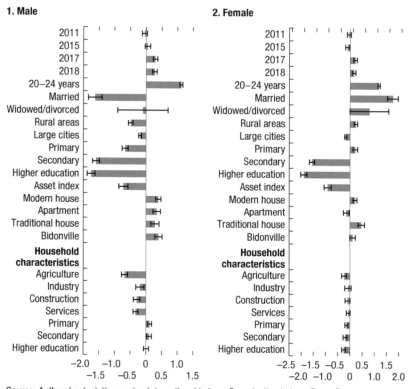

1. Male   **2. Female**

Source: Authors' calculations using International Labour Organization Labour Force Surveys, 2010–18.
Note: In panel 1, dependent variable is the not in employment, education, or training (NEET) binary variable (NEET = 1, non-NEET = 0); number of observations = 94,287; Wald χ^2 = 5,117.66 (p = 0.00); pseudo R^2 = 0.0844. In panel 2, dependent variable is the NEET binary variable (NEET = 1, non-NEET = 0); number of observations = 100,322; Wald χ^2 = 20,375.69 (p = 0.00); pseudo R^2 = 0.2846.

Figure 8.6 shows the results by dividing the sample into males and females to better explore the role of gender differences. Because the regressors are the same as those used in the whole sample, it is worth commenting only on the key aspects that differ in the two subgroups.

- *Marital status* seems to matter differently, because married men have a lower probability of being NEET, whereas the opposite can be observed for women. These results suggest that once married, it is even harder for women to enter the labor market. They often must rely economically on their husbands' income.

- *Higher education* seems to matter more for women than men in determining the risk of becoming NEET (having higher education reduces the probability of being NEET more for women than for men).

TABLE 8.4.

NEET and Non-NEET Rates in 2010, 2011, 2014, 2016, and 2018
(Percent)

Years/Status		2011		2014		2016		2018	
		Non-NEET	NEET	Non-NEET	NEET	Non-NEET	NEET	Non-NEET	NEET
2010	Non-NEET	88.48	11.52	74.53	25.47	71.63	28.37	69.13	30.87
	NEET	22.95	**77.05**	52.25	**47.75**	60.15	39.85	63.04	**36.96**

Source: Authors' calculations using International Labour Organization Labour Force Surveys, 2010–18
Note: Values in boldface refer to the results discussed in the text. NEET = not in employment, education, or training.

- The *household head education variables* remain significant and negative for women only, suggesting that family background matters more for women than for men. This is further confirmed by the size of the marginal effect of the Asset Index, as well as by most of the housing quality variables: in absolute value, they are bigger for women than for men and are always negative and significant.

- Finally, results by *area of residence* show different effects for men and women. For men, living in rural areas reduces the probability of being NEET, whereas for women the effect is the opposite. This may be because in rural areas men can often find work in agriculture or can undertake jobs that require high levels of physical effort.

MARKOV CHAIN MATRICES

In the preceding section, a static snapshot of the NEET condition was captured, but it is also important to understand the dynamics of the phenomenon, especially the probability of moving in or out of a NEET position and for how long. The lack of panel data over a period longer than 1 year limits the possibility to undertake a meaningful analysis: 1 year is not enough, for example, to gauge whether or not a person is stuck in the NEET condition. A longer time span is clearly needed. With the adaptation of a Markov chain method to the analysis, it was possible to overcome this limitation and estimate 2010–18 transition matrices.[4] Table 8.4 shows the percentage of those NEET/non-NEET in 2010 who changed status or remained in the same position after 1, 4, 6, and 8 years (2011, 2014, 2106, and 2018), and Table 8.5 splits the sample between men and women.

There are two main results that are worth highlighting:

- *First, the NEET condition tends to persist* (see Table 8.4). About 37 percent of those who were NEET in 2010 are likely to still be NEET after 8 years. In other words, more than one-third of NEETs tend to remain in the same condition after 8 years and see their chances of entering the labor market dramatically diminish. On the other hand, even though 70 percent of those non-NEET in 2010 did not change their status (were still non-NEET after 8 years), the risk increases over time: whereas only 12 percent are likely to become NEET in 2011, in 2018 that probability is almost tripled (31 percent).

---

[4] See Annex 8.1 for more details.

TABLE 8.5.

NEET and Non-NEET Rates in 2010, 2011, 2014, 2016, and 2018 by Gender
(Percent)

Years/Status		2011		2014		2016		2018	
		Non-NEET	NEET	Non-NEET	NEET	Non-NEET	NEET	Non-NEET	NEET
2010 Female	Non-NEET	81.20	18.80	61.82	38.18	56.91	43.09	53.03	46.97
	NEET	15.49	84.51	39.07	**60.93**	44.71	55.29	46.21	**53.79**
2010 Male	Non-NEET	88.48	11.52	87.34	12.66	87.00	13.00	85.70	14.30
	NEET	22.95	77.05	80.10	**19.90**	85.11	14.89	85.16	**14.84**

Source: Authors' calculations using International Labour Organization Labour Force Surveys, 2010–18
Note: Values in boldface refer to the results discussed in the text. NEET = not in employment, education, or training.

- *Second, the chances for NEETs to transition out of their status are concentrated in the early years* (see Table 8.4). There is a bigger drop in the probability to transition out of the NEET position between 1 and 4 years (from 77 percent to 47.8 percent) than between 4 and 8 years (from 47.7 percent to 37 percent). This most likely reflects the depreciation of human and social capital associated with being in a NEET status.

- *Persistence is higher for women than for men* (see Table 8.5). Only men see a reduction in the share of those persistently in the NEET status as time passes. Whereas the number of men with NEET status in 2010 remaining NEET in 2014 drops to about 20 percent, the number of women in the same condition is estimated at about 61 percent. After 8 years, the share for men declines to 15 percent, whereas for women it remains above 50 percent. These results confirm that the NEET condition has strong gender connotations, and it is generally women paying the larger costs of labor market inefficiencies (see also Lopez-Acevedo and others 2021).

CONCLUSION

Young people unemployed, outside the school system, and not undergoing any training—the so-called NEETs—form about 30 percent of the Moroccan population between ages 15 and 24, above the average for the MENA region (ILO 2019).

Subsequent rounds of Moroccan labor force surveys have already presented the opportunity to develop a clearer profile of NEETs in the country. What is missing, however, are the data to examine how the circumstances of people in the NEET condition have evolved over a reasonably long period of time. This analysis was able to overcome the data limitations and to provide helpful insights into NEET dynamics in the last decade.

The first part of the analysis showed the key determinants of the NEET condition. As expected, individual characteristics play an important role. The probability of becoming NEET is higher for women—particularly those married and/or with children—and for young men and women with lower levels of education. A higher concentration of NEETs is also more likely in medium-sized towns than in big towns or in rural farming areas. In big towns, it is easier for young people to continue schooling or find a job, whereas in rural areas every household member is typically involved in some farming activities. The family context also influences the probability of being NEET. Higher parental education and better economic conditions tend—all other things being equal—to decrease the probability of young household members becoming NEET.

In the second part, the results are presented on NEET dynamics using estimated transition matrices. It was found that 37 percent of those who were NEET in 2010 tended to remain outside both the labor market and education even after 8 years, with very little chance of moving out. For a woman, the chance of remaining NEET after 8 years becomes 54 percent.

These preliminary results can already provide some initial suggestions for policy intervention. On one side, it would be important to work on "prevention" measures, because initial conditions tend to largely dictate a young person's future trajectory. This means improving the quality of education, reducing the likelihood of early dropouts, and financially supporting those whose initial relatively disadvantaged background might preclude continuing with formal academic studies or vocational skills training.

Ex-post interventions are also necessary. One important aspect stressed throughout the chapter is the persistent disadvantaged position of women. This is true for those analyzed as NEET (that is, between ages 15 and 24) but it also applies to those older than 24. According to the latest figures, more than 8 million Moroccan women are not active in the labor market (Lopez-Acevedo and others 2021). Among these, almost 2 million have more than a secondary level of education—a significant underutilization of human capital. Developing incentives and providing services to encourage Moroccan women to enter or remain in the labor market should be a top priority in the country's agenda of structural reforms.

ANNEX 8.1. ANALYSIS METHODOLOGY

Following Bilgen Susanli (2016), the probability of being NEET was estimated using a simple logit model based on a set of individuals (age, gender, and level of education) and household characteristics, geographical location, and housing conditions.

$$logit(p_{i,t}) = \beta_t x_{i,t} + \varepsilon_{i,t} \qquad (8.1.1)$$

The model calculates the probability that the dependent variable acquires value 1:

$$E[Y_{i,t,h} = 1 | X = x] = P(Y_{i,t,h} = 1) \qquad (8.1.2)$$

where $P(Y_{i,t,h} = 1)$ represents the probability of observing the condition of success for the i-th individual given a particular value of X.

All the independent variables are dummies or categorical variables: female (1 = female, 0 = male); age group (1 = 19–24, 0 = 15–19); marital status (married or widower/divorced, with being single as the omitted reference case); education attainment (Koranic school, primary school, secondary school, and tertiary education, with no-education as the omitted reference case); housing characteristics (villa, apartment, traditional Moroccan house, modern Moroccan house, with rural house as the omitted reference case); and two geographical areas, namely urban or rural regions (with urban as the omitted reference case) and macro-regions (less-developed regions and more-developed regions, with the former as the omitted reference case).

An asset index is constructed to capture household wealth. As suggested by Filmer and Pritchett (2001), a principal-components analysis was used to calculate the weights of the index. The first principal component—the linear combination capturing the greatest variation among the set of variables—is converted into factor scores, which serve as weights. The rationale for using this index is that it captures the household's permanent welfare dimension better than simple consumption data and can provide more reliable rankings among households.

For the logit regression model, the 2010, 2011, 2015, 2017, and 2018 survey rounds were used. The choice depended on whether a complete set of data required to perform the analysis was available. The regression results are shown in Annex Table 8.1.1 and Figure 8.5 (where significant results are indicated by the bar being

ANNEX TABLE 8.1.1.

Marginal Effects of the Logit Model: Full, Male, and Female Models

	N2010_2018 Total		M2010_2018 Male		F2010_2018 Female	
	Coeff.	SE	Coeff.	SE	Coeff.	SE
2011	−0.00719	0.00412	−0.00404	0.00378	−0.0117	0.00777
2015	−0.00546	0.00437	0.00472	0.00417	−0.0264**	0.0081
2017	0.0432***	0.00398	0.0290***	0.00378	0.0535***	0.00703
2018	0.0357***	0.004	0.0270***	0.00381	0.0385***	0.00709
Female	0.298***	0.0023				
20–24 years	0.182***	0.0023	0.102***	0.00217	0.278***	0.00423
Married	0.282***	0.00516	−0.0827***	0.00267	0.407***	0.00538
Widowed/Divorced	0.143***	0.0222	−0.00879	0.0345	0.194***	0.0257
Rural area	−0.0112**	0.00366	−0.0446***	0.00339	0.0569***	0.00703
Large cities	−0.0297***	0.00242	−0.0175***	0.00223	−0.0444***	0.00445
Primary school	−0.0218***	0.00464	−0.0631***	0.00484	0.0517***	0.00854
Secondary school	−0.227***	0.00356	−0.118***	0.00348	−0.343***	0.00691
Higher education	−0.212***	0.00239	−0.0966***	0.00205	−0.367***	0.00574
Asset index	−0.140***	0.00774	−0.0654***	0.00683	−0.226***	0.0141
Modern house	0.0406***	0.00379	0.0362***	0.00382	0.0495***	0.00764
Apartment	0.0000634	0.00621	0.0354***	0.00687	−0.0369***	0.011
Traditional house	0.0639***	0.00768	0.0298***	0.00758	0.115***	0.0126
Bidonville	0.0308***	0.00652	0.0424***	0.00703	0.0260*	0.0118
Household characteristics						
Unemployed	0.0772***	0.00593	0.0784***	0.00714	0.0603***	0.0096
Industry	0.0475***	0.00756	0.0533***	0.00869	0.0403**	0.0125
Construction	0.0382***	0.00555	0.0402***	0.00629	0.0358***	0.00995
Services	0.0348***	0.00379	0.0308***	0.00368	0.0418***	0.00764
Primary school	−0.00594	0.0032	0.0115***	0.0031	−0.0351***	0.00622
Secondary school	−0.0115**	0.004	0.00971*	0.00391	−0.0485***	0.00755
Higher education	−0.0229***	0.00386	0.00105	0.00369	−0.0629***	0.00736

Source: Authors' calculations using International Labour Organization Labour Force Surveys, 2010–18

Note: Coeff. = coefficient; F2010_2018 = female-only model pooling data from 2010 to 2018; M2010_2018 = male-only model pooling data from 2010 to 2018; N2010_2018 = full model pooling data from 2010 to 2018; SE = standard error.
*$p < .05$, **$p < .01$, ***$p < .001$.

away from zero and the symbol describing the confidence interval not including the zero value).

Although the annual labor market survey used in the chapter has a rotating panel component that allows the creation of year-over-year transition matrices, any longer-term analysis of labor-force transition is not feasible. However, the majority of the analyses of the Moroccan labor market conducted so far (HCP-WB 2017) indicate that the duration of inactivity or unemployment tends to be particularly long. To get a longer-term perspective on Moroccan labor market outcomes, Markov chain theory was used to obtain the probabilities of transitioning from one condition to another for longer time intervals.

Using Markov chains, the one-step probability of transitioning from state i to state j, for all $t \geq 0$ and all states $i, j, i_0, i_1, ..., i_{t-1}$, is

$$p_{t,i,j} = \Pr(X_{t+1} = j | X_t = i) \tag{8.1.3}$$

which depends on time t. The matrix $P(t)$, whose elements are the one-step transition probabilities in equation (8.1.3), is called the *transition matrix at time t*. Higher-order (multistep) transition probabilities can be derived through matrix multiplication as follows (Brémaud 2020; Miller and Childers 2012):

$$P(t, s) = P(t) \times P(t + 1) \times ... \times P(s - 1) \tag{8.1.4}$$

with $s > t \geq 0$. Therefore, in the following section, current panel data modules are first used to calculate year-over-year transition matrices. From these, the transitions over the longer period 2010–18 are derived by chaining (multiplying) the one-step transition matrices until the transition matrix $P(2010,2018)$ is reached.

REFERENCES

Abayasekara, Ashani, and Neluka Gunasekara. 2019. "Sri Lanka's NEETs: An Analysis of Youth Not in Education, Employment or Training." Working Paper 30, Institute of Policy Studies of Sri Lanka.

Akinyemi, Babatope E., and Abby Mushunje. 2017. "Born Free but 'NEET': Determinants of Rural Youth's Participation in Agricultural Activities in Eastern Cape Province, South Africa." *International Journal of Applied Business and Economic Research* 15: 521–33.

Alfani, Federica, Fabio Clementi, Michele Fabiani, Vasco Molini, and Enzo Valentini. 2020. "Once NEET, Always NEET? A Synthetic Panel Approach to Analyze the Moroccan Labor Market." Policy Research Working Paper 9238. World Bank, Washington, DC. http://hdl.handle.net/10986/33747.

Bilgen Susanli, Z. 2016. "Understanding the NEET in Turkey." *Eurasian Journal of Economics and Finance* 4: 42–57.

Brémaud, Pierre. (2020). "Non-homogeneous Markov chains." In *Markov Chains: Texts in Applied Mathematics*, Volume 31. Cham: Springer. https://doi.org/10.1007/978-3-030-45982-6_12.

Cabral, François J. 2018. "Key Drivers of NEET Phenomenon among Youth People in Senegal." *Economics Bulletin* 38: 248-61.

Doss, Cheryl R., Jessica Heckert, Emily Myers, Audrey Pereira, and Agnes R. Quisumbing. 2018. "Gender, Rural Youth, and Structural Transformation." Background Paper for the Rural Development Report 2019. IFAD, Rome.

Filmer, Deon, and Lant H. Pritchett. 2001. "Estimating Wealth Effects without Expenditure Data or Tears: An Application to Educational Enrollments in States of India." *Demography* 38: 115–132.

Haut-Commissariat au Plan (HCP) and World Bank (WB). 2017. "Le Marché du Travail au Maroc: Défis et Opportunités." https://www.hcp.ma/Le-marche-du-travail-au-Maroc-Defis-et-opportunites_a2054.html.

International Labour Organization (ILO). 2015. *World Employment and Social Outlook: Trends for Youth 2015.* Geneva: International Labour Office, Economic and Labour Market Analysis Department. https://doi.org/9789221301080.

International Labour Organization (ILO). 2017. *World Employment and Social Outlook: Trends for Women 2017.* Geneva: International Labour Office, Economic and Labour Market Analysis Department.

International Labour Organization (ILO). 2019. *World Employment and Social Outlook: Trends 2019.* Geneva: International Labour Office, Economic and Labour Market Analysis Department.

Lopez-Acevedo, Gladys, Gordon Betcherman, Ayache Khellaf, and Vasco Molini. 2021. *Morocco's Jobs Landscape: Identifying Constraints to an Inclusive Labor Market.* International Development in Focus. Washington, DC: World Bank. doi:10.1596/978-1-4648-1678-9.

Miller, Scott L., and Donald Childers. 2012. *Probability and Random Processes: With Applications to Signal Processing and Communications.* Amsterdam: Elsevier Academic Press.

Organisation for Economic Co-operation and Development (OECD). 2016. *Society at a Glance 2016: OECD Social Indicators.* Paris: OECD Publishing. http://www.oecd.org/social/society-at-a-glance-19991290.htm.

Organisation for Economic Co-operation and Development (OECD). 2018. "CO3.5: Young People Not in Education or Employment." Child Outcomes Indicator. OECD Family Database. www.oecd.org/els/family/database.htm.

Quintano, Claudio, Paolo Mazzocchi, and Antonella Rocca. 2018. "The Determinants of Italian NEETs and the Effects of the Economic Crisis." *Genus* 74. https://doi.org/10.1186/s41118-018-0031-0.

Ranzani, Marco, and Furio C. Rosati. 2013. "The NEET Trap: A Dynamic Analysis for Mexico." Understanding Children's Work (UCW) Programme Working Paper. http://www.ucw-project.org/attachment/NEET_youth_TRAP_MEXICO_final_sept12[1]20121123_111408.pdf.

Recensement Général de la Population et de l'Habitat (RGPH). 2014. "Annuaire Statistique du Maroc, année 2014." https://www.hcp.ma/file/235420/.

Verme, Paolo, Abdoul Gadiry, and Jamal Guennouni. 2016. "Female Labor Participation in the Arab World: Evidence from Panel Data in Morocco." *Labour* 30: 258–84.

Verme, Paolo, Abdoul Gadiry, Jamal Guennouni, and Mohamed Taamouti. 2016. "Labor Mobility, Economic Shocks and Jobless Growth: Evidence from Panel Data in Morocco." *Middle East Development Journal* 8: 1–31.

CHAPTER 9

Implications of Gender Inequality for Growth in Morocco

Lisa Kolovich and Anta Ndoye

INTRODUCTION

Despite the various progress recorded over the last decades, Morocco is still experiencing significant gender gaps. According to the United Nations Development Programme Gender Inequality Index, in 2019, Morocco ranked 111 out of 162 countries—below other Middle East, North Africa, Afghanistan, and Pakistan (MENAP) region countries such as Tunisia (65), Algeria (103), and Jordan (109).[1] Female labor force participation remains low at 21 percent in 2021 and lags behind other countries at a similar income level. There are also gender gaps in education and literacy rates, particularly in secondary education and rural areas.

This is a cause of concern because countries with high gender inequality are, on average, poorer and grow more slowly. Several studies have highlighted the various channels through which significant gender gaps can hinder output growth. For example, having more women in the labor force increases the pool of talent that employers can hire, as well as the number of potential entrepreneurs. This implies a more efficient allocation of resources and hence higher productivity and growth (Cuberes and Teignier 2015). Moreover, women are more likely to invest a larger share of their household income in the education of their children (Elborgh-Woytek and others 2013). Gender inequality is also associated with higher income inequality, which itself has been shown to be a drag on growth (Ostry and others 2014). An IMF study (Gonzales and others 2015b) shows that the MENAP region could have gained $1 trillion in cumulative output—equivalent to twice the average real GDP growth during the past decade—if the gender gap in the labor force participation rate had narrowed from triple to double the average for other emerging market and developing countries during the past decade.

---

[1] This index measures gender inequality of outcomes (the gap between male and female labor force participation rates and the share of women's seats in parliament) as well as inequality of opportunity (gender gaps in education and indicators of female health, such as the maternal death ratio and adolescent fertility).

The chapter first provides an overview of trends in Morocco's gender gaps both over time and compared to peer countries. It also offers estimates of GDP losses due to gender gaps based on IMF research (Dadam and others 2017) and concludes by discussing policies to reduce gender gaps in Morocco.

A FEW FACTS ON GENDER GAPS IN MOROCCO

Education

Much progress has been made in Morocco in closing gender gaps in education enrollment over the past few decades, but challenges remain, particularly in rural areas. The female-to-male ratio of primary school enrollment rates jumped from about 70 percent in the mid-1990s to 97 percent in 2020. The gender gap for the secondary level also narrowed significantly and stands at 95 percent. Meanwhile, for tertiary education, the gender gap favors women rather than men because it is now over 100 percent. Nonetheless, Morocco is being outperformed by comparator regions and peer countries on secondary education (Figure 9.1). Gender gaps in the adult literacy rate have also narrowed, but Morocco is being outperformed by peer countries.

Moreover, these improvements have been driven by the urban areas, where gender gaps in primary and secondary education enrollment have narrowed significantly. Rural girls' secondary school enrollment (12–14 years old) trailed urban girls' rates by 14 percentage points, and for girls aged 15–17, this gap jumped to 53 percentage points. Within the rural regions, gender gaps were 13 percentage points for 12–14-year-olds and 14 percentage points for 15–17-year-olds (Figure 9.2).

Labor Markets

Gender gaps in the Moroccan labor market are particularly large. At 21 percent in 2021, the rate of women's participation in the labor force lags other countries at a similar income level and has been falling since 2004 (Figure 9.3). Frequent profiles of inactive workers suggest that women with low levels of education residing in urban areas are the most numerous of those who are neither working nor looking for work (Lopez-Acevedo and others 2021). Several factors explain the low level of female labor participation in Morocco (Box 9.1). Although the gender gap in urban areas is wider than in rural areas, female labor force participation has been relatively stable in urban areas, whereas it has declined in rural areas over the past decade (DEPF and UN Women 2021).

There are also some gender disparities in employment rates. The unemployment rate for women is higher than the unemployment rate for men in Morocco. Labor market skills mismatches and government regulations are known to be impediments to employment in Morocco, and their impact is more acute on women. Indeed, Angel-Urdinola and others (2016) showed that high minimum wages and payroll taxes are associated with higher unemployment rates and lower formality rates in Morocco, especially among youth and women in Morocco. Low levels of education also limit women's chances for active participation in the economy; many of the less educated find work in informal, low-quality jobs (Figure 9.4).

Figure 9.1. Education and Literacy in Morocco

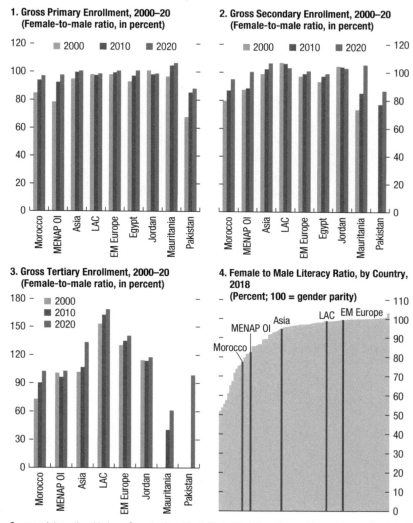

1. Gross Primary Enrollment, 2000–20
(Female-to-male ratio, in percent)

2. Gross Secondary Enrollment, 2000–20
(Female-to-male ratio, in percent)

3. Gross Tertiary Enrollment, 2000–20
(Female-to-male ratio, in percent)

4. Female to Male Literacy Ratio, by Country, 2018
(Percent; 100 = gender parity)

Sources: International Labour Organization; World Bank, World Development Indicators; and IMF staff calculations.
Note: In panels 1 and 2, the latest available data for Egypt, Mauritania, and Pakistan are from 2019. In panel 3, the latest available data for Pakistan are from 2019. EM = emerging market; LAC = Latin America and the Caribbean; MENAP = Middle East, North Africa, Afghanistan, and Pakistan; OI = oil importers.

Figure 9.2. Secondary School Enrollment Rates
(Percent)

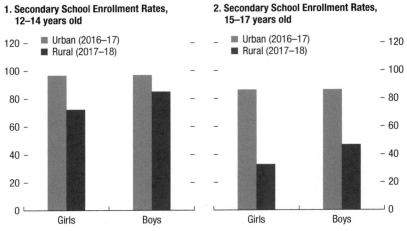

Source: Loi des Finances 2019.

Figure 9.3. Female Labor Force Participation Gaps
(Percent)

Sources: International Labour Organization; World Bank; and IMF staff calculations.
Note: Panel 2 shows male minus female participation rates. EMs = emerging markets; LAC = Latin America and the Caribbean; MENA = Middle East and North Africa; MENAP = Middle East, North Africa, Afghanistan, and Pakistan; OI = oil importers.

Box 9.1. Drivers of Female Labor Force Participation in Morocco

There are important regionally specific factors, such as history, religion, and culture, as well as social norms that can help explain the low level of female labor force participation in the Middle East and North Africa region. In the case of Morocco, several articles (Verme and others 2014; Lopez-Acevedo and others 2021) argued that jobless growth—coupled with factors such as marriage, education, household composition, perceptions of the role of the women in the household, and society's values regarding gender issues—tend to disproportionally influence female labor force participation.

Verme and others (2014) highlighted that the slow pace of structural transformation has not allowed sufficient creation of manufacturing jobs where women with a secondary school education could be employed. They also find that marriage and household composition also influence the probability of participation. Educated women are likely to marry educated men who have done better than women in the labor market and may be able to support their families on their own.

A recent study (DEPF and UN Women 2021) reached similar conclusions and noted that several factors such as gender norms, the legal framework, the structure of the economy, the labor market, and human capital explained the low level of female labor force participation. They also found that in urban areas, the proportion of women in the household positively affects female labor force participation.

Further evidence on the role that attitudes and marital status play in the decision to join the labor force can be seen in the chart below. In the World Values Survey (see Figure 9.1.1), Moroccan men and women were asked whether they agreed with the statement "Men should have more right to a job than women when jobs are scarce." More than three-quarters of married men and 86 percent of divorced or widowed men agreed. For never-married men, the share stood at 70 percent. On the other hand, only half of married women and slightly less than half of women who have never married agreed. The highest share of women who agreed was divorced or widowed women, at 56 percent. These responses reflect a large gender gap in attitudes on working, ranging from 24 percentage points to 30 percentage points.

Figure 9.1.1. Attitudes toward Female Work

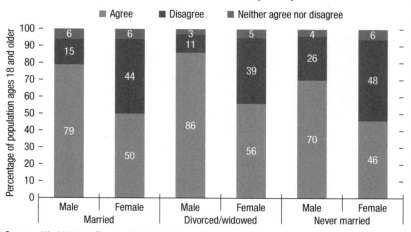

Responses to statement "Men should have more right to a job than women."

Sources: World Values Survey, 2011; Arab Barometer.

Sources: Lopez-Acevedo and others (2021); World Values Survey, 2011; Arab Barometer.

Figure 9.4. Labor Force Participation and Employment Levels by Education, Gender, and Sector
(Percent)

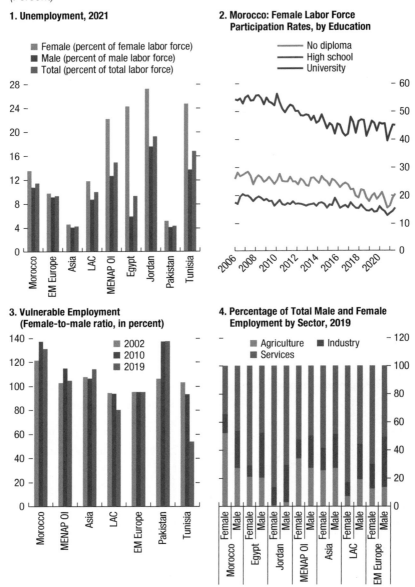

Sources: Haut Commissariat au Plan; International Labor Organization; and IMF staff estimates.
Note: Panel 3 shows the ratio of females to males, in percent. EM = emerging market; LAC = Latin America and the Caribbean; MENAP = Middle East, North Africa, Afghanistan, and Pakistan; OI = oil importers.

Legal Barriers

Morocco has made substantial progress over the last decade in promoting gender equality in its legal framework by allowing women to be head of a household in the same way as a man and by introducing criminal penalties for gender-based violence. The World Bank's (2015) "Women, Business and the Law" report tracked legal barriers that impact women's economic empowerment and calculated an index for 190 countries. The index measures gender discrimination in eight key areas: mobility, workforce, pay, marriage, parenthood, entrepreneurship, assets, and pension. As can be seen in Figure 9.5, Morocco's legal reforms have boosted its overall performance on the index to a level well above that of its peers in the region.

Changes to the Family Code in 2004 underlie the largest jump in the Women, Business, and the Law index. More recently, in 2021, the Moroccan Parliament adopted legal reforms aimed at promoting higher levels of women on corporate governance bodies and set mandatory quotas for women on boards of publicly traded companies. This reform addresses an important gender gap in the country because women are vastly underrepresented in managerial and board positions. In fact, as Mouline, Ozlu, and Herzog (2022) pointed out, in 2019 women led only 13 percent of businesses, held only 23 percent of public sector managerial positions, and comprised only 21 percent of regional and local board members.

Although female representation in parliament also remains well below gender parity, there has been an upward trend in the share of seats held by women (Figure 9.6). Women represented less than 1 percent of parliamentarians in 1997, but by 2020 women held just over 20 percent of the seats. This is almost 2 percentage points higher than the share of its regional emerging market peers.

Figure 9.5. Legal Barriers, as Measured by World Bank Women, Business, and the Law Index, 1990–2022

(WBL Index, 100 = gender equality)

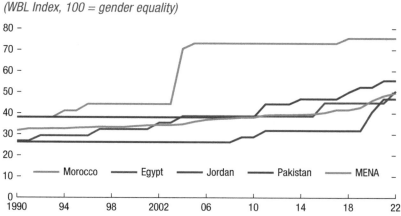

Sources: World Bank Group, *Women, Business, and the Law*; and IMF staff calculations.
Note: MENA = Middle East and North Africa.

Figure 9.6. Percentage of Seats Held by Women in National Parliaments

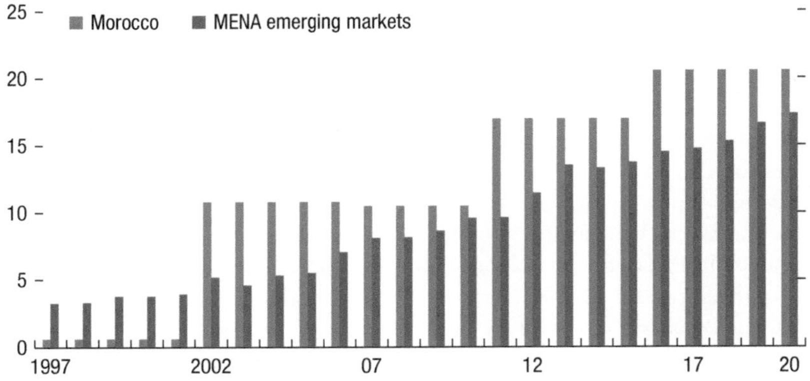

Sources: Inter-Parliamentary Union; and IMF staff calculations.
Note: For 1998, the data are as of August 10, 1998. MENA = Middle East and North Africa.

COVID-19 and Gender Gaps

The Moroccan government acted swiftly in introducing a state of health emergency at the start of the pandemic. Although this helped mitigate the initial health impact of COVID-19, poverty, employment, and gender equality were negatively affected. Unemployment rates in urban regions increased by 4 percentage points (9.1 percent in 2019 versus 13.0 percent in 2020), whereas in rural regions the unemployment rate more than doubled, from 3.4 percent in 2019 to 7.2 percent in 2020 (Abouzzohour 2020). A joint study from Morocco's High Commission for Planning, the UN Development System, and the World Bank (2020) also showed that a larger share of women reported a decline in their income during the COVID-19 crisis. Informal sector workers, who are disproportionately women, suffered higher rates of job losses than formal sector workers. The study also estimated that the poverty rate would increase from 4.8 percent in 2014 to 6.6 percent in 2020, and during the lockdown period, women's time spent on domestic work increased by about 33 minutes per day. Domestic violence reports also increased.

QUANTIFYING THE IMPACT OF GENDER GAPS ON GROWTH

An IMF research paper (Dadam and others 2017) quantified the effect of gender inequality on output growth in Morocco. The paper used cross-country growth regressions to estimate the impact of gender inequality on growth while controlling for the impact of variables such as initial income, investment, education, infrastructure, terms of trade, and institutional quality. The sample consisted of 103 countries from regions including MENA, Latin American countries, sub-Saharan Africa, and

Asia as well as selected advanced economies over the period 1990–2014. Consistent with previous studies (for example, Hakura and others 2016), the results showed that gender inequality has a negative impact on growth and this impact is more striking for countries in their early stages of development. The paper then quantified the extent to which the differences in average real GDP per capita growth rates between Morocco and four benchmark groups can be explained by differences in gender gaps.[2] This approach reveals that income inequality, years of education, and gender gaps can explain a significant share of Morocco's real GDP per capita shortfall compared to benchmark groups. In particular, reducing gender inequality and improving education to the levels of the Asian, emerging Europe, and Latin American benchmark countries could boost real GDP per capita growth rates relative to these countries by 1 percent, 1.5 percent, and 0.75 percent, respectively.

Dadam and others (2017) also used an occupational choice model, following Cuberes and Teignier (2016), to quantify income losses due to the misallocation of women in the labor force. The results showed that Morocco is losing a significant share of income due to gender gaps in the labor market. The costs associated with gender gaps in labor force participation and entrepreneurship are as high as 46 percent of income per capita compared to a situation where women have the same level of labor force and entrepreneurship participation as men.

Reducing gender gaps would also help offset the impact of the demographic transition on growth. Simulating the implication of an increase in the dependency ratio for men and women suggests that policies to eliminate gender gaps could offset those negative effects. This in turn may lead to overall income gains of about 22 percent in 2040 if gender gaps were to be closed in 50 years. These gains in GDP decrease with the increase in the time it takes to eliminate gender gaps. For instance, the results show that GDP gains would be 14 percent if gender gaps were to be eliminated in 100 years, and 9 percent were they to be eliminated in 150 years (Figure 9.7).

More recent work by Bargain and Lo Bue (2021) examining the impact of closing employment gender gaps provided further evidence on the large GDP losses. The authors followed the method in Ostry and others (2018) to analyze and estimate the complementarities between female and male labor market participation. The approach relies on firm-level data, which are often scarce for non–advanced-market countries, to calculate the potential gains from a small and a complete reduction in gender gaps in employment. That is, if only one-quarter of the gender gap were to be closed, GDP per capita could be increased by between 6 percent and 13 percent, whereas eliminating the gender gap[3] could lead to GDP per capita gains between 22 percent and 39 percent.

---

[2] MENAP oil importers (Egypt, Jordan, Mauritania, Tunisia, and Pakistan), Asian countries (Korea, Singapore, Malaysia, Thailand, and China), Latin American countries (Argentina, Bolivia, Colombia, Costa Rica, Dominican Republic, Ecuador, Mexico, Panama, and Peru), and European countries (Turkey, Bulgaria, Hungary, Ukraine, and Romania).

[3] The authors use a female labor force participation rate of 70 percent, which is also close to the approximate rate in advanced markets.

Figure 9.7. Demographic Transition in Morocco

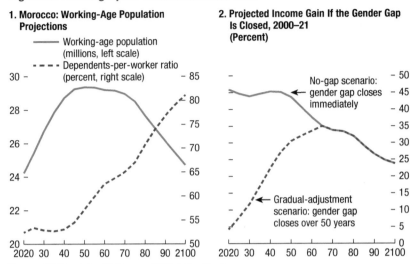

Sources: UN Population Division; and IMF staff estimates.
Note: In panel 1, dependents are those younger than 15 or older than 64; working-age population includes those aged 15–64. In panel 2, the baseline assumes continuation of the current gender gap and a medium level of fertility.

GOVERNMENT POLICIES TO REDUCE GENDER INEQUALITY

Research by the IMF shows that policies can have an impact on closing gender gaps regardless of country-specific circumstances and cultural norms. For example, Christiansen and others (2016) examined the drivers of female labor force participation in Europe and found that demographics and women's self-reported attitudes toward the desirability of formal labor force participation are key predictors of women's decision to join the labor force. However, policies matter as well, and tax distortions, childcare provisioning, and parental leave are additional factors that can have a positive impact on female labor force participation. Fabrizio and others (2020) offered further evidence on the relationship between social norms and policies. Using a model-based framework, the authors estimated the potential GDP gains from gender-responsive fiscal policy measures. They then modeled the reduction of social bias against women and found that their estimates on GDP gains could be further increased by up to 5 percent.

Cultural norms and attitudes in Morocco likely play a role in creating and sustaining gender gaps, as in many other countries. Thus, the country's past and recent efforts to introduce gender-responsive policies and legal framework reforms are welcome. Below, key milestones are summarized and suggestions for additional policies and programs are presented.

- *Legal framework.* There are several laws in Morocco that promote gender equality, including the (revised) Labor Code (2004);[4] the 2011 constitution, which provides for equality for Moroccan citizens; and the Family Code, which was revised in 2004 with a view to expanding the rights of women in areas such as guardianship, marriage, child custody, and access to divorce. In 2017, the Act on the Authority for Equality and Fight Against All Forms of Discrimination Against Women was adopted, and in 2018, a law aimed at reducing gender-based violence was adopted. Notably, the country has also introduced programs and policies to help with the effective implementation of these laws, including by providing support to domestic violence centers and introducing media programs to combat gender-based stereotypes.

- *Gender budgeting.* Morocco is notable for having the first and most developed gender budgeting initiative in the Middle East and Central Asia region. Box 9.2 gives an overview of Morocco's achievements in this area.

- *Maternity leave and protection.* Morocco increased maternity leave in 2004. It now offers 14 weeks of maternity leave, at 100 percent of a woman's wages payable from a national social security fund, thereby meeting the International Labor Office standards on duration of maternity leave. Paid paternity leave is also available; increasing paternity leave, which is currently one of the lowest in the world (3 days), could contribute to gender equality at work and intra-household equality. Replacing maternity and paternity leave with parental leave options could also help break down gender stereotypes and encourage female labor force participation. Moreover, there is no legal prohibition on dismissing pregnant workers.

- *COVID-19 measures.* In an effort to address the negative impacts on women and girls during the pandemic, the Moroccan government introduced several gender-sensitive policy measures. For example, according to the UN Women/United Nations Development Programme COVID-19 policy tracker, the Public Prosecutor's Office strengthened domestic violence victims' ability to access courts. The government also established a mobile/toll-free counseling platform to allow domestic violence victims access to remote help and introduced awareness raising campaigns. A guarantee mechanism was established to provide financing options for very small and small and medium enterprises, many of which were headed by women. Hygiene kits were provided to vulnerable populations, including pregnant women, female victims of domestic violence, and teachers. Although the authorities have taken several measures to reduce gender gaps, some could be expanded or complemented by additional policies such as the following:

  - *Legal restrictions.* Providing for equality in inheritance rights can create opportunities for women to own housing or land (World Bank 2015) and

---

[4] In 2004, a new labor law went into effect in Morocco that extended maternity leave from 12 weeks to 14 weeks and provided time allowances for breast-feeding.

Box 9.2. Gender Budgeting in Morocco

Fiscal policies can play an important role in promoting gender equality and women's development. Gender budgeting allows fiscal authorities, at any level of government, to assess the needs of men and women; identify key outcomes or goals; plan, allocate, and distribute public funds; and monitor and evaluate achievements. More than 100 countries have introduced gender budgeting initiatives. Whereas the focus for most countries tends to be on using spending policies to address gender inequality, some countries have introduced changes to tax policies. Gender budgeting may emphasize administrative changes to expenditure tracking and monitoring systems.

Morocco is notable for being one of the early adopters and leaders of gender budgeting in the Middle East and Central Asia regions. The Council of Government approved in 2014 an organic finance law with two key components designed to strengthen the initiative. First, the law requires that gender equality be considered when defining performance objectives, results, and indicators in all line budgets. Second, the law dictates that the Gender Report be included as part of each year's finance bill (UN Women 2014). In 2015, the country introduced a law on adopting performance-based budgeting for all ministries, requiring that each public program objective takes gender into consideration.

The 2019 Gender Report, published by the Ministry of Economy and Finance, covered 28 ministries and highlights key gender equality goals, recent accomplishments, and remaining challenges. It was redesigned, with support from UN Women, to become a tool for accountability, monitoring, and evaluation. For example, the report included an analysis on barriers to female employment, finding that care responsibilities, husband's/father's lack of approval, and own unwillingness to work are among the top reasons women do not join the labor force.

The 2020 Gender Report further supported gender budgeting performance reporting, by offering a more standardized template for reporting and improved guidelines and examples for ministries. Moreover, the 2020 report includes an analysis of the macro-criticality of gender equality and an analysis of ministerial efforts to address gender equality in program performance, including whether the ministry/department has a gender strategy, what its gender-sensitive programs/goals are, and the number of gender-sensitive indicators for each goal. Beginning in 2002, Morocco's efforts on gender budgeting focused on meeting the Millennium Development Goals, increasing women's public employment, and collecting gender-disaggregated data.

The 2021 Gender Report includes analyses examining the impact of COVID-19 on male and female (1) frontline workers, (2) beneficiaries of public assistance, and (3) time spent on unpaid work, among others. It also included a summary and statistics on gender-based violence.

Policy measures in the report call for generating new gender disaggregated data, adopting gender-sensitive responses to the pandemic, increasing women and girls' access to digital technologies, reducing violence against women, and ensuring that women participate in developing pandemic response measures.

Source: Authors.

---

lead to smaller gender gaps in labor force participation (Gonzales and others 2015a). As noted previously in this chapter, Morocco has made substantial progress in legal reforms over the last two decades, but there are several areas where legal inequalities remain. The World Bank's 2022 "Women, Business and the Law" report notes that the legal framework still allows for gender inequality in pay, marriage-related constraints, property and inheritance laws, and pensions. Women also face barriers should they choose to work after having children.

o *Infrastructure.* Safe public transportation and improved road accessibility would decrease women's travel time and therefore reduce the costs related to work and going to school outside the home (World Bank 2016). Investing in public childcare facilities could free women's time to go to school and join the labor market, because women are in most cases the main providers of household work in Morocco and caring for children/home was listed as the primary reason for women not working in the analysis included in the 2019 Finance Bill. Lack of access to transportation was also included as a reason that women, especially rural women, were not able to access healthcare services during the COVID-19 pandemic (Ministry of Economy and Finance of Morocco 2022).

o *Education gaps.* The Strategic Vision of Reform 2015–2030 (Royaume du Maroc 2015) aims to establish, among other components, universal preschool education, apply positive discrimination in rural/suburban areas to help close the existing gaps, encourage girls and other marginalized groups to attend and complete school, and upgrade the quality of schools and technology. In 2019, The World Bank introduced a $500 million program to improve the performance and efficiency of the school system and help the government achieve its goal of universal preschool education by 2027. Still, social norms and stereotypes need to be addressed as the International Labor Office (2019) noted that these could limit the educational options offered to boys and girls and serve as a barrier to training for women in rural areas.

   The pandemic also posed challenges for gender equality in education. A joint survey conducted by the Morocco High Commission for Planning and UN Women examined the barriers to distance learning and found that female-headed households were more likely than male-headed households to report that their children were not participating in distance learning. Lack of access to computers and the internet as well as the higher rate of illiteracy for women compared to men (42 percent versus 22 percent) all posed challenges for distance learning (Ministry of Economy and Finance of Morocco 2022).

o *Gender budgeting.* The authorities have continued to push forward with their gender budgeting efforts, introducing improvements to their annual Gender Report and expanding their focus on monitoring and evaluation. For example, in the 2019 Finance Bill Gender Report, the Department of National Education published targets for a broad range of education-related goals for girls. Including such targets increases transparency and accountability and provides a base for developing further monitoring and evaluation efforts. Not all departments and ministries have completed a gender-sensitive analysis (according to the 2022 Gender Budgeting Report Summary), and this could impact their ability to set appropriate targets and develop and fund the associated programs.

CONCLUSION

The chapter documented key stylized facts and trends regarding gender gaps in Morocco. Despite some progress over time, gender gaps in education, labor force participation, and employment still exist. At 21 percent in 2021, female labor force participation lags behind other countries at a similar income level and has been falling since 2004. Improvements in education enrollment rate have been driven by the urban areas. At the secondary level, rural girls' secondary school enrollment rate trailed urban girls' rates and female adult literacy. Gender gaps in the adult literacy rate remain significant. There are also gender disparities in employment rates, with women more likely than men to work in low-quality, informal jobs.

Using the results of existing regression analyses relating gender gaps to GDP losses, the chapter found that closing the overall gender gap could help Morocco close its GDP per capita gap with benchmark countries in other regions by up to 1.5 percentage points. Simulations also show that gradually closing gender gaps in the labor force participation rate could lead to significant income gains over the long term.

With the potential gains from greater gender equality clear, the chapter summarizes the progress Morocco has made in terms of legal and policy reforms aimed at closing gender gaps. Moreover, it also spotlights the critical role that policies can play, particularly when social norms and attitudes are driving factors behind long-standing gender gaps.

Finally, the chapter points to several areas for additional reforms and policy changes going forward. For example, legal barriers that hinder equal opportunities in labor force participation should be removed. The Moroccan government should continue its long-standing efforts to create a comprehensive gender-budgeting framework. Rural and urban divides need to be considered, and gendered analysis that allows for additional demographic information can help better inform policy and budgetary decisions. Ensuring equal access to education and redoubling efforts to close literacy gaps will be crucial for building a highly skilled labor force.

REFERENCES

Abouzzohour, Y. 2020. *Coping with COVID-19's Cost: The Example of Morocco.* Washington, DC: Brookings Institution.

Angel-Urdinola, Diego F., Abdoul Gadiry Barry, and Jamal Guennouni. 2016. "Are Minimum Wages and Payroll Taxes a Constraint to the Creation of Formal Jobs in Morocco?" Policy Research Working Paper 7808. World Bank, Washington, DC. https://openknowledge.worldbank.org/handle/10986/25053.

Bargain, Olivier, and Maria C. Lo Bue. 2021. "The Economic Gains of Closing the Employment Gender Gap: Evidence from Morocco." Working Paper 2021/79, The United Nations Institute for Development Economics Research (UNU-WIDER), Helsinki.

Christiansen, Lone, Huidan Huidan Lin, Joana Pereira, Petia Topalova, and Rima Turk. 2016. "Individual Choice or Policies? Drivers of Female Employment in Europe." IMF Working Paper 16/49. International Monetary Fund, Washington, DC.

Cuberes, David, and Marc Teigner. 2015. "Aggregate Effects of Gender Gaps in the Labor Market: A Quantitative Estimate." Working Paper 2015/308, UB Economics, Barcelona.

Cuberes, David, and Marc Teigner. 2016. "Aggregate Effects of Gender Gaps in the Labor Market: A Quantitative Estimate." *Journal of Human Capital* 10 (1): 1–32.

Dadam, Vincent, Lisa Kolovich, and Anta Ndoye. 2017. "Implications of Gender Inequality for Growth in Morocco." Selected Issues Paper, International Monetary Fund, Washington, DC.

DEPF (Direction des Etudes et des Prévisions Financières) and UN Women. 2021. "Coûts Économiques des Inégalités de Genre dans le Marché du Travail au Maroc." Kingdom of Morocco.

Elborgh-Woytek, Katrin, Monique Newiak, Kalpana Kochhar, Stefania Fabrizio, Kangni Kpodar, Philippe Wingender, Benedict Clements, and Gerd Schwartz. 2013. "Women, Work, and the Economy: Macroeconomic Gains from Gender Equity." IMF Staff Discussion Note 13/10, International Monetary Fund, Washington, DC.

Fabrizio, Stefania, Anna Fruttero, Daniel Gurara, Lisa Kolovich, Vivian Malta, Marina Mendes-Tavares, and Nino Tchelishvili. 2020. "Women in the Labor Force: The Role of Fiscal Policies." IMF Staff Discussion Note 20/03. International Monetary Fund, Washington, DC.

Gonzales, Christian, Sonali Jain-Chandra, Kalpana Kochhar, Monique Newiak, and Tlek Zeinullayev. 2015a. "Catalyst for Change: Empowering Women and Tackling Income Inequality." Staff Discussion Note 15/20, International Monetary Fund, Washington, DC.

Gonzales, Christian, Sonali Jain-Chandra, Kalpana Kochhar, and Monique Newiak. 2015b. "Fair Play: More Equal Laws Boost Female Labor Force Participation." Staff Discussion Note 15/02, International Monetary Fund, Washington, DC.

Hakura, Dalia S., Mumtaz Hussain, Monique Newiak, Vimal V. Thakoor, and Fan Yang. 2016. "Inequality, Gender Gaps and Economic Growth: Comparative Evidence for Sub-Saharan Africa." IMF Working Paper 16/111, International Monetary Fund, Washington, DC.

International Labour Office. 2019. *Morocco: Young Women's Employment and Empowerment in the Rural Economy.* Geneva: International Labour Office. https://www.ilo.org/wcmsp5/groups/public/—ed_emp/documents/publication/wcms_622767.pdf.

Lopez-Acevedo, Gladys, Gordon Betcherman, Ayache Khellaf, and Vasco Molini. 2021. "Morocco's Jobs Landscape: Identifying Constraints to an Inclusive Labor Market." International Development in Focus. World Bank. https://openknowledge.worldbank.org/handle/10986/35075.

Ministry of Economy and Finance of Morocco. 2013. "Governmental Plan for Gender Equality (2012–2016)." http://www.slideshare.net/Gobernabilidad/2-presentationmarocco-eng.

Ministry of Economy and Finance of Morocco. 2019. "Finance Bill for the Budget Year 2019." https://cebsg.finances.gov.ma/uploads/fichiers/d5t-R91DrGxukOuV.pdf.

Ministry of Economy and Finance of Morocco. 2022. "Summary of the 2022 Gender Responsive Budgeting Report." https://www.finances.gov.ma/Publication/db/2022/DEPF_SyntheseRBG2022_ANGLAIS.pdf.

Morocco High Commission for Planning, UN Development System, and World Bank Group. 2020. "The Social and Economic Impact of the Covid-19 Crisis in Morocco." Washington, DC.

Mouline, Samia, Onu Ozlu, and Lucas Herzog. 2022. "A Big Step Forward for Women's Leadership in Morocco." World Bank Blogs. https://blogs.worldbank.org/arabvoices/big-step-forward-womens-leadership-morocco.

Ostry, Jonathan, Jorge Alvarez, Raphael A. Espinoza, and Chris Papageorgiou. 2018. "Economic Gains from Gender Inclusion: New Mechanisms, New Evidence." IMF Staff Discussion Note 18/06, International Monetary Fund, Washington, DC.

Royaume du Maroc. 2015. "A Strategic Vision of Reform 2015–2030." https://www.csefrs.ma/wp-content/uploads/2015/05/Re%CC%81sume%CC%81-vision-Anglais.pdf

UN Women. 2014. "Budgets Respond to the Needs of Women in Morocco." New York. http://www.unwomen.org/en/news/stories/2014/3/budgets-respond-to-the-needs-ofwomen-in-morocco.

Verme, Paolo, Abdul Gadiry, and Jamal Guennouni. 2014. "Female Labor Participation in the Arab World: Some Evidence from Panel Data in Morocco." Policy Research Working Paper Series 7031, World Bank Group, Washington, DC.

World Bank Group. 2015. "Women, Business and the Law 2016: Getting to Equal." Washington, DC.

World Bank Group. 2016. "Morocco: Mind the Gap. Empowering Women for a More Open, Inclusive and Prosperous Society." Washington, DC. https://openknowledge.worldbank.org/handle/10986/22274.

CHAPTER 10

Financial Inclusion in Morocco

Lorraine Ocampos

INTRODUCTION

Morocco's financial system is comparatively deep and well developed. As of 2020, Morocco's value of the IMF Financial Development Index is somewhat higher than the average for MENA and emerging markets (Figure 10.1).[1] Morocco has a relatively well-capitalized and sophisticated banking system, with a credit-to-GDP ratio that, at about 91 percent in 2020, is above the average for MENAP (Middle East, North Africa, Afghanistan, Pakistan) and emerging market and developing economy (EMDE) countries, although below the average for upper middle-income economies (143.8 percent).

The Global Competitiveness Ranking (WEF 2019) shows a more mixed picture (Figure 10.2). Morocco scores better than the median for MENAP countries on the overall indicator of financial systems, driven by higher values for financial depth and stability. However, the scores for domestic credit to the private sector and small and medium enterprise (SME) financing are lower than the median for MENAP countries. Moreover, competitive indicators that are key for the development of the financial system, such as adoption of information and communications technology, and innovation capacity (to be discussed below), score lower than the MENAP average.

Other indicators point to a low level of financial inclusion:

- *Large segments of the population still have relatively low access to financial services.* As of 2021, 44 percent of adults (aged 15+) have an account in financial institutions versus 58 percent on average for other EMDE countries (Figure 10.3, panel 1). Women, young adults, and the poorest have even

---

[1] This index is constructed for 183 countries on an annual frequency between 1980 and 2020. Financial development is defined as a combination of *depth* (size and liquidity of markets), *access* (ability of individuals and companies to access financial services), and *efficiency* (ability of institutions to provide financial services at low cost and with sustainable revenues, and the level of activity of capital markets). The index summarizes how developed financial institutions and financial markets are in terms of their depth, access, and efficiency. Financial institutions include banks, insurance companies, mutual funds, and pension funds. Financial markets include stock and bond markets. See Sahay and others 2015 for more details.

Figure 10.1. Financial Development Index, 2020
(Index, normalized, 0–1; higher value = greater financial development)

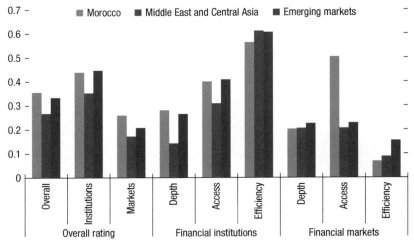

Source: IMF, Financial Development Index.

Figure 10.2. Competitiveness Gap: Morocco versus MENAP
(Index, 0–100, unless noted otherwise)

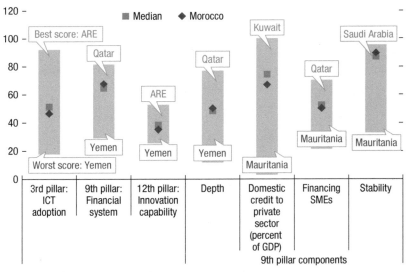

Source: World Economic Forum (2019).
Note: Figure presents best, median, and worst scores on the Global Competitiveness Index (GCI), by index pillar or pillar component. Tops and bottoms of bars show best and worst scores, respectively, on a particular index pillar or pillar component. ICT = information and communications technology; MENAP = Middle East, North Africa, Afghanistan, and Pakistan; SMEs = small and medium enterprises.

Figure 10.3. Percentage of Adult Population with a Bank Account, 2021
(Percent)

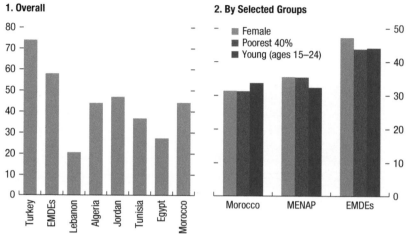

Sources: World Bank, Global Findex Database 2021; and IMF staff calculations.
Note: "Adult" is defined as ages 15 and older. EMDEs = emerging market and developing economies; MENAP = Middle East, North Africa, Afghanistan, and Pakistan.

lower shares (Figure 10.3, panel 2). For example, only 31 percent of women had a bank account versus 53 percent of men, a larger gender gap than in peer countries (61 percent versus 70 percent). The last Report on Financial Inclusion from Morocco's central bank and Ministry of Economics and Finance (BAM and MEF, 2021) shows a positive trend, though: the gap in terms of bank account ownership between Moroccan young and adults has fallen from 52 percent in 2017 to 28 percent in 2021, below the objective set by the authorities (of 38 percent).

- *Small and micro firms have relatively low access to credit.* According to the World Bank Enterprise Survey (2019a), only 21 percent of SMEs have a line of credit, which is below the average for MENA and middle-income economies. Only 6 percent of micro-enterprises in Morocco have access to bank financing, with micro-credit representing 0.7 percent of GDP compared to 1.7 percent to 3.4 percent of GDP in countries like Bolivia or Romania (Figure 10.4). The estimated finance gap for micro, small, and medium enterprises (MSME)—quantified by International Finance Corporation (2017) at about US$14 billion or 13.5 percent of GDP, larger than in peer economies—suggests a relatively high degree of credit concentration toward large and medium enterprises, including state-owned enterprises.

Figure 10.4. Outstanding Loans with Micro-financial Institutions
(Percent of GDP)

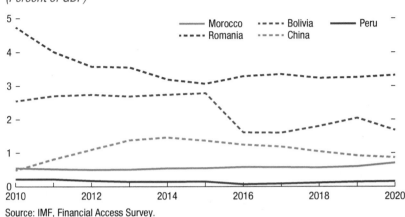

Source: IMF, Financial Access Survey.

A FEW CONSTRAINTS TO FINANCIAL INCLUSION

The low level of financial inclusion in Morocco reflects both supply and demand factors:

- *On the demand side,* insufficient funds are mentioned as the main reason for not having a bank account (52 percent of the World Bank 2021 Global Findex Database respondents). This might be explained by the existence of a large informal sector in Morocco (see Cardarelli and others 2022)—the Global Findex survey shows that only half of Moroccan SMEs have the necessary documentation, proper accounting systems, and ability to provide high-quality collateral, which makes it difficult for them to access traditional banking.

- *On the supply side,* despite the rapid expansion of the banking system, "bancarization" of the economy is still low. Between 2004 and 2017 the number of branches of commercial banks per 1,000 km² increased from 5 to 14, and the number of ATMs expanded from 4 to 16 (IMF 2017). However, bank density in rural areas remains low, with 65 percent of the Moroccan rural population without close access points (BAM, MEF 2018).

Morocco has implemented several measures to boost credit to SMEs. Greater information on credit history is a key factor for SME access to formal financing because it reduces collateral requirements and borrowing costs. The introduction of two new credit bureaus in 2009 and 2018 has allowed the gathering of more information on borrowers' history, but the number of individuals and firms listed in the credit bureau's database was still low in 2020, at about 30 percent of the adult population (Peru and Uruguay are close to 100 percent; Figure 10.5). Recent measures aimed at expanding the coverage include the introduction of credit scores in 2017 and the set-up of a National Electronic Registry of Movable

Figure 10.5. Credit Bureau Coverage, 2015 and 2020
(Percent of adults)

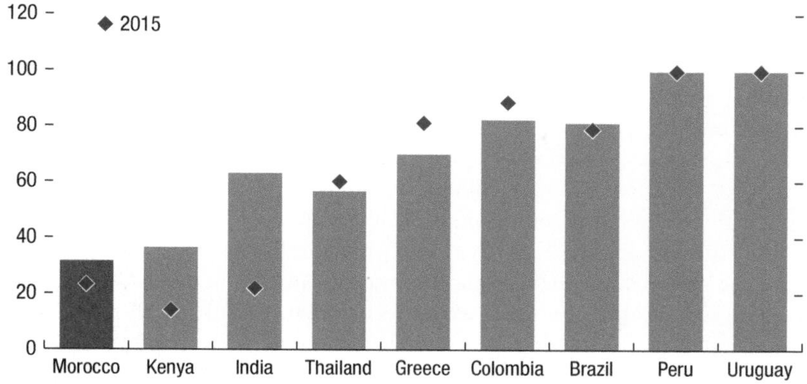

Source: World Bank, *Doing Business.*

Assets in 2020, which should make it easier for MSMEs to access credit by using movable assets (such as machinery and inventories) as collateral.

Public guarantees have been extended for bank loans to MSMEs through the newly established (in 2020) *Société Nationale de Garantie et de Financement des Entreprises* (known commercially as *Tamwilcom*).[2] Since 2013, the Central Bank has also offered a refinancing facility for banks' lending to MSMEs. Nonetheless, before the COVID-19 crisis, its coverage had remained limited because bank credit remained concentrated on companies with an existing revenue stream and a track record of at least three years (World Bank 2018).[3] High and costly collateral requirements have also made it difficult for small enterprises to obtain loans (in Morocco, the value of collateral needed for a loan has been estimated at an average of 165.7 percent of the loan amount, higher than in peer economies) (World Bank 2019b).

A few regulatory constraints may hinder faster development of micro credit. A main constraint to micro-finance is its generally small scale, which makes it time consuming and labor intensive. The increase of the cap on the loan size (from US$5,000 to US$15,000) in 2019 should therefore help support this type of credit. However, limiting micro credit to productive purposes only does not necessarily correspond to the needs of low-income groups, which may also need financing for education or insurance purposes. Moreover, regulatory caps on interest rates may

---

[2] These subsidized financing schemes have been vastly expanded on the wake of the COVID-19 crisis. Schemes like "*Damane Oxygene*" and "*Damane Relance*" were set up to help struggling businesses cover their working capital needs. In 2021, about 75,640 enterprises have benefited from these guarantees, for a total of MAD 50.6 billion (or about 4 percent of GDP).

[3] As a response to the COVID-19 crisis in 2020, Morocco's central bank greatly increased its liquidity provision to the banking sector by expanding the range of collateral accepted for repos to include public and private debt instruments, lengthening refinancing operations, and providing foreign exchange swaps to domestic banks.

not fully reflect the high operational costs and risks of this type of financing. Finally, the legal form of micro-finance institutions as "associations" may limit their ability to diversify and strengthen funding sources. It should be noted, however, that the new micro-finance law of 2020 has introduced, in addition to micro-finance associations, micro-finance institutions under the status of credit institutions (banks or financing companies, able to collect deposits and provide micro-insurance) in the form of limited companies. This should help make their business model (generally based on proximity, close follow-up, and cash flow–based lending) better suited to assess their needs and risks and allow them to play a stronger role in meeting the financing needs of low-income groups (World Bank 2018).

Alternative and technologically innovative financing schemes are still developing. Despite the rapid changes and innovations in technology, digitalization in Morocco remains low compared to peer economies. Even if the mobile penetration rate (number of SIM cards relative to population) reached 124 percent in 2018, only 6 percent of adults have a mobile-money account compared to an average of 23 percent in EMDEs (Figure 10.6). As of 2021, about 74 percent of payments in Morocco were in cash compared to 20.5 percent worldwide. Utility bills are mostly paid in cash, and less than one-third of remittances are received or paid in cash rather than being transferred through the banking system.

This may in part reflect limited access to broadband internet (World Bank 2018). The telecommunications sector suffers from reduced competition, incomplete and inefficient regulation, and underinvestment in fixed infrastructure.

Figure 10.6. Percentage of Population Using Mobile Accounts or the Internet, 2021

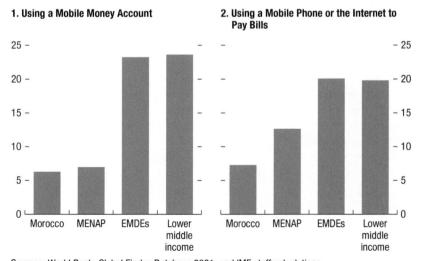

1. Using a Mobile Money Account

2. Using a Mobile Phone or the Internet to Pay Bills

Sources: World Bank, Global Findex Database 2021; and IMF staff calculations.
Note: Figure depicts data for population ages 15 and older. EMDEs = emerging market and developing economies; MENAP = Middle East, North Africa, Afghanistan, and Pakistan.

Figure 10.7. Access to Telecommunication Services, 2020

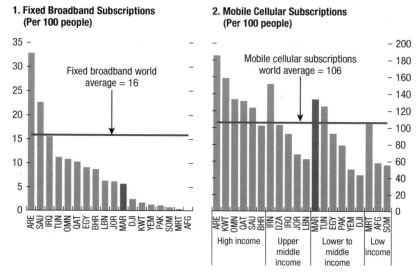

1. Fixed Broadband Subscriptions (Per 100 people)

2. Mobile Cellular Subscriptions (Per 100 people)

Source: International Telecommunication Union, World Telecommunication/ICT [Information and Communication Technologies] Indicators Database.
Note: AFG = Afghanistan; ARE = United Arab Emirates; BHR = Bahrain; DJI = Djibouti; DZA = Algeria; EGY = Egypt; IRN = Iran; IRQ = Iraq; JOR = Jordan; KWT = Kuwait; LBN = Lebanon; MAR = Morocco; MRT = Mauritania; OMN = Oman; PAK = Pakistan; QAT = Qatar; SAU = Saudi Arabia; SOM = Somalia; TUN = Tunisia; YEM = Yemen.

Maroc Télécom still holds over 99 percent of the ADSL (fixed broadband) market and is mainly responsible for investing in the fiber-optic network. As a result, Morocco lags the MENA region regarding fixed broadband subscriptions (estimated at 4.3 per 100 people in 2020) (World Bank 2020) (Figure 10.7). High-speed internet is unaffordable for the bottom 60 percent of Morocco's population, and the broadband market is limited to the country's main urban centers, deepening the digital divide between urban and rural populations.

MOROCCO'S NATIONAL STRATEGY FOR FINANCIAL INCLUSION

Morocco's National Strategy for Financial Inclusion, launched in 2019, builds on efforts made in the past and seeks to expand financial services to SMEs and excluded populations. Key aspects of the strategy are (1) expanding mobile payments; (2) boosting micro-finance by expanding its clientele to 3 million by 2030 through increased credit ceilings and relaxed interest rate caps; (3) encouraging bank penetration, including through postal agencies with their extensive regional and rural presence, and through more flexible regulatory requirements for reserve requirements for deposits in rural areas, for credits to small and micro enterprises, and for underserved segments (for example, women, micro enterprises, rural areas); (4) using innovative schemes to reach small and micro enterprises and households by developing new credit scorings systems (for example, big data analytics based on data from utility bill payments); (5) accelerating digital payment systems, including BAM's commitment to promote innovative payments (M-Wallet and Mobile Payment through regulatory easing and a communication strategy); and (6) promoting financial literacy.

The National Strategy for Financial Inclusion is a commendable initiative that should help reduce Morocco's financial inclusion gap vis-à-vis peer countries. The strategy is appropriately comprehensive, builds on international best practice, and is associated with clear objectives and specific action plans. In particular, its fintech component will benefit from an effective payments infrastructure to increase competition and diversify financing sources in the economy. Given the importance of informality in the economy, its financial literacy component will also be particularly important.

Changes in the regulatory framework have been encouraging. The new law extending the array of assets that can be pledged for a loan, including moveable assets, would facilitate financing to SMEs through more flexible collateral requirements. The bankruptcy law approved in April 2018 would also enhance the insolvency regime by reducing time and increasing efficiency. Moreover, the planned securitization schemes for nonperforming loans should revamp credit provision. More efforts to support the financing needs of start-ups and companies in their early development stages through programs like INTELAKA and FORSA are also initiatives in the right direction.[4]

In parallel to these initiatives, the government should accelerate its digital strategy (Maroc Digital 2020), including programs such as e-payment and digital platforms, while strengthening the Agence de Developpement du Digital. Of utmost importance is to increase access to existing broadband infrastructure (via the sharing of infrastructure among telecom companies) by ensuring greater regulatory clarity and transparency (World Bank 2018).

SMALL AND MEDIUM ENTERPRISE FINANCIAL INCLUSION, OUTPUT, AND JOBS

The 2019 IMF Departmental Paper "Financial Inclusion of Small and Medium-Sized Enterprises in the Middle East and Central Asia" (Blancher and others 2019) showed that greater financial inclusion of SMEs would significantly boost

---

[4] The INTELAKA program was adopted in 2020 to facilitate the financing of about 13,500 micro enterprises per year through subsidized loans (interest rate of 2 percent in urban areas and 1.75 percent in rural areas) and technical support to ensure the sustainability of businesses. The FORSA program, launched in 2022, aims at encouraging entrepreneurship by supporting business plans from initial stages to the actual implementation, and it includes subsidized loans for a maximum of DH100,000 to be reimbursed in 8 years, with a grant component of DH10,000.

Figure 10.8. Growth with Access to Formal Finance

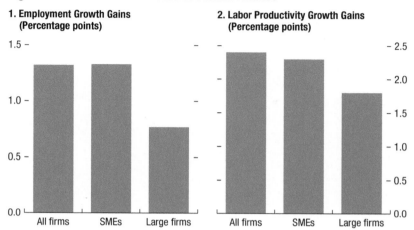

**1. Employment Growth Gains
(Percentage points)**

**2. Labor Productivity Growth Gains
(Percentage points)**

Sources: International Labour Organization; World Bank, Enterprise Surveys; and IMF staff calculations.
Note: The analysis is drawn using the firm-level data. SMEs = small and medium enterprises.

output and employment in Middle East and Central Asia (MCD) economies. The paper used a variety of analytical methods:

- Using firm-level data from the World Bank Enterprise Surveys, the paper showed that greater access to formal finance increases the rate of employment and productivity growth for an average firm in the MCD region by 2 and 1 percentage points, respectively, with most of these gains coming from SMEs (Figure 10.8).[5] Building on these estimates, a simple growth accounting exercise indicates that SME financial inclusion could boost GDP growth for MCD economies by about 1 percent.[6]

- Estimates based on cross-country regression suggest that closing the SMEs' financial inclusion gap in MCD economies with respect to emerging market and developing economies would help increase annual economic growth in MCD countries by an average of 0.3 percentage point (Figure 10.9).

- Finally, the paper used a dynamic stochastic general equilibrium model to assess the impact on growth and employment from relaxing constraints that may force SMEs to operate at a suboptimal scale due to limited access to credit. The paper showed that removing these constraints could yield long-term cumulative growth benefits of about 5 percent in certain MENAP and Caucasus and Central Asia countries.

---

[5] See also Ghassibe, Appendino, and Mahmoudi (2019).

[6] This assumes a labor share equal to two-thirds and that SMEs represent about half of the economy.

Figure 10.9. Benefits from Financial Inclusion of Small and Medium Enterprises

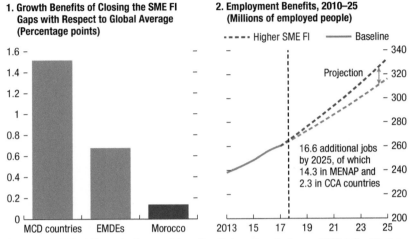

1. Growth Benefits of Closing the SME FI Gaps with Respect to Global Average (Percentage points)

2. Employment Benefits, 2010–25 (Millions of employed people)

Sources: World Bank Enterprise Surveys; International Labour Organization; and IMF staff estimates.
Note: In panel 2, the baseline employment projection follows the average annual growth rate from 2012 to 2017; projection of 1.3 percent additional growth in employment is due to higher small and medium enterprise financial inclusion (SME FI). CCA = Caucasus and Central Asia; EMDEs = emerging market and developing economies; MCD = Middle East and Central Asia; MENAP = Middle East, North Africa, Afghanistan, and Pakistan.

The estimated growth and employment benefits are somewhat lower for Morocco, but they are still significant. Blancher and others (2019) showed that closing the SMEs' financial inclusion gap with the rest of the world would boost growth in Morocco by 0.15 percentage point (Figure 10.9). The reason this is lower than the average for MCD and EDMEs is that Morocco's financial inclusion gap is estimated to be relatively smaller (consistent with the Financial Development Index in Figure 10.1). The paper also suggested that greater SME financial inclusion in Morocco could create potentially about 680,000 additional jobs by 2025 (Figure 10.9). The estimated benefits could be much larger if the informal sector and micro enterprises were also included in the calculations. The results mentioned above are based on data for formal enterprises and may therefore underestimate the absolute degree of SME financial exclusion because the informal sector and micro enterprises represent a large share of enterprises and employment in Morocco (Cardarelli and others 2022).

Blancher and others (2019) suggested that increasing SME access to financing would require a comprehensive approach (Figure 10.10). Partial approaches, such as policies focusing solely on direct public financing or guarantees, are unlikely to yield large benefits. Rather, meaningful and sustainable SME access to financing requires establishing proper macroeconomic and institutional policy frameworks, as well as legal and regulatory conditions that are critical to developing a strong SME credit culture and risk management practices. This approach can also trigger

Figure 10.10. Framework for SME Financial Inclusion

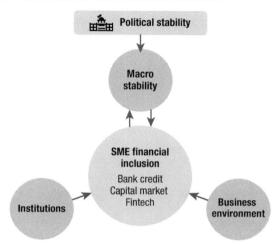

Source: Blancher and others (2019).
Note: SME = small and medium enterprise.

a virtuous circle of greater SME transparency and reduced informality, bringing about broader benefits to the economy and stronger demand for credit.

The development of new technologies could greatly accelerate financial inclusion. Financial transactions can now be performed in a relatively inexpensive and reliable way, eliminating spatial and temporal barriers (Lukonga 2020). Digital wallets are further reducing the use of cash and related costs and inefficiencies, providing a cheaper and more efficient payment system for micro and small business.[7] Digitalization helps create credit histories and reduce financial and administrative costs linked to extending micro credit. In some countries (for example, China) micro credit is being offered via mobile money, and cloud-based funding platforms are allowing companies to launch new models of "crowd-funded mortgages."

Developing fintech in Morocco would require further investment in digitalization. Affordable high-speed internet, a labor force that has digital skills, and digital platforms to connect businesses with consumers are all essential to boost fintech in Morocco. Deploying infrastructure for rural coverage is also an economic challenge so as to close the rural-urban digital divide. For instance, the lack of internet connectivity in rural areas is still a barrier because about 50 percent of the rural population uses internet (compared to 75 percent in urban areas).[8]

---

[7] Digital payments in China rose from 4 percent of all payments in 2012 to 34 percent in 2017 (*The Economist* 2019, 9).

[8] Arab Barometer 2020; https://www.arabbarometer.org/.

CONCLUSION

Despite significant improvements in recent years, financial inclusion in Morocco continues to lag peer economies and contrasts with its well-capitalized and sophisticated banking system. Small and micro firms have a relatively low access to credit, and large segments of the population—mostly female, the poor in rural areas, and young adults—still have low access to financial services.

The National Strategy for Financial Inclusion is a welcome initiative that would require Morocco's financial system to be strengthened through a more comprehensive, holistic approach. Accelerating fintech development will allow the development of alternative ways of saving and lending while closing the financial inclusion gap. Digitalization will be crucial to make the leap from payment systems to credit provision and will provide an innovative technological solution for surmounting the shortcomings of traditional financial services for the provision of credit to MSMEs, in particular by facilitating credit information and reducing the financial and administrative costs linked to their low amounts and perceived risks.

To speed up the digitalization process, expanded access to broadband connectivity and affordable high-speed internet is needed. Efficient digital ecosystems are needed for payment and credit systems to grow in digital platforms that connect businesses with consumers (e-commerce) and the provision of digital financial services at the time of improving digital skills in the labor force.

REFERENCES

Bank Al-Maghrib (BAM), Ministère de l'Economie et des Finances (MEF). 2018. "Stratégie Nationale d'Inclusion Financière (SNIF). Note de Synthèse." September. https://www.bkam.ma/Inclusion-financiere/Note-de-synthese-de-la-strategie-nationale-d-inclusion-financiere

Bank Al-Maghrib (BAM), Ministère de l'Economie et des Finances (MEF). 2021. "Stratégie Nationale d'Inclusion Financière." n.3.

Blancher, Nicolas R., Maximiliano Appendino, Aidyn Bibolov, Armand P. Fouejieu, Jiawei Li, Anta Ndoye, Alexandra Panagiotakopoulou, Wei Shi, and Tetyana Sydorenko. 2019. "Financial Inclusion of Small and Medium-Sized Enterprises in the Middle East and Central Asia." IMF Departmental Paper 2019/002, International Monetary Fund, Washington, DC.

Cardarelli, Roberto, Hippolyte W. Balima, Chiara Maggi, Adrian Alter, Jérôme Vacher, Matthew Gaertner, Olivier Bizimana, Azhin Abdulkarim, Karim Badr, Shant Arzoumanian, Mahmoud Harb, Mariam El Hamiani Khatat, Priscilla S. Muthoora, and Aymen Belgacem. 2022. "Informality, Development, and the Business Cycle in North Africa." IMF Departmental Paper 2022/011. Washington, DC.

The Economist. 2019. "Digital Payments. The Dash from Cash." August 3.

Ghassibe, Mishel, Maximiliano Appendino, and Samir Elsadek Mahmoudi. 2019. "SME Financial Inclusion for Sustained Growth in the Middle East and Central Asia." IMF Working Paper 19/209, International Monetary Fund, Washington, DC.

International Finance Corporation. 2017. "MSME Finance Gap. Assessment of the Shortfalls and Opportunities in Financing Micro, Small, and Medium Enterprises in Emerging Markets." World Bank Group, Washington, DC.

International Monetary Fund (IMF). 2017. "Financial Access Survey (FAS)." Washington, DC.

Lukonga, Inutu. 2020. "Harnessing Digital Technologies to Promote SMEs and Inclusive Growth in the MENAP Region." IMF Working Paper 20/135, International Monetary Fund, Washington, DC.

Sahay, Ratna, Martin Čihák, Papa N'Diaye, Adolfo Barajas, Ran Bi, Diana Ayala, Yuan Gao, and others. 2015. "Rethinking Financial Deepening: Stability and Growth in Emerging Markets." IMF Staff Discussion Note 15/08, International Monetary Fund, Washington, DC, and updated 2020 version with 2018 data.

World Bank. 2018. *The Global Findex Database 2017. Measuring Financial Inclusion and the FinTech Revolution.* Washington, DC.

World Bank. 2019a. *Morocco 2019 Country Profile: Enterprise Surveys.* Washington, DC.

World Bank. 2019b. *Support for Small and Medium Enterprises. A Synthesis of Evaluative Findings.* Washington, DC, September.

World Bank. 2020. *Morocco Database.* Washington, DC.

World Bank. 2022. *The Global Findex Database 2021. Financial Inclusion, Digital Payments, and Resilience.* Washington, DC.

World Economic Forum (WEF). 2019. "The Global Competitiveness Report 2019." https://www3.weforum.org/docs/WEF_TheGlobalCompetitivenessReport2019.pdf.

CHAPTER 11

Efficiency of Public Spending on Education

Dominique Fayad, Gregory Auclair, and Ananta Dua

INTRODUCTION

Over recent decades, Morocco has made significant progress in improving access to education (Figure 11.1). In the late 1980s only 55 percent of children aged 6–11 were enrolled in (primary) school in Morocco. In 2014 that percentage had risen to 98 percent (Benkassmi and Abdelkhalek 2020). Other age groups recorded similar improvements.[1] These improvements benefited mostly disadvantaged groups, particularly girls (+25.7 percentage points in primary school) and rural populations (+30 percentage points in primary school). The number of young people enrolled in vocational training and higher education also increased dramatically.

Figure 11.1. School Enrollment
(Percent)

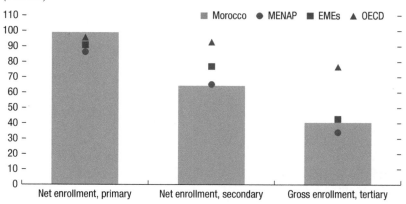

Sources: IMF, Expenditure Assessment Tool; World Bank; and IMF staff calculations.
Note: Figure shows latest values available for each country or country group. EMEs = emerging market economies; MENAP = Middle East, North Africa, Afghanistan, and Pakistan; OECD = Organisation for Economic Co-operation and Development.

---

[1] Net enrollment rates rose from 58.1 to 86.1 percent for the age group 12–14 years (lower secondary), from 35.5 to 59.2 percent for the age group 15–17 years (upper secondary), and from 10.4 to 22.1 percent for the age group 19–23 years (tertiary).

However, Morocco's education system is still facing several important challenges. Learning outcomes, as measured by the test scores of Moroccan students on international tests, are among the lowest in the MENA region. Early dropout rates are still high, and 72 percent of all students leave the education system without any qualification (Higher Council of Education, Training, and Scientific Research 2014). The majority of Moroccan students choose to follow studies in social sciences at the expense of technical sciences, engineering, and business. Low average education quality and skill mismatches are widely recognized as impediments to the youth population gaining a foothold in the labor market. The Education's Strategic Reform Vision 2015–2030 launched in 2014 and the New Model of Development report published in 2021 (which has given new emphasis to the reform of the education system) both emphasize the need for deep reforms to adapt Morocco's education system to a fast-changing world with shifting demographics and rapid technological advances changing the nature of jobs (Cardarelli and others 2022).

Improving the efficiency of public spending on education is key to boosting education results to better prepare young Moroccans to find jobs. Government spending on education in Morocco has been increasing and was about 5.9 percent of GDP in 2019, accounting for about one quarter of total government spending. Even if spending does not appear as high once expressed as a ratio to students, the poor educational outcomes and the lack of fiscal space in the aftermath of the COVID-19 crisis suggest it is crucial for Morocco to improve the efficiency of public spending is this area.

This chapter focuses on the efficiency of public spending on education in Morocco. Adopting an efficiency frontier analysis, an IMF research paper found that Morocco can significantly improve learning outcomes through a series of reforms that would improve the efficiency of public spending (Auclair and Fayad 2016). Potential reform measures include improving the quality of budget management, enhancing teachers' incentives and overall education levels, and strengthening institutional and governance quality. The reforms announced by Morocco under the Education's Strategic Reform Vision 2015–2030 and envisaged in the New Model of Development Report (2021) address some of these issues and, if well implemented, promise to improve the efficiency of public spending on education.

LABOR MARKET, EDUCATION, AND PUBLIC SPENDING IN MOROCCO

Morocco's unemployment rate has decreased considerably since 1990 but remains elevated, particularly among youth. Although it has fallen below the average for oil-importing countries in the region, the unemployment rate is still high, at 9 percent in 2021, and major groups are still excluded from this trend. In particular

- *Youth unemployment has increased over the last 10 years and approached 30 percent in 2021.* Moreover, this figure may underestimate the size of the problem because a high level of labor market dropout fuels inactivity—over the past decade, the NEET (young people not in education, employment, or training) rate has remained at about 29 percent (about 4.5 million in 2019), among the highest rate in the Middle East and North Africa (see Chapter 6).

- *Youth unemployment is particularly high in urban areas,* where the unemployment rate remains steadily above 14 percent at the end of 2021 and is particularly high among the highly educated population (in 2021 the unemployment rate was about 30 percent for those with a diploma or more education compared to 2.1 percent for the population without a diploma).

- *Labor market participation rate for young people has been decreasing* particularly for those who are highly educated (with a university degree), and unemployment is particularly high for women with more education.

At least to a certain degree, these trends reflect a few characteristics and developments of Morocco's education system. In particular:

- Despite the increase in enrollment rates, they remain below the regional average and other developing regions for secondary and tertiary education. Moreover, significant differences remain between urban centers and rural areas. For instance, in 2016–17, secondary education rates were about 97 percent for urban children (with parity between boys and girls) but only 76 percent for their rural counterparts. The gaps are higher for high school education—the high school enrollment rate in urban centers is 86 percent, whereas it drops substantially in rural areas to 49 percent for males and 32 percent for females (Higher Council of Education, Training, and Scientific Research, 2018).

- *The dropout rate is high.* Although Morocco has succeeded in lowering primary school dropout rates (to around 2 percent in cities and 5 percent in urban regions), the rate is much higher in secondary education (reaching 13 percent in urban centers and 17 percent in rural areas) (Higher Council of Education, Training, and Scientific Research 2018). Some 432,000 students dropped out of public-school programs in 2018 without obtaining a diploma, of which 78 percent were in primary and college education programs.

- *Higher education is mainly on non-STEM (science, technology, engineering, mathematics) subjects.* Looking at the details of higher education enrollment shows that the majority of Moroccan students choose to follow studies in social sciences at the expense of technical sciences, engineering, and business. As a result, the number of registrations in the first set of subjects exceeds universities' capacity (Figure 11.2). The high level of unemployed university graduates could reflect the fact that tertiary education does not seem to provide training in the skills and needs most in demand by the labor market.

Morocco lags other countries on international indicators of education outcomes, including the following:

- *Average years of schooling.* Despite the increase since 2010, with slightly less than 6 years of schooling on average, Morocco still lags other countries in 2019 (average for MENAP region is 7.4 years) (Figure 11.3).

Figure 11.2. Morocco: Under- and Overenrollment by Field of Study, 2013
(Percentage of capacity)

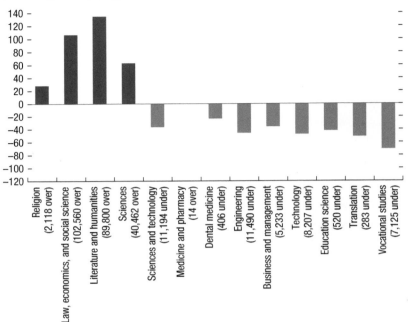

Source: Ministry of Higher Education.
Note: Numbers in parentheses in the horizontal-axis labels specify the amount of under- or overenrollment.

- *Average teacher-to-student ratio.* With 3.7 teachers per 100 students at primary level and 5.1 at secondary level (in 2018), Morocco is lagging other regions (average for MENAP is 4.3 and 6.3 for primary and secondary levels, respectively) (Figure 11.3).

- *Learning outcomes.* International benchmarking data show that despite some improvements over the past decade, Morocco's learning outcomes remain below that of other countries. This is the case if looking at PISA scores (based on 2018 data), as well as 2016 PIRLS reading and literacy test scores and 2019 TIMSS mathematics and sciences test scores (Figure 11.4).[2]

---

[2] PISA (Programme for International Student Assessment) is run by the Organisation for Economic Co-operation and Development and tests the skills and knowledge of 15-year-old students in reading, mathematics, and science. TIMSS (Trends in International Mathematics and Science Study) and PIRLS (Progress in International Reading Literacy Study) are produced by the International Association for the Evaluation of Educational Achievement, an international cooperative of national research institutions, governmental research agencies, scholars, and analysts working to research, understand, and improve education worldwide.

Figure 11.3. Education Indicators

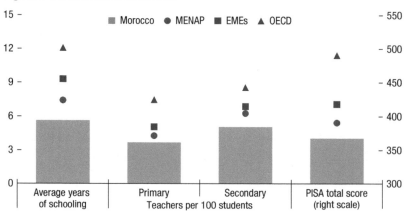

Sources: IMF, Expenditure Assessment Tool; World Bank; and IMF staff calculations.
Note: Figure shows latest values available for each country or country group. EMEs = emerging
market economies; MENAP = Middle East, North Africa, Afghanistan, and Pakistan;
OECD = Organisation for Economic Co-operation and Development; PISA = Programme for
International Student Assessment.

Public spending on education has increased since 2005 and is quite high as a
share of GDP (Figure 11.5). However, public spending *per student* is relatively
low, particularly for primary and secondary levels, as youth represent a large share
of the Moroccan population. Although regional disparities in school infrastructure and education services are important, the regional budget allocation in
pre-graduate education has remained stable across regions since 2006.

ASSESSING EFFICIENCY OF SPENDING ON EDUCATION: A FRONTIER APPROACH

The persistent weakness of Morocco's indicators of educational outcomes in
the face of rising spending suggests an efficiency problem. Addressing the
challenges faced by Morocco's education system requires continued public
investments in education. However, because Morocco (like many other countries) is facing fiscal pressures from the higher level of public debt after the
2020 recession and competing spending needs, improving spending efficiency
has become essential.

The literature typically indicates large inefficiencies in the education sector. The
literature on efficiency of public spending in education generally adopts a production function approach, which links inputs (such as public education spending) and
outputs (such as school enrollment rates and test scores). The "efficiency frontier"
is defined by those countries that achieve the best education outcomes with the
same levels of input (or the same outcomes with the least costs).[3] The efficiency

---

[3] Gupta and others (2007), Gupta and Verhoeven (2001), Herrera and Pang (2005), Jayasuriya and
Wodon (2003).

Figure 11.4. Morocco: Comparative School Indicators and Test Outcomes

1. PIRLS: Mean Reading Achievement Score

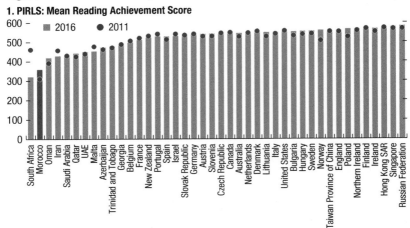

2. TIMSS: Mean Fourth-Grade Math Score

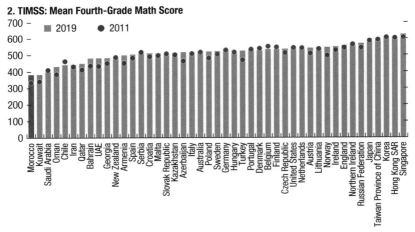

3. TIMSS: Mean Eighth-Grade Math Score

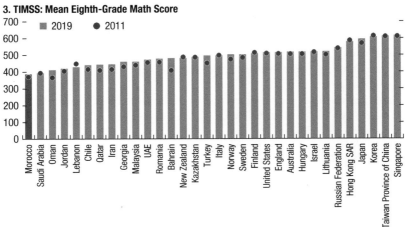

Figure 11.4. *(continued)*

4. TIMSS: Mean Eighth-Grade Science Score

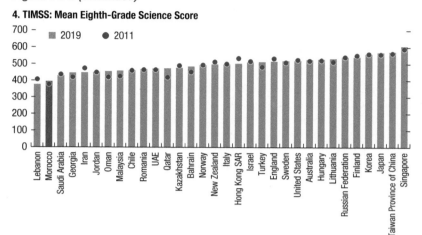

Sources: 2011 and 2016 Progress in International Reading Literacy Study (PIRLS); 2011 and 2019 Trends in Mathematics and Science Study (TIMSS); and IMF staff calculations.
Note: In panel 1, comparative scores for 2011 are not available for Bahrain, Chile, Egypt, Kazakhstan, Kuwait, Latvia, and Macao SAR. UAE = United Arab Emirates.

Figure 11.5. Government Expenditure on Education

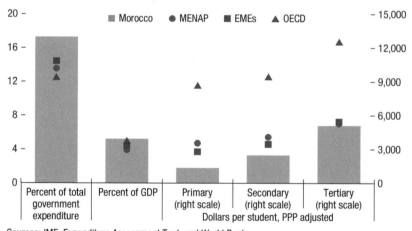

Sources: IMF, Expenditure Assessment Tool; and World Bank.
Note: EMEs = emerging market economies; MENAP = Middle East, North Africa, Afghanistan, and Pakistan; OECD = Organisation for Economic Co-operation and Development; PPP = purchasing power parity.

frontier can be estimated using parametric methods (such as stochastic frontier analysis [SFA]; Kumbhakar and Knox Lovell 2000) and nonparametric methods (such as data envelope analysis or the free disposal hull technique), with each having its advantages and disadvantages (Kapsoli and Teodoru 2017). The efficiency scores from this analysis indicate the efficiency of a country relative to that of the best-performing countries (the frontier).

The literature is not conclusive on the relationship among public spending in education, educational outcomes, and level of development. Herrera and Pang (2005) used gross primary enrollment and completion rates as outputs, and public expenditures as an input, and found a positive relationship between expenditure and level of development. Gupta and Verhoeven (2001) used a free disposal hull technique to assess the education sector's performance by taking expenditure in purchasing power parity as an input and gross enrollment rate in primary and secondary schools as output. The authors noted that adding GDP per capita lowers or cancels the significance of the impact of expenditure on educational output and concluded that African countries are less efficient than countries in Asia and in the Western Hemisphere. Gupta and others (2007) used a data envelope analysis to evaluate the efficiency of education expenditure. By taking public expenditure on education in purchasing power parity terms as an input and primary net enrollment and youth literacy rates as output, they found no clear relationship between income per capita and the efficiency of education spending. The performance of poor countries varies widely depending on the output indicator. Jayasuriya and Wodon (2003) used an SFA technique to estimate education efficiency frontiers using the primary enrollment rate as the output variable and real GDP per capita, adult illiteracy, and education expenditure per capita (private and public) as input variables. The findings showed that neither education expenditure nor regional differences have a statistically significant impact on net primary enrollment.

An IMF research paper estimated the efficiency of public spending on education in Morocco using an SFA (Auclair and Fayad 2016). The SFA has the advantage to estimate the inefficiency term, although at the cost of imposing constraints on the production function.[4] The paper used the PIRLS and TIMSS indicators of students' performance in order to assess the efficiency frontier for a panel of 34 countries. The main dependent variable is the eighth grade TIMSS scores averaged across math and sciences from the 2003, 2006, and 2011 surveys. The main explanatory variable is educational expenditure in primary and secondary education per student (in US dollar purchasing power parity basis) averaged for the 4 preceding years to reflect the lagged

---

[4] The nonparametric methods do not isolate the error term that becomes part of the inefficiency and are extremely sensitive to the presence of outliers (see also Grigoli 2014, and Grigoli and Kapsoli 2013).

effects of public spending on education. The paper also used a number of control variables:

- The *Gini index* to control for income inequality, with greater inequality possibly an obstacle to school attainment.

- The *population density* to control for regional disparity in accessing education infrastructures (which tend to be higher in urban areas).

- The *number of books at home*, a proxy for adult literacy and parents' education level, to further control for socioeconomic determinants.

The results of the analysis show the existence of significant inefficiency in Morocco's education spending. The paper found that Morocco ranks third in terms of inefficiency gap (defined as the difference between actual and potential education outcomes under current education spending). Using the efficiency frontier regression to estimate the predicted TIMSS score for Morocco shows that the inefficiency in spending plays a significant role in explaining Morocco's low score (the fifth lowest in the sample) (Figure 11.6). Morocco could have scores closer to the middle of the sample if it succeeded in closing the gap with the estimated efficiency frontier.

In order to identify the determinants of the inefficiency, the IMF paper regressed the inefficiency gap on a set of fiscal, institutional, and educational variables (see Table 11.1). The paper estimated the determinants of the gap using pooled ordinary least squares with fixed effects on univariate and multivariate regressions. The fiscal variables were *governance efficiency, ethics and corruption, wastefulness of public spending*, and *diversion of public funds*. As institutional variables, the paper used an indicator of *decentralization* (the ratio of central budget over total budget), the ratio of capital to current expenditure, the ratio of wage to current expenditure, and the ratio of teacher wage to average wage. Finally, the indicators relative to education were the *number of students in private schools, teachers' education level*, the *number of teachers trained*, the *student-to-teacher ratio*, a *student absenteeism index*, a *teacher absenteeism index*, and an *index of student intimidation* as an indicator of the school climate.

The results showed that spending inefficiency in Morocco is linked to a series of factors. In particular, the main determinants of the efficiency gap are the ethics and corruption indicators, diversion of public funds,[5] teacher training, and teacher wages relative to the average wage in the economy (Table 11.1). Indeed, Morocco is lagging other countries mainly based on indicators of teacher training and teacher education and teachers' and students' absenteeism (Figure 11.7). Hence, progress in these areas would be particularly important.

---

[5] Diversion of public funds is an indicator from the World Economic Forum that assesses how common the reallocation of public funds is to companies, individuals, or groups due to corruption.

Figure 11.6. Morocco: Comparative Inefficiency Term for TIMSS Scores

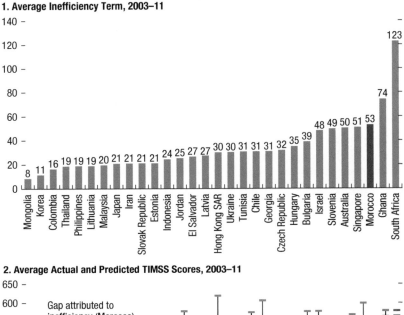

1. Average Inefficiency Term, 2003–11

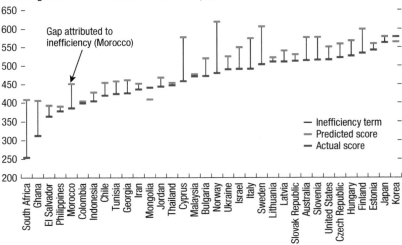

2. Average Actual and Predicted TIMSS Scores, 2003–11

Source: IMF staff calculations based on Trends in Mathematics and Science Study (TIMSS) scores for math and science.
Note: Morocco ranks third in terms of inefficiency gap (defined as the difference between actual and potential education outcomes under current education spending).

TABLE 11.1.

Gap Analysis Results

	(1)	(2)	(3)	(4)	(5)	(6)	(7)	(8)	(9)
Wastefulness of public spending	−10.80								−16.55**
Government efficiency	0.79								
Ethics and corruption	−21.73**	−26.10**	−26.96**	−26.11**	−25.54**	−25.72	−31.42***	−32.86***	
Diversion of public funds	−17.17**								
Decentralization	1.70	0.97							
Ratio of capital to current expenditure	−35.71		−12.94	−20.58					
Ratio of wage to current expenditure	−2.79*				−2.67*	−1.76			−2.21
Ratio of teacher wage to average wage	13.21						19.84	12.37	
Percentage of students in private schools	0.72			0.85			1.68		
Teacher education level	16.72***					16.77			
Teacher training	−27.04**								
Student-to-teacher ratio	−0.25								0.29
Student absenteeism	−5.52							−6.65	
Student intimidation	3.42								
Number of countries	29	28	24	24	25	25	18	18	21
Number of observations	55	52	40	40	49	48	35	35	37

Source: IMF staff calculations.
*p < .05; **p < .01; ***p < .001.

Figure 11.7. Morocco: Comparative Education Indicators

1. Teacher Training
(Percent of teachers with university-level degree in education or subject area)

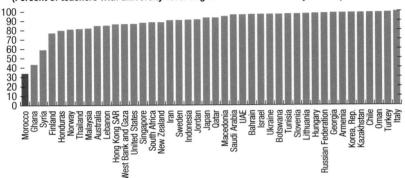

2. Teacher General Education Level
(International Standard Classification of Education Scale, 0–8; score of 5 or higher indicates university or advanced education)

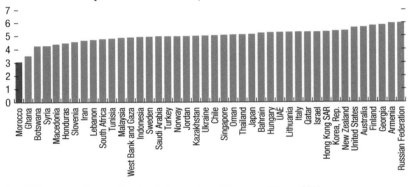

3. Staff Compensation per Teacher in Comparison to Average Wages, 2011

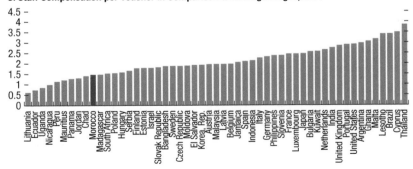

Figure 11.7. *(continued)*

4. Diversion of Public Funds
(Scale, 0–7, with 7 best)

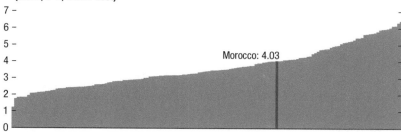

Morocco: 4.03

5. Wastefulness of Government Spending
(Scale, 0–7, with 7 best)

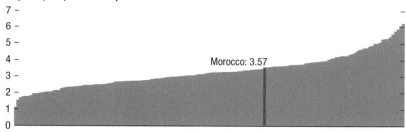

Morocco: 3.57

6. Government Efficiency
(Scale, 0–7, with 7 best)

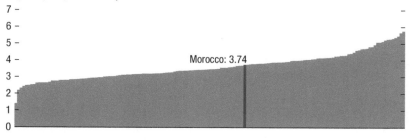

Morocco: 3.74

7. Ethics and Corruption
(Scale, 0–7, with 7 best)

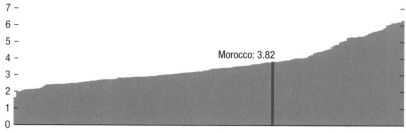

Morocco: 3.82

(continued)

Figure 11.7. *(continued)*

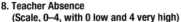

8. Teacher Absence
(Scale, 0–4, with 0 low and 4 very high)

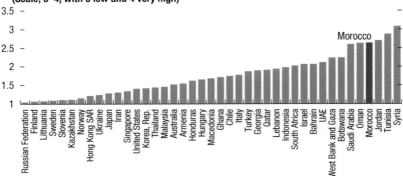

9. Intimidation among Students
(Scale, 0–4, with 0 low and 4 very high)

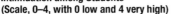

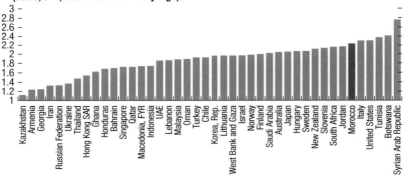

10. Student Absence
(Scale, 0–4, with 0 low and 4 very high)

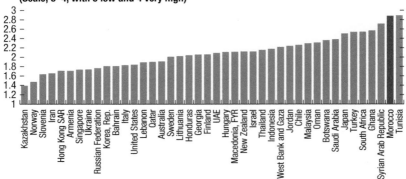

Sources: Haut Commissariat au Plan; International Labour Organization, *Global Wage Report*; 2011 Trends in International Mathematics and Science Study teacher background questionnaire; United Nations Educational, Scientific and Cultural Organization; World Economic Forum, *Global Competitiveness Report*; and IMF staff estimates.

Note: Panel 3 shows per-teacher compensation as a multiple of average salaries in each country depicted. Panels 4–7 rank all countries, lowest to highest, based on the latest values available for each country. Values for Morocco are based on 2009 data. In panel 3, wages in education are calculated as total compensation of education employees divided by the number of teachers. UAE = United Arab Emirates.

The results of the gap analysis suggest that fiscal reforms greatly improve the efficiency of Moroccan public spending in education. For the same amount of public spending per student, the TIMSS test score would increase by 53 points by (1) improving the quality of budget management through a better allocation of public spending and lower diversion of public funds, (2) enhancing teachers' incentives and improving the overall education level of teachers, and (3) strengthening institutional and governance quality.

POLICY IMPLICATIONS

The result of the IMF paper suggests that the efficiency of public spending on education in Morocco would benefit from the following:

- *A better allocation of responsibilities between the central government and subnational authorities.* The ongoing decentralization process may increase the efficiency of public spending unless it is poorly designed and/or not completely achieved. Beyond the transfer of responsibilities, subnational authorities should manage financial and human resources. This would increase the efficiency in the allocation of public spending resources because educational needs may differ among geographical areas. Moreover, the transfer of competencies should be supported by incentive-based policies.

- *More managerial autonomy at the school level,* which would also improve the quality of resource allocation through allowing more flexibility in the wage-setting process, budget allocation, and teaching methods. Also, greater decision-making autonomy could improve the capacity to monitor student performance and allow for more benchmarking among schools. It would also help enhance teachers' motivation and incentives to take initiatives and responsibilities in improving educational output quality.

These conclusions are consistent with the authorities' diagnosis of the education system. In particular, the education framework law approved in 2019 allows the implementation of the proposals of the Education's Strategic Reform Vision 2015–2030 to increase the quality and accessibility of Morocco's education system. The law introduces several important changes to the structure of Morocco's education system, including by making primary education available to pupils as young as 4 years old (previously, primary education began at age 6). More recently, the New Model of Development report (2021) called for reforms to reinforce and complement Vision 2030 and the related framework law. It placed its emphasis on (1) enhancing teachers' pedagogical skills, investing in their training and motivations; (2) the creation of an efficient guidance system to optimize the chances of success at school and reduce the risk of dropping out; (3) an upgrading of school programs and pedagogical approaches; and (4) more accountability for educational institutions, including through assessing their compliance with good management practices.

CONCLUSION

This chapter shows that more efficient public spending could help improve the quality of education and help remove the distortions that boost youth unemployment in Morocco. Although public spending on education has increased substantially over the past decade, the quality of education in Morocco (as measured by students' scores on international tests) is lagging many emerging countries, and skill mismatches are widely recognized as a key factor behind the high level of unemployment.[6] This chapter shows that there is significant scope to improve efficiency of public spending in education in Morocco. A broad reform of the national education system to strengthen the general level of education is ongoing, and measures to make the public education sector more efficient should be at its core. This would help to give students the necessary background and skills they need to continue their studies and, ultimately, to attain successful and productive roles in the Moroccan job market.

REFERENCES

African Development Bank. 2014. "Diagnostic de Croissance du Maroc: Analyse des Contraintes à Une Croissance Large et Inclusive." https://www.afdb.org/fileadmin/uploads/afdb/Documents/Generic-Documents/Diagnostic_de_croissance_du_Maroc_%E2%80%93_Analyse_des_contraintes_%C3%A0_une_croissance_large_et_inclusive_-_version_FR.pdf

Auclair, Gregory, and Dominque Fayad. 2016. "Efficiency of Public Spending on Education." IMF, Selected Issues Papers, IMF Country Report No. 16/36.

Benkassmi, Mohamed, and Touhami Abdelkhalek. 2020. "Building Human Capital: Lessons from Country Experiences—Morocco." World Bank, Washington, DC.

Cardarelli, Roberto, Mercedes Vera Martin, and Subir Lall (editors). 2022. *Promoting Inclusive Growth in the Middle East and North Africa: Challenges and Opportunities in a Post- Pandemic World*. International Monetary Fund, Washington, DC.

Higher Council of Education, Training, and Scientific Research. 2014. *La Mise en Oeuvre de la Charte Nationale d'Education et de Formation 2000–2013. Acquis, Déficits et Défit*. December.

Higher Council of Education, Training, and Scientific Research. 2018. *L'Atlas Territorial de l'Abandon Scolaire*.

Grigoli, Francesco. 2014. "A Hybrid Approach to Estimating the Efficiency of Public Spending on Education in Emerging Economies." IMF Working Paper 14/19, International Monetary Fund, Washington, DC.

Grigoli, Francesco, and Javier Kapsoli. 2013. "Waste Not, Want Not: The Efficiency of Health Expenditures in Developing Economies." IMF Working Paper 13/187, International Monetary Fund, Washington, DC.

Gupta, Sanjeev, Gerd Schwartz, Shamsuddin Tareq, Richard Allen, Isabell Adenauer, Kevin Fletcher, and Duncan Last. 2007. "Fiscal Management of Scale-Up Aid." IMF Working Paper 07/222, International Monetary Fund, Washington, DC.

Gupta, Sanjeev, and Marijn Verhoeven. 2001. "The Efficiency of Government Expenditure. Experiences from Africa." *Journal of Policy Modelling* 23: 433–67.

---

[6] African Development Bank (2014); International Bank for Reconstruction and Development (2014); and Sutherland and others (2009).

Herrera, Santiago, and Gaobo Pang. 2005. "Efficiency of Public Spending in Developing Countries: An Efficiency Frontier Approach." World Bank Policy Research Working Paper 3645, World Bank, Washington, DC.

International Bank for Reconstruction and Development. 2014. "Revue des Dépenses Publiques, Tome II: Secteur de l'Education."

Jayasuriya, Ruwan, and Quentin Wodon. 2003. "Efficiency in Reaching the Millennium Development Goals." World Bank Working Paper 9, World Bank, Washington, DC.

Kapsoli, Javier, and Iulia Ruxandra Teodoru. 2017. "Benchmarking Social Spending Using Efficiency Frontiers." IMF Working Paper No. 17/197, International Monetary Fund, Washington, DC.

Kumbhakar, Subal C., and C.A. Knox Lovell. 2000. *Stochastic Frontier Analysis.* Cambridge University Press.

Sutherland, Douglas, Robert Price, and Frederic Gonand. 2009. "Improving Public Spending Efficiency in Primary and Secondary Education." *OECD Journal: Economic Studies 2009.* https://www.oecd.org/economy/growth/46867041.pdf.

Index